W9-BVJ-295

CITY COLLEGE LIBRARY
1825 MAY ST.
BROWNSVILLE, TEXAS 78520

POPULATION POLICIES
and
ECONOMIC DEVELOPMENT

POPULATION POLICIES
and
ECONOMIC DEVELOPMENT

A World Bank staff report

Coordinating author: Timothy King

Contributors:
   Roberto Cuca
   Ravi Gulhati
   Monowar Hossain
   Ernest Stern
   Pravin Visaria
   K. C. Zachariah
   Gregory Zafros
   B. Meredith Burke (consultant)
   Bonnie Newlon (consultant)
   Robert Repetto (consultant)

Published for the World Bank
by
THE JOHNS HOPKINS UNIVERSITY PRESS
Baltimore and London

CITY COLLEGE LIBRARY
1825 MAY ST.
BROWNSVILLE, TEXAS 78520

Copyright © 1974
by the International Bank for Reconstruction and Development
All rights reserved

Manufactured in the United States of America

Text prepared for publication
with the assistance of
Shirley Sirota Rosenberg.

Library of Congress Catalog Card Number 74-12786
ISBN 0-8018-1675-0 (cloth bound)
ISBN 0-8018-1676-9 (paper bound)

TABLE OF CONTENTS

TEXT FIGURES

TEXT TABLES

INTRODUCTION

In 1972 the World Bank published a paper on Population Planning which summarized the world population outlook and described the Bank's initial efforts to help member countries reduce their rates of population growth. The paper also set out the Bank's program of assistance as then envisaged. For the five years, 1969–1973, the Bank estimated that it would commit $67 million for work in this sector.[1] Actually, during the five-year period ending in fiscal year 1973, $84 million was lent for population projects in seven developing countries, including two of the largest, India and Indonesia.

The primary objective of Bank Group assistance in this field is to help countries establish sound organizations and programs that will be effective in reducing population growth rates. Bank projects have been used to finance a wide range of activities including construction of health facilities and training schools; the provision of transport and data-processing equipment; the execution of management studies; the conduct of experimental and pilot projects; the preparation of information and education materials; the training of health-service staff and demographers; and the conduct of sample surveys and research to find out which program activities are effective and which are not.

Based on the experience gained in these operations, the population lending program proposed for the Bank for the five-year period, fiscal years 1974–1978, has been expanded substantially. It envisages lending $375 million for projects in twenty-three countries.

The rapid expansion of the Bank Group lending program in the population field reflects the increasing importance we attach to moderating population growth rates. Compared to even a decade ago, considerable progress has been made in understanding the interaction of population growth and development, establishing family planning programs, and adopting policies intended to reduce the rate of population growth. Yet, as the projections in Chapter 1 show, a continued and rapid expansion of population in all developing countries seems inevitable. The social and economic cost of absorbing this addition to population is immense, and the burden is heaviest in the large and poor countries in South Asia and in the lowest income groups within each

---

[1] Unless otherwise specified, all money amounts in this study are in current U.S. dollars.

The term *World Bank* refers to the *International Bank for Reconstruction and Development* (*IBRD*).

1

country. Even if we could be sanguine about the ultimate carrying capacity of the earth, which we cannot, we could not be indifferent to the consequences for economic growth and social equity which are implicit in current demographic trends.

Past rapid rates of population growth have created a young age structure which provides a built-in momentum for future growth. Even with the most antinatalist policies conceivable, fertility will not drop to replacement levels quickly. Even when it does, population will continue to expand for approximately seventy years. For instance, even if fertility in the eight largest developing countries were to drop to replacement level today—and it is not likely to reach that for some time—their combined population would be about 60 percent larger 70 years from now. Thus policymakers must take a very long-term view of the relation between population size and resources, even in countries which do not seem densely populated today.

Essentially, the rapid rate of population growth in the developing countries has been the result of stable birth rates combined with plummeting mortality rates. The experience of industrialized countries suggests that a low population growth rate eventually is restored as fertility rates decline. In these countries both mortality and fertility declined as development progressed and incomes rose; in the developing countries mortality levels have been reduced by public health measures well below levels to be expected solely in relation to socio-economic indicators. This raises the central question whether public policies and programs can reduce fertility rates as well as mortality rates.

The question is crucial because, as I said earlier, the cost of rapid population growth is large, and it falls most heavily on the poorest. High rates of fertility increase the number of children that the labor force must support. Some of these costs are borne by the individual household, though often only by depriving the younger children in the family of minimal nutritional support and health care. Other costs, such as education, are borne by society. For instance, the level of expenditure needed to provide full enrollment to the 6–14 year age group by the year 2000 under a low fertility assumption would be 30 percent less than the amount needed if no decline in fertility takes place. Without a decline in fertility, increased expenditures are necessary merely to provide the same inadequate level of instruction to larger numbers of students.

Rapid population growth also means a rapidly growing labor force. A major constraint on increasing productivity in developing countries is the scarcity of capital. Yet at present almost half of the funds available for fixed capital investment is required merely to hold constant the amount of capital invested per worker, leaving little capital for investment to increase the output per worker.

2

Whatever the national views on the appropriate ultimate size of the population, the economic and social costs of different population growth rates must be measured against other objectives. Differences in population growth rates have major implications for resource use and productivity in every sector of the economy. Moreover, these costs are not evenly distributed. Rapid population growth is an important cause of income inequality. Growth of the labor force provides a downward pressure on wages, and leads to unemployment; in agriculture, the effect is often land fragmentation among small farmers and growing landlessness. Where social services or rates of job creation are inadequate, lower income groups have less access to such public services as education and health and, being generally less skilled, suffer most from low wages and high unemployment.

This study also presents evidence that the reverse is true. Low levels of income and, particularly, the maldistribution of income, contribute to high rates of fertility. Thus, development programs dealing directly with the poor are an essential part of any attempt to reduce the rate of population growth. High fertility is part of the socio-economic environment in which a high proportion of babies die in infancy or childhood, parents expect children to contribute to the family income rather than be educated, women remain illiterate, and support for the aged and the disabled must be provided by the extended family. Efforts to accelerate economic growth and improve the distribution of income are critical to the goal of reduced fertility.

Some countries have arrived at a point where fertility rates are declining; in others there is evidence that this point may soon be reached. Many factors—social, cultural, religious, economic—affect the size of a family. Sometimes parents misjudge current mortality levels so that they end up with more children than they actually desire. Other factors involve social and cultural values which change slowly as income levels rise, education spreads, and the country develops. The evidence suggests that, as incomes rise, fertility declines through increased age at marriage, reduced incidence of marriage, and increased costs of raising children compared to their contribution to family welfare. While public policy necessarily affects these factors only gradually, redistributive policies may make a significant contribution to reducing fertility. For instance, the birth rates of many Latin American countries are higher than might be expected at their overall levels of socio-economic development, and a major part of the explanation seems to lie in the inequitable distribution of income. The converse is true in some Eastern European countries. Reduced inequality in income distribution seems to be strongly related to reductions in fertility.

However, even at present levels of socio-economic development, the potential demand for family planning services is far greater than the level now being provided. Estimates of abortions, no matter how deficient, are ample evidence of this. Present family planning programs have made important contributions to reducing fertility rates, but in most countries they are not of a size commensurate with the problem.

More adequate programs require:

- better information and motivation activities
- more convenient access to services
- more and better trained manpower
- improved technology
- increased financing.

Motivation requires extensive use of mass media, but this must be supplemented, particularly in rural areas, by personal contact. The most effective contacts have been made by peer group members, even though these individuals may have little professional training. Reliance on direct contact requires large numbers of participants and puts a strain on scarce managerial talent. Yet programs of direct contact with potential family planning practitioners should be expanded well beyond present levels.

Expenditure on family planning programs is still very low and does not reflect the priority that governments have assigned to the reduction of population growth rates. Shortage of funds means inadequate manpower and facilities and, consequently, fewer individuals who accept family planning services. Not only do budget allocations not provide for sufficient expansion of services, but family planning budgets are often the first to be cut in times of austerity.

Despite accumulated evidence that personnel with limited training can provide many family planning services, too much reliance is still placed on the use of physicians and paramedical personnel. Highly trained personnel are scarce and their number cannot be increased quickly. Delivery systems can and should be designed to include easily trained auxiliaries and lay persons so as to enable programs to expand, while retaining medical supervision where needed.

The present technology is far from adequate yet there is too little support of research. While no "optimal" technique of fertility control may be in sight, there is considerable scope for improving present methods. Given the importance of the problem to the world, total public funding of contraceptive research of approximately $60 million annually is grossly inadequate. Moreover, too little account is taken of the relative effectiveness of present techniques. For example, sterilization is many times more effective than other means, but few programs offer it and too often it is available only to those who can afford private care.

4

The precise impact of family planning programs on fertility and family size is still a matter of uncertainty. In some cases, the programs are too young to assess their effectiveness; in others, it is difficult to disentangle the effects of changing socio-economic conditions. Continuing evaluation of the effectiveness of present efforts must be a feature of all projects and programs. However, there is little doubt that well-run family planning programs are an essential element in any national fertility control program.

The analysis of population policies and programs in this report was prepared for internal use as part of the World Bank's effort to define better the relationship between population growth and development, the impact of higher incomes on fertility, and the motivational and operational issues which seem to limit the effectiveness of family planning programs. This evaluation is essential both to the Bank's own activities and to our understanding of the longer-term social and economic prospects for developing countries. The importance of the two-way relationship between population growth and poverty reinforces one of the major objectives of the Bank's overall lending program, which is to direct an increasing part of Bank Group lending towards raising the productivity and living standards of the poorest members of the population. Because of the special interest in this subject during the World Population Year, the report is being published and made available to a wider audience.

Robert S. McNamara
President
International Bank
for Reconstruction and Development

Chapter 1

RECENT DEMOGRAPHIC TRENDS AND FUTURE PROSPECTS

DEMOGRAPHIC TRENDS in the developing countries are characterized by two contrasting features. On the one hand, the recent rate of population growth is unprecedented. Within many national boundaries population is already pressing on the margins of available land. Moreover, the current age composition of the population implies a continuing rapid growth for at least several decades, with a world population approaching 6,500 million by the year 2000. On the other hand, there are concurrent signs that, following similar past experience in the now developed countries, some reduction in fertility is taking place in developing countries.[1] This, if strengthened and accelerated by proper policies and programs, holds promise that the alarming demographic prospects may be moderated.

RECENT POPULATION GROWTH

The population of the world is now 3,900 million. It increased by more than 1,000 million people between 1950 and 1970; the increase between 1930 and 1950 was only 400 million. (Table 1.) The rate of population growth has increased steadily to the unprecedented current level of nearly 2 percent per year, which would lead to a doubling of

---

[1] In this report, fertility refers to the frequency of live births in a particular segment of the population observed during a specified period of time (usually expressed as an annual rate per thousand). The *birth rate* is the number of births per thousand persons in the total population; the *general fertility rate* is the number of births per 1,000 women in the reproductive ages 15 to 49; and the *age-specific fertility rates* refer to births per 1,000 women of a particular age or age-group. The total fertility rate is the sum of the age-specific fertility rates and represents the total number of births that a hypothetical group of one thousand women would bear if they reproduce according to a given set of age-specific rates throughout the reproductive years. This is frequently expressed per woman. The *gross reproduction rate* (GRR) and *net reproduction rate* (NRR) are derived from the total fertility rate. The GRR (expressed per woman) represents the total fertility rate in terms of female births alone. The NRR adjusts the GRR for the fact that, in reality, not all women would survive through the reproductive years, and is therefore smaller than the gross reproduction rate. In effect, the net reproduction rate measures the extent to which the female population would replace itself, and the "replacement level" of fertility is given by NRR = 1.

7

Table 1

World Population 1930–2000

	Population (millions)			Years required to double population at average annual growth rate during the period		
Period	World	Developed countries	Developing countries	World	Developed countries	Developing countries
1930	2,044	759	1,285	—	—	—
1950	2,486	858	1,628	71	114	59
1970	3,621	1,084	2,537	32	61	32
1990	5,346	1,282	4,064	35	83	30
2000	6,407	1,368	5,039	39	108	32

Source: United Nations. May 3, 1973. *Demographic Trends in the World and its Major Regions, 1950–1970.* E/Conf. 60/BP/1. Table 1. p. 4. New York City: U.N. Also unpublished population projections. 1974.

the total population within approximately 35 years. The previous doubling took about 50 years; the doubling before that, 110 years.

In 1930, 63 percent of the world's population lived in countries which are currently classified as developing.[2] These countries accounted for 78 percent of the world's population growth between 1930–50, 80 percent of the growth between 1950 and 1970, and are likely to account for about 88 percent of the expected population increase between 1970–90. Although the annual rate of population growth during 1950–70 was twice that during 1930–50 in both industrialised and developing countries (Figure 1), the demographic causes differ. Changes in population growth rates in developed countries have reflected movements in fertility which, in Western Europe and North America, reached their lowest levels in the 1930s, then rose until the late 1950s, and have since fallen again. In developing countries, the acceleration of population growth since 1920 has resulted from a welcome decline in mortality without a compensating fall in fertility.

The recent United Nations projections given in Table 1 envisage some decline in fertility in all developing countries during the next three decades. These declines will compensate for the expected fall in mortality and reduce the annual growth rate from 2.4 percent during 1970–75 to 2.1 percent during 1995–2000.[3] The lower fertility implies

---

[2] In this report, classification of countries into *developing* and *developed* is based on definitions used in U.N. population statistics. Thus, Southern European countries and Argentina, Uruguay, and Chile are classified as developed countries, chiefly because their demographic characteristics are much closer to those of economically more advanced countries than of the countries which are less economically developed. South Africa is classified as a developing country.

[3] The projections assume that GRR (a measure of fertility, defined in foot-

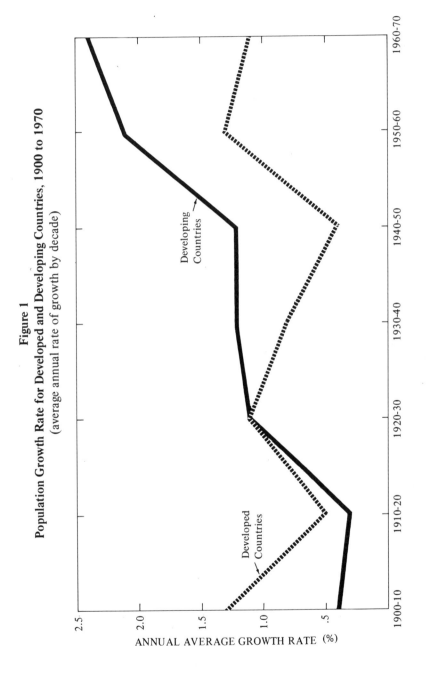

Figure 1
Population Growth Rate for Developed and Developing Countries, 1900 to 1970
(average annual rate of growth by decade)

that the total population of developing countries in the year 2000 would be about 760 million less than if fertility remained unchanged. At the end of the century, the growth rate of developed countries is expected to be 0.6 percent and that of the world as a whole is expected to be 1.8 percent.

Recent population growth has been concentrated in eight large developing countries [4] inhabited by about 1,800 million people representing nearly 70 percent of the population of the developing countries. Although the growth rate of these eight countries has been slightly lower than that of the rest of the developing world, these countries added nearly 600 million people to the world during the 20 years between 1950 and 1970. Even if their fertility rates continue to decline as expected, these countries are likely to add another 950 million people, contributing 55 percent of the expected growth in total world population during the next 20 years.

Of these eight large countries, only three—Brazil, China and Mexico—have attained death rates below 13 per thousand. Mortality has also fallen in the other five countries, but death rates are still above 16. These death rates are expected to continue to fall; unless fertility also declines, their growth rates could rise significantly.

Vital Rates

In Annex Table 1, countries are classified according to levels of birth and death rates.[5] About 40 percent of the world's population live in countries with both high birth and death rates. The remainder are divided equally between (a) countries which have low mortality but high birth rates, and (b) those which have low birth as well as death rates. No country has a birth rate below 30 and a death rate above 15; it appears that birth rates fall to low levels only after a decline in death rates.

Europe and North America, excluding Mexico, have attained low birth and death rates. In Africa both mortality and fertility continue to be high. In Asia about half of the population is in countries which

---

note 1) would decrease from 1.13 during 1970–75 to 1.10 during 1995–2000 in the developed countries and from 2.60 to 1.89 in the developing regions. The expectation of life at birth would increase by about 2 years (from 71 to 73) in the developed countries and by about 10 years (54 to 64) in the developing countries.

[4] People's Republic of China, India, Indonesia, Brazil, Bangladesh, Pakistan, Nigeria, Mexico.

[5] The relative level of vital rates can be used to assess the stage of demographic transition reached by a country, i.e., how far it has progressed from the high fertility-high mortality situation characterizing the least developed countries to the low fertility-low mortality situation which characterizes developed countries. A further discussion of the conceptual framework of demographic transition is contained in Chapter 3.

have achieved low mortality. Most Latin American countries already enjoy low mortality, and their birth rates are on a downward course; ten of the thirty countries in Latin America have already achieved birth rates low enough to yield relatively low growth rates.

MORTALITY TRENDS AND PROSPECTS

While fertility rates have remained relatively stable or have declined only slowly since 1950, an unprecedented decline in mortality rates has taken place in all developing countries until the current average death rate of the world is about 13 per 1,000 population: 9 in developed and 14 in developing countries. Life expectancy at birth is currently about 71 years for developed and 54 years for developing countries. Annex Table 2 shows how it has risen since the 1930s.

Among developing countries, Latin America has the lowest mortality level; the average death rate in this region is 9 per 1,000, the same as developed countries, and the life expectancy is 62 years. Africa has the highest average death rate of around 20 per 1,000, and a life expectancy of about 45 years. The low death rates in some of the developing countries compared to those in developed countries are partly a reflection of the youthful age structure of the populations of the former and the fact that the high and rising proportion of old people in developed countries limits a decline in death rates, even under the best health conditions.

Infant mortality rates indicate that substantial mortality differences still exist between developing countries where they are estimated to be around 140 per 1,000 live births, and developed countries where they are about 27. The difference in the infant mortality rate alone accounts for as much as 6.4 years of the difference in average life expectancy between developed and developing countries. Table 2 shows infant mortality rates for 111 political entities, where about 64 percent of the world's people live. All but three of the African countries have an infant mortality rate above 100. Twenty-one have a rate above 150. In three countries—Niger, Guinea, and Gabon—the rate is probably above 200. In striking contrast, Sweden, Finland, and the Netherlands have infant mortality rates of about 11–12.

Recent mortality reduction in the developing countries has been achieved principally through low cost, efficient public health and disease control measures which have been largely independent of economic development. For example, significant mortality declines have occurred both in Mexico, which has experienced rapid economic growth, and in Sri Lanka, a country with relatively slow economic growth.

Although disease control will undoubtedly be still further expanded, much of the future progress in reducing mortality will depend on improving socio-economic conditions which govern nutritional standards,

Table 2

Countries by Infant Mortality Rates, About 1972

Infant mortality rate [b]	Number of Countries [a]				
	All regions	Africa	Asia	Latin America	Europe N. America Oceania
Below 25	26	—	5	—	21
25–49.9	27	—	3	13	11
50–74.9	8	2	1	5	—
75–99.9	6	1	—	4	1
100–124.9	11	8	3	—	—
125–149.9	12	8	4	—	—
150+	21	21	—	—	—
	111	40	16	22	33

[a] The 111 countries include only about 64 percent of the population of the world; 69 percent in Africa, 47 percent in Asia, 56 percent in Latin America and 100 percent in Europe, North America and Oceania.

[b] Infant mortality rate is the number of deaths before age one per 1,000 live births.

Source: Population Reference Bureau. *1973 World Population Data Sheet.* Washington, D.C.: P.R.B.

environmental sanitation, and medical care systems. For example, serious obstacles to further improvement in mortality reduction are posed by slow rates of increase in per capita food production in Asia and Africa during the decade 1960–70, and possible declines in food intake and nutrition levels in recent years, particularly among low income groups. It therefore seems quite likely that even very recent projections, such as those in Table 1, are based on assumptions on the course of mortality in developing countries which may prove over-optimistic.

RECENT FERTILITY TRENDS

The principal determinant of future population growth is the birth rate. Table 3 shows the small but steady decline in the birth rate that has taken place in developed countries since the 1930s, and in the developing countries since about 1960.

The most conspicuous demographic difference between high income countries and low income countries is in the level of fertility. The average birth rate shown in Table 4 and Annex Table 3, and the average gross reproduction rate (GRR) of low income countries are about twice those of high income countries.

Although the current birth rates of developing countries differ by region, they not only are higher than the recent rates of developed countries but also exceed the rates reported by developed countries through-

Table 3
Birth Rates in Developed and Developing Countries, 1935–1970

	Birth rate per 1,000 population				
	1935–1939	1950–1955	1955–1960	1960–1965	1965–1970
WORLD TOTAL	34–38	36.7	36.4	35.1	33.8
Developed regions	24.9	22.9	21.9	20.5	18.6
Developing regions	40–45	43.9	43.6	42.0	40.6

Source: Annex Table 3.

Table 4
Vital Rates by Per Capita GNP

Income range (U.S. dollars)	Average income (U.S. dollars)	Birth rate	Death rate	Rate of natural increase	Percent of total population
		Per 1,000 population			
0–299	136	38.9	16.3	22.6	58.8
300–599	374	41.4	13.2	28.2	8.9
600–899	695	33.3	10.9	22.4	3.7
900+	2561	17.3	9.1	8.2	28.6
All incomes	873	33.0	14.0	19.0	100.0

Source: Population Reference Bureau. *1973 World Population Data Sheet.* Washington, D.C.: P.R.B.

out the last 150 years. Towards the end of the last century, the average birth rate of Europe was about 35; around 1800, it was probably not more than 39. The main reasons for the difference are the relatively early age at marriage and the near universality of marriage in most developing countries.[6] The dramatic differences between developed and developing countries are shown in Table 5. The average age at marriage of females in the Asian developing countries around 1960 ranged from less than 16 to nearly 23 years. In Europe around 1900, the age of marriage was between 25 and 29 years, and about 10 to 20 percent of European women remained unmarried throughout their reproductive years. In developing countries, the corresponding proportion of unmarried women has been less than 4 percent. (Table 6.)

[6] According to Hajnal, "the marriage pattern of most of Europe as it existed for at least two centuries up to 1940 was, so far as we can tell, unique or almost unique in the world. There is no known example of a population of non-European civilization which has had a similar pattern. . . . The distinctive marks of the 'European Pattern' are (1) a high age at marriage and (2) a high proportion of people who never marry at all." (Hajnal 1965. p. 102)

13

Table 5

Average Age of Females at Marriage in Selected Countries

Asian countries	Year	Age	European countries around 1900	Age
Sri Lanka	1963	22.1	Denmark	24.9
Taiwan	1956	21.1	England and Wales	25.5
India	1961	15.8	France	22.9
Iran	1966	18.5	Iceland	28.7
Korea, Rep. of	1960	21.3	Netherlands	25.4
Malaysia (West)	1957	18.4	Norway	26.9
Nepal	1953	15.0	Sweden	26.3
Pakistan	1961	15.9	Austria	26.2
Philippines	1960	22.2	Germany	25.0
Thailand	1960	22.0	Ireland	27.4

Sources: International Institute for Population Studies. October 1969. *Newsletter.* No. 30. Bombay.

Hajnal, J. 1965. European Marriage Pattern in Perspective. In *Population in History.* Eds. D. V. Glass and D. E. C. Eversley. Chicago: Aldine Publishing Company.

Hajnal, J. 1953. Age at Marriage and Proportion Marrying. In *Population Studies.* Vol. 7.

Bogue, D. J. 1969. *Principles of Demography.* New York City: John Wiley and Sons.

Table 6

Percentage of Never-Married Females in the Age Group 45–49 in Selected Countries

Asian and African countries	Year	Percent	European countries around 1900	Percent
Morocco	1952	2	Iceland	29
Algeria	1948	2	Portugal	20
Tunisia	1946	4	Sweden	19
Egypt	1947	1	Norway	17
Turkey	1935	3	Ireland	17
India	1961	0.5	Belgium	17
Pakistan	1961	0.9	Great Britain	15
Philippines	1960	7	Finland	15
Korea, Rep. of	1960	1	Holland	14
Thailand	1947	3	Denmark	13
Malaysia	1947	1	Austria	13
Taiwan	1930	0	France	12
Sri Lanka	1953	4	Italy	11

Sources: Hajnal, J. 1965. European Marriage Pattern in Perspective. In *Population in History.* Eds. D. V. Glass and D. E. C. Eversley. Chicago: Aldine Publishing Company.

Hajnal, J. 1953. Age at Marriage and Proportion Marrying. In *Population Studies.* Vol. 7.

Bogue, D. J. 1969. *Principles of Demography.* New York City: John Wiley and Sons.

Income and Fertility

The birth rate distribution is highly bimodal, falling in two distinct groups. Countries with a per capita Gross National Product (GNP) below $600 have an average birth rate of 39.2 and a GRR of 2.7; in countries with a per capita GNP above $600, the birth rates and GRR are half this average. The major exceptions are five oil rich countries—Venezuela, Libya, United Arab Emirates, Qatar, and Kuwait with a per capita GNP above $900—and Mexico, South Africa, Gabon and Jamaica with per capita GNP of $600–$900. Except for three countries —Barbados, Republic of China (Taiwan), and Mauritius—no country with a per capita GNP below $600 has a birth rate below 30. Few countries have a birth rate in the intermediate range; most have birth rates above 40 or below 25. Of 150 countries with available data, only fifteen have birth rates in the range 25–34; eighty-two have birth rates of 40 or above; and forty-one have rates of 20 or below.

Apparently, when fertility begins to fall and the birth rate reaches a level of about 35, the fertility decline gathers momentum and the birth rate falls sharply until it drops below 25. If this is a general behavior pattern, it would have considerable significance for those developing countries that have participated in the global trend toward declining birth rates during 1960–70. As shown in Table 7, fertility has declined in rich countries as well as in some poorer ones, in countries with high birth rates as well as in those with low birth rates, and in most countries of Europe and North America, several countries in Latin America, and a few in Asia and Africa. Indeed, the extent of fertility decline in the developing countries included in Table 7 has been greater than in the developed countries. It is impossible, however, to generalize from these statistics because the developing countries, especially the largest, are inadequately represented in the available data.[7]

Demographic Factors Affecting Fertility

Age structure. The principal determinant of a population's age structure is its past fertility. Except for countries which have experienced heavy external migration, drastic changes in fertility rates, or war, classifying countries by age structure is broadly equivalent to classification by fertility. Where fertility rates have been high, the proportion of children will be relatively high and the proportion of older persons rela-

---

[7] The 82 countries with reliable vital statistics have only about one-third of the world's population. They include almost all countries in Europe and North America, 37 percent in Latin America, 19 percent in Africa and 6 percent in Asia. Conspicuous among countries not included are the People's Republic of China, India, Indonesia, Pakistan, Bangladesh, Nigeria, and Brazil, which together account for two-thirds of the people in developing countries.

15

Table 7

Percentage Change in Birth Rates [a]

	Average percentage change in birth rate, 1966–1969	Percent of population
GNP per capita (U.S. dollars)		
$ 0–299	−12.1	3.9
300–599	−8.6	2.3
600–899	−5.6	10.1
900+	−6.6	83.7
All groups	—7.1 [b]	100.0
Birth rate, 1966		
45 or more	−6.7	0.7
35–44.9	−9.3	9.9
25–34.9	−10.2	3.3
Less than 25	−5.1	86.1
All groups	—7.3	100.0
Regions		
Africa	−8.4	5.4
Asia	−4.7	8.3
Latin America	−9.4	10.8
Europe, USSR North America Oceania	−6.3	57.4
All regions	—7.3	100.0

[a] The data pertain to eighty-two populations with reliable vital statistics, comprising about 34 percent of the world's population. See footnote 7 above.

[b] Average for seventy-six populations only.

Source: United Nations. 1966–1971. *Demographic Year Books.*

tively low. In the Philippines, for example, about 45 percent of the population is under 15 years of age; in East Germany, children under 15 constitute less than 22 percent of the total. In Mexico only 3.5 percent of the population is over 64 years; in the United Kingdom, the comparable proportion is 12 percent.

Under normal circumstances, the age-sex composition of a population does not change significantly in short periods of time and, therefore, does not play a major role in changes in birth rate during five- or ten-year periods. Annex Table 4 shows that, for the few developing countries with good data, the influence on fertility of changes in sex-age structure has been most significant in Jamaica during 1960–70, Hong Kong during 1961–65, and Sri Lanka during 1953–63—three countries with small populations and/or considerable external migration. Elsewhere changes in marital status and fertility have been major factors in birth rate declines.

Marital status. Countries with traditionally early and almost universal marriage go through a stage of demographic change when the decline in the proportion of married persons is observed largely among girls 10 to 15 years old. However, since these girls have few children in the early years of marriage, reduction in the marriage rate of 10–15 year old girls has little impact on fertility. But in circumstances where marital fertility is high, increases in the average marriage age can produce significant declines in the birth rate. For this reason, delaying the age of marriage within the 15–24 age group reduces fertility significantly.[8] In developed countries, variations in marriage age are not likely to be significant since contraception controls fertility. In general, the older the average age of the mother at each birth, the longer the average age of each generation. As a result, the birth rate tends to fall, especially during the period of transition from younger to older marriage ages of females. As Annex Table 4 shows, a reduction in the proportion married has been an important fertility determinant in several Asian countries. In Tunisia, the lower proportion of married women in the 15–24 year group accounted for half the decline in fertility from 1965–68. Data are not available for the People's Republic of China, which has reportedly been very successful at promoting late marriage.

Changes in marital fertility. Changes in marital fertility have been a significant demographic factor affecting overall fertility in several countries, and the relative impact has tended to increase where declines in birth rates have continued for an extended period of time. This is illustrated by data on Hong Kong and Sri Lanka in Annex Table 4. In Latin America, most of the observed decline in fertility is attributable to reduced fertility within sexual unions, including both informal and consensual unions as well as marriage, rather than to changes in age-sex composition or marital structure (Conning 1973).

Although with an increase in age at marriage marital fertility is often found to increase in the younger age groups, its effect is not enough to offset the fall in fertility due to a declining percentage of women married. Annex Figures 1 and 2 illustrate the combined effect of marital fertility and the proportion married on age-specific fertility rates in selected countries. In general, fertility declines have been greater at older ages—above 30 years—than at younger ages. (Annex Table 5.)

---

[8] In West Malaysia for example (Palmore and bin Marzuki 1969), the completed fertility of women who married before reaching 15 exceeded by only 0.2 children that of women married between 15 and 20 years, and that of women married above age 20 by 0.8 children. The maximum differential in cumulative fertility between those who married early and those who married later was observed when the latter had been married for only a few years. Over the course of the reproductive span, other factors evidently offset a great deal, but not all, of the fertility effect of earlier marriage.

CITY COLLEGE LIBRARY
1825 MAY ST.
BROWNSVILLE, TEXAS 78520

Population Growth and Urbanization

Many governments regard the spatial distribution of population and especially the rate and pattern of urbanization as their most serious population problem. During the 20 years between 1950 and 1970, the urban population of the world increased by 655 million—almost as much as in the entire previous history of the world. (Annex Table 6.) The average annual urban growth rate was 3.3 percent. Urban growth in developing countries was twice as fast (4.6 percent) as in developed countries (2.3 percent). Rates appear to have slowed down slightly in the 1960s in comparison with the previous decade. By 1970, roughly 37 percent of the world's population, or 1,358 million people, was classified as urban,[9] with the urban population making up 65 percent of the total in developed countries and about 25 percent in developing countries.

Urban growth results from natural increase in urban areas as well as from rural-urban migration. Historically, natural increase, which is the difference between births and deaths, has not been a major factor in urban growth. It has now become more important, especially in countries where the level of urbanization is high. In 1960 the rate of natural increase (2.2 percent) of the urban population in the developing countries was about the same as that of the rural population because the lower urban birth rate was offset by the lower urban death rate. (Table 8.)

Table 8

Urban and Rural Vital Rates

(per 1,000 population)

Rates in 1960	Developed countries		Developing countries	
	Rural	Urban	Rural	Urban
Birth rate	23.3	20.1	44.1	37.9
Death rate	9.3	8.9	21.7	15.4
Rate of natural increase	14.0	11.2	22.4	22.5

Source: United Nations. May 1973. *Demographic Trends in the World and its Major Regions, 1950–1970.* E/Conf. 60/BP/1. Table 12.

Rural-urban migration has been, and perhaps still is, the principal cause of urban growth. Although its relative importance has diminished from 60 percent in the 1950s to 55 percent in the 1960s, the absolute volume of rural-urban migration has increased considerably. Migration added 55 million to urban populations in developing countries in the 1940s, and more than 100 million in the 1960s (United Nations Social and Economic Council 1969). This movement of rural population to

---

[9] Definition of "urban" varies considerably among countries.

urban areas is accompanied by an increase in the proportion of the urban population living in the very large cities.

Urbanization in the developing countries of today differs markedly from similar rapid urbanization undergone by developed countries a century ago. As in the case of mortality decline, the basic difference lies in the relatively weak link between urbanization and economic development. At an early stage of development in now developed countries, the percentage of work force engaged in manufacturing industry was higher than the proportion of population living in large towns and cities. In today's developing countries, the situation appears to be just the opposite. Similarly, major changes in agricultural productivity preceded the growth of the industrial cities in Europe. But in the developing countries at present, food production barely keeps pace with the population growth.

In the developing countries, the rate of natural increase in the urban areas is as high as in rural areas. These rates are almost twice the rate of natural increase in developed countries when they underwent rapid urbanization. Even without any fresh rural-urban migration, the current urban rate of natural increase of 2.2 percent means that the urban population of developing countries would increase by 160 million during 1970–1980. A lowering of both urban and rural fertility rates would not only reduce the urban rate of natural increase, but, by reducing population pressure on arable land, could also slow down rural-urban migration. These two effects could narrow the widening gap between urbanization and urban development.

FUTURE GROWTH PROSPECTS

The explosive population growth potential of current fertility rates may be seen by comparing the population projection in Table 9 for

Table 9

Future Population Assuming Unchanged Fertility Rates [a]

(millions)

Country	1970	2070
Brazil	93	2,121
United Kingdom	56	97

[a] The assumptions about mortality changes are given below:

Country	Expectation of life at birth in				
	1970	2000	2025	2050	2070
Brazil	63	72	75	75	75
United Kingdom	70	75	75	75	75

Source: World Bank projections.

19

Brazil, which has fertility and mortality patterns similar to many developing countries, and the United Kingdom, an example of a developed country.

If current fertility rates remain unchanged and mortality rates fall as generally expected, in 100 years the population of Brazil would increase 23-fold to 2,100 millions, while the population of the United Kingdom would not even double.

Differences in population growth rates between developed and developing countries also reflect differences in age structure and, therefore, both past and current fertility. Even given the impossible—immediate equalization of fertility between both groups of countries—substantial differences in population growth rates would still result. For example, if the current age distribution of the United States were replaced by the current Indian age distribution, and current U.S. fertility and mortality rates were held constant for this new population structure, the birth rate would increase by one point and the death rate would fall by 5 points. Consequently, the growth rate would increase immediately from about 0.9 percent to 1.5 percent. Over the 30-year period, 1970–2000, the United States, with presently projected fertility and mortality rates but still with the Indian age distribution, would have 23 percent more people than is now foreseen.[10]

The same point can be illustrated dramatically by calculating future growth on the assumption that, in each country, fertility rates would decline to replacement level (NRR = 1) immediately and then remain at that level indefinitely. Under such conditions, the total population would continue to grow for about 70 years or more, depending on the current demographic picture, because of the existing built-in momentum for population growth generated by many young people. Population growth would level off at about 70–100 percent above the current population numbers in developing countries, but at only about 5–30 percent above the present population in developed countries. Table 10 compares relative population growth in Brazil and the United Kingdom if replacement level fertility had been achieved in 1970.

The above illustration of the continuation of current fertility rates or an immediate decline to replacement levels shows the two extremes of population growth. Two more likely courses are that the rates of decline in fertility rates depend on their current level [11] or that fertility rates will

---

[10] Similarly, by exchanging age structure with the U.S., the Indian population in 2000 would be 23 percent lower than now estimated for India.

[11] It was observed above that relatively few countries have a birth rate in the intermediate range; most have rates above 40 or below 20. This peculiar distribution could be the result of differential rates of decline in birth rates. The speed of decline in birth rates tends to be slow initially but gathers momentum when the rate declines to about 35, and the birth rate falls sharply until it goes

Table 10

Index of Population Growth with Fertility at Replacement Level[a]

	Year			
Country	1970	2000	2050	2070
Brazil	100	144	174	175
United Kingdom	100	109	117	117

Source: World Bank projections.

[a] The mortality assumptions are the same as in Table 9 above.

decline steadily until they reach replacement level in the year 2000. Although both these assumptions about rates of fertility decline seem optimistic today, the Brazilian population will increase 3.3 times over the next 100 years from about 100 million to more than 300 million under the first assumption, and to 260 million under the second assumption.

Table 11

Percentage Growth of Functional Groups in Brazil and United Kingdom, 1970–2000

(percent)

Groups	Brazil	United Kingdom
Total population	94	11
Pre-school children (0–4 years)	32	—4
School age population (5–14 years)	54	1
Working age population (15–64 years)	125	13
Old age population (65+ years)	177	19

Note: The percentages have been calculated from projections which assume the decline in fertility rates to vary according to the current level of GRR. See footnote 11 above.

Source: World Bank projections.

Table 11 shows the implications of the first assumption about fertility decline for prospective growth rates in the different age groups in the two countries. The expected total population growth over the next 30 years would be 94 percent in Brazil and 11 percent in the United Kingdom. Growth rates of the various age groups would also vary widely. In

below 25. The rate of decline slows down once again when the birth rate is below 20. It is assumed, therefore, that the gross reproduction rate would decline by one percent per year when it is below 1.5 or above 3.0; by two percent when it is between 1.5 and 2.0, or between 2.5 and 3.0; and by three percent when it is at the intermediate level of 2.0 to 2.5.

general, the higher the average age of a group, the higher its rate of growth; thus, in Brazil, while the number of children in pre-school ages would increase by only 32 percent, the group aged 65 and above would increase by 177 percent.

CONCLUSION

The world's population is now increasing at a rate which would double every 35 years. The world will achieve a total of more than 6,000 million by the end of this century.

Most of this potential increase is concentrated in the developing countries which accounted for 80 percent of the increase in world population between 1950 and 1970, and will account for almost 90 percent in the next two decades. Within the developing countries, the People's Republic of China, India, Indonesia, Brazil, Bangladesh, Pakistan, Nigeria, and Mexico account for the bulk of the world's population growth. They now contain 1,800 million people; they contributed 600 million of a total increase of 1,135 million people in 1950–70; even if their fertility rates decline, they will contribute 950 million people in 1970–90.

The rapid rise in world population has resulted from relatively stable birth rates and a rapid decline in death rates. This decline in mortality has been the result largely of public health measures and eradication of major diseases rather than major improvements in living conditions.

The principal demographic determinants of family size—age at marriage, the proportion of women married and marital fertility—are at very different levels in the developing countries than existed in Europe as recently as 70 years ago. There is some evidence that these factors are changing and that, in some countries, fertility is declining. Nevertheless, present fertility rates in developing countries have a potential for future population growth that is explosive. The key questions are whether the determinants of fertility can be influenced by specific policies and whether a more rapid decline in fertility can be achieved by effective family planning programs. The urgency of these questions is inherent in both the projected size and geographical distribution of world population and in the effects of high fertility on social and economic development. These effects are discussed in Chapter 2.

Chapter 2

THE EFFECT OF POPULATION GROWTH
ON ECONOMIC DEVELOPMENT

THE RAPID RATES of population growth and the projected total world population may by themselves appear adequate cause for concern. But global aggregates may seem a remote issue for individual nations, and the prospect of overcrowding or the fear of food shortage may appear unimportant in sparsely populated countries. Much of the controversy about the economic effects of population growth has centered on its impact on growth of total or per capita income. This chapter, however, suggests that the effect of population growth on the quality of development—as measured by such social indicators as the number of people who are adequately fed, become literate, share equitably in income growth, and are productively employed—is more important than its effect on the growth of average income.

While the relevance of assessing the effects of population growth on development may be obvious for the heavily populated, poor countries of Asia, the need may appear to be less important for those countries in Latin America or Africa which are not only less densely populated but may also have higher income levels. For all countries undergoing rapid population growth, however, an understanding of economic prospects or the selection of economic policies requires a knowledge of the economic effects of population growth. Even in countries where a larger population may be an explicit national objective, it will, nevertheless, be necessary to assess the cost of achieving that objective against other social goals. In contemporary developing countries, where both incomes and population are growing fast by historical standards and where widespread poverty exists, the welfare of both the existing and projected population must always be considered. As indicated in Chapter 1, virtually no developing country need be concerned that its population will stagnate. Fertility in developing countries is well above replacement levels, and the young age structure provides an inbuilt momentum to keep population growth high for several decades after fertility falls to replacement.

The use of per capita income as a criterion in evaluating the impact of higher rates of fertility on development appears to give equal weight to an increase in income and a decrease in population of similar proportion. A declining population, however, is obviously not a satisfactory substitute for a rise in total income. Although other objectives of modernization and welfare are more or less correlated with income gains, these objectives would not be attained simply by a drop in population size. Reducing rates of population growth is an aid to and a consequence of economic development. But it is not a substitute. In this chapter, the effects of population growth on development are considered only under assumptions of alternative positive rates of growth of both population and income. In these circumstances, per capita income appears to be a widely accepted and commonsense criterion.

Per capita income cannot, of course, be the sole guide to population policy. One limitation is that it ignores the non-economic benefits that children provide for their families. High levels of fertility are the result, to a considerable degree, of deliberate decisions by parents about family size. If parents also bore the full costs of having children, it could be argued that the lower per capita income in the family is voluntarily accepted in return for the benefits and pleasure that children provide. Some of the costs of children, however, are met through public expenditure. Other costs are borne by members of the same generation competing for educational opportunities, land or jobs. Eventually, similar costs will also be imposed on members of future generations, whose numbers will be affected by current patterns of fertility.

Population growth in one economy might be lower than in another because of differences in mortality or in fertility or both. In the following analysis, only differences in fertility are considered. It is true that in many countries mortality also remains a variable, and that governments can devote more or less resources to trying to accelerate mortality decline. In general, however, mortality reduction is a common objective. Differences in mortality between developed and developing countries are greatest at young age groups; it is probable that, in developing countries, the economic effect of a reduction in mortality would be largely similar to an increase in fertility—at least in the short run. This is not the full story, however. There is evidence that such changes in mortality and fertility are causally interrelated and to some extent will take place in the same direction. This interrelationship is discussed in Chapter 3.

ECONOMIC EFFECTS OF POPULATION GROWTH

Although rates of population growth and size of the population are related, it is useful to distinguish between their different effects. The issues revolving around population growth rates turn mostly on the fact that in a high fertility society, the age structure will be younger and the demands made upon resources to feed, clothe, house, educate, and equip the increasing numbers, will be greater than in a low fertility society.

Issues of population size involve analysis of the results of the pressure of a larger population on fixed supplies of land and natural resources. This distinction is important because countries which are not "over-populated"—a size concept—in relation to natural resources still must deal with the economic costs imposed by the rate of population growth.

It is important to bear in mind that the context of the following discussion is the present rates of population growth in contemporary developing countries. Sometimes the view that costs are imposed by population growth has been countered with the argument that the continued progress of mankind requires pressures of the sort provided by population growth. For example, it has sometimes been argued that population pressure can stimulate technological change in agriculture (Boserup 1965). At the present time, however, the difficult food supply situation in many countries, massive malnutrition, and several more decades of population growth seem to provide sufficient pressure on agriculture to increase productivity. It has also been argued that the rapid growth of the labor force provides an economic benefit by facilitating adjustment to technological change. New entrants into the labor force may find it easier than older workers to learn and adjust to new techniques of production. This argument may have validity under certain circumstances. But the current youthful age structure and high levels of fertility mean that no plausible rate of fertility decline will lead to a shortage of potential young workers in the foreseeable future.

Population pressure may have sometimes provided a stimulus to aggregate demand; in some economies, this may have served to keep up levels of investment and economic growth. Good government fiscal and expenditure policies, however, can obviate the need to rely on population pressure to maintain high levels of aggregate demand. A population-induced stimulus to investment may have tended to offset adverse effects of population growth on development in the past, and be one factor explaining why there seems to have been little negative correlation between population growth rates and rates of growth of total or per capita income. In some cases, faster economic growth may have encouraged a decline in mortality, which could also contribute to this lack of a negative correlation. As suggested later in this chapter, the impact of population growth is strongest among the poor who account for a relatively small proportion of total income growth. In any case, the absence of correlation does not establish that population growth is unimportant, but rather suggests that it is only one influence, among many others, on any variable in an economic system. Furthermore, any of the consequences of population growth can be magnified or reduced by economic policies which make it difficult to distinguish the past economic effects of population growth from those of policy.

Effect of Population Growth on Per Capita Income

It is important to keep in mind the distinction between total income, income per member of the labor force and per capita income. Economies can have identical production structures and the same output per worker and, therefore, the same total output, but have different per capita incomes because of different age structures. Alternatively, the differences between the two situations may result from differences in output per worker; for example, faster growth of the labor force would normally be expected to yield a higher growth of total output, and yet lead to a relatively lower output per worker.

The Dependency Burden

A major reason for expecting a high fertility economy to have a lower per capita income than a low fertility economy is that, *other things being equal,* the proportion of persons of working age will be substantially lower in the higher fertility economy. Data in Annex Table 8 show that in developed countries, the dependency ratio—the ratio of the population under 15 and over 65 to the population in the ages 15–64—increased from 55.0 percent in 1950 to a peak of 59.0 in 1960; it has since declined to 57.4 percent. In developing countries, the ratio increased from 78.7 percent in 1950 to 81.4 in 1960; it has since declined slightly to 80.8 percent in 1970. In other words, the difference between developed and developing countries in output per person of working age is much less than differences in per capita income. For example, the 1970 per capita GNP of Mexico at (US) $668 was 35 percent of that of Japan ($1,910); per person of working age, it was 49 percent or $1,356 as compared with $2,783.

Population Growth, Investment, and Employment

Output per worker may also be affected directly by population growth. First, lower fertility and, therefore, reduced dependency might provide an opportunity for increasing the savings rate and so lead to larger investment and an opportunity for faster growth in total income. Second, slower population growth would affect the composition of expenditure, especially investment and public expenditure. Slower growth in numbers would mean that a lower proportion of this expenditure is required to provide each added person with the average amount of physical capital and social services and so more is available to increase the amount per person. For example, a lower proportion of investment could go to equipping new workers, thus permitting an increase of capital per worker. Less education expenditure would be needed to maintain minimal education standards per child; more could go to improving standards. Third, the rate of growth of labor force, together with the volume and composition of investment, will affect the pattern of employment and amount of unemployment, and also wage levels and the distribution of income.

Population Growth and Personal Savings

The proportion of its income that an economy diverts from consumption and uses for savings and investment is determined simultaneously by the activities of both savers and investors. Any effect of population growth on savings is on the potential for savings and investment. The simplest view is that by lowering the dependency burden, lower fertility frees resources from use in child support for use in investment.

This plausible effect of reduced fertility is supported by a study for the United States (Eizenga 1961) which showed that, for individual families, savings significantly diminished as family size increased. The evidence, however, is insufficient to establish that this relationship holds true for developing countries. Moreover, the relationship ignores other demographic factors such as the rising proportion of retired people with lower fertility. Although *numerically* this increase does not offset fully a drop in the number of children, each retired person is likely to be a more important source of dissaving than a child.[1]

The fact is that relatively little is known about household savings behavior in developing countries. Consequently it is not possible to be definite about the impact of population growth on such behavior. It is possible that households which do the most saving are not representative of the general population; they may be more forward-looking and more ambitious, and already inclined to have fewer children. Some savings theories emphasize the source of income—as distinct from level of income—as an important determinant of the amount saved on the assumption that income derived from profits is more likely to be saved than income from wages or rents. A study of personal savings in several Asian countries suggested that the marginal propensity to save out of profits was much higher than that out of employment income (Williamson 1968). As discussed later in this chapter, labor force growth is likely to

---

[1] A cross section study by Leff (1969) examined the association between aggregate as well as per capita savings ratios on the one hand, and on the other, the young and old-age dependency, both separately and together, in forty-seven developing countries, twenty developed Western countries, and seven East European countries in 1964. The investigator concluded that the dependency ratios have "a statistically distinct and quantitatively important influence on aggregate savings ratios" in all the countries and also within the two groups of developed and developing countries considered separately. It appears, however, that eliminating four rather demographically atypical countries—Israel, Puerto Rico, Spain and Greece—would substantially reduce the significance of the correlation (Bilsborrow 1973). A more satisfactory cross-section approach needs to recognize that savings and investment are simultaneously determined. Econometric techniques to try to take this into account involve some cost in precision.

have the effect of lowering wages per worker relative to profits and rents. But since, in this case, the number of workers will be larger, it is not clear in what direction, if at all, the relative shares of wages, rents, and profits in total income would change in response to different rates of labor force growth. But even if more were known about household savings behavior, conclusions about levels of national savings and investment would still be difficult to reach, since households usually provide only a relatively small share of total savings. Governments and corporations are frequently more important savers.[2]

The Composition of Expenditure

Through its effects on both total and per capita income, population growth affects the pattern of demand and hence investment. On balance, lower per capita incomes are likely to lead to relatively more expenditures on food, which is produced under conditions of diminishing returns—i.e., additional labor and capital provide diminishing increments to output as land is farmed more intensively—and relatively less on manufactured goods where economies of scale are more important. It has sometimes been argued that population growth may be needed to provide a satisfactory market for some industries producing at optimum scale, or at least to permit a reasonable degree of competition among a sufficient number of efficient firms. Fortunately, as the economic success of countries like Luxembourg, Norway, and Hong Kong demonstrates, opportunities for international trade prevent this from being a serious handicap to development. Even domestically, market size is more a question of aggregate income than population size.

The more rapidly a labor force grows, the more investment will be required to maintain the average capital stock per worker, allowing less of an increase in capital per worker and thereby dampening the growth of productivity. This phenomenon is sometimes described as capital "widening" rather than "deepening." Some idea of the importance of this effect for investment in physical capital is given in Table 12.[3] The

---

[2] In seven out of the eleven Latin American countries for which a comparison was possible, government savings—excluding public corporation savings—exceeded household savings, including unincorporated enterprises, averaged for each country for six- to ten-year periods between 1955 and 1967 (King 1971). Corporate savings, public and private, exceeded households savings in six out of eleven countries. In four out of ten countries, household savings were more important than the total of corporate plus government savings.

[3] The concept used in Table 12 is the "demographic investment" of Sauvy (1969). This is not quite the same as the investment needed for capital widening, which strictly speaking should be the investment needed to keep the capital-labor ratio constant. Because of changing participation rates and arbitrary definitions of labor force, this number is more difficult to calculate than demographic

Table 12
Percentage of Fixed Capital Formation Required to Maintain Current Level of Per Capita Income

Country/Region	Rate of population growth 1965–70	Required demographic investment[a] Percent of GDP	Rate of fixed capital formation 1966–68	Demographic investment as percent of fixed capital formation
Developing countries	2.4	7.2	17.4	42.5
India	2.6	7.8	16.5	47.3
Indonesia	2.9	8.7	8.8	98.9
Brazil	2.8	8.4	17.2	48.8
Bangladesh	3.0	9.0	12.3[b]	73.2
Pakistan	3.2	9.6	14.3[c]	67.1
Nigeria	2.5	7.5	12.3	61.0
Mexico	3.4	10.2	15.6	65.4
Developed market economies	1.0	3.0	24.0	12.5
France	0.9	2.7	25.4	10.6
West Germany	0.6	1.8	24.3	7.4
Japan	1.1	3.3	32.9	10.0
United Kingdom	0.5	1.5	19.0	7.9
United States	1.1	3.3	16.7	19.8

[a] Demographic investment is defined as that part of capital formation which is required to maintain the current level of per capita income, with assumed incremental capital output ratio of 3.0.

[b] The figure is an average for the three years 1966–67, 1967–68, and 1968–69, calculated on the basis of current prices.

[c] The figure represents an average for 1969–70 and 1970–71, and shows fixed capital formation as percentage of gross national product at current market prices.

Sources: United Nations. 1973. *World Population Prospects as Assessed in 1968.* New York City: U.N.

United Nations. 1971. *World Economic Survey, 1969–1970; The Developing Countries in the 1960s: The Problem of Appraising Progress.* New York City: U.N.

estimates, based on an assumed capital-output ratio of 3.0, suggest that the proportion of investment needed to keep the ratio of capital per person constant averaged 42.0 percent for the developing countries as a group.[4] For the eight largest countries, it ranged from 47.0 percent for India to nearly 99.0 percent in Indonesia. Demographic investment is a much smaller proportion of total investment in developed countries.

investment in Sauvy's sense and for countries where there has been no marked change in fertility, the estimates should not be very different.

[4] The estimates would, of course, vary according to the assumptions about the value of the incremental capital-output ratio, which depends on the pattern and productivity of investment and which varies from country to country as well as over time. But the incremental capital-output ratios in eighteen developing countries during 1965–1968 have averaged about 3.0 (United Nations 1971, p. 81).

Assuming a similar capital-output ratio, the equivalent figure for most major developed countries was only 7 to 10 percent, except in the United States where it was almost 20 percent.

The effect of population growth in requiring capital widening rather than deepening extends well beyond conventional investment. It also means that resources committed to human capital, such as in education, nutrition, and other health expenditures, must be spread more thinly over growing numbers of people. Population growth also creates substantial additional demand for infrastructure investments, particularly housing. Less investment or public expenditure per person may not mean that each person gets proportionately less; it may mean that distribution of expenditures is less even. One consequence can be high levels of unemployment, illiteracy, and malnutrition among the poor. Inequalities thus created can be a manifestation of the effect of population growth on income distribution, discussed later in this chapter.

Education. In most developing countries, education is the most important item of public expenditure on human capital. The following illustration of the effects of population growth on educational growth could readily be extended to other social services. Most developing countries have set ambitious educational targets that reflect both earlier neglect and rising levels of public demand for education. As a result, educational expenditures in most countries have increased as a proportion of total public expenditure. School and university enrollments at all levels, especially at higher ones, have grown considerably faster than population growth. For example, in India the proportion of the appropriate age group enrolled has doubled since 1950 for lower primary schools, tripled for higher primary, quadrupled at the secondary level, and has gone up eight times at the university level. In Mexico during the 1960s, primary enrollment rose by 6.5 percent per year, secondary enrollment by 16.3 percent a year and university enrollment by 7.8 percent. In much of Africa, enrollment growth rates have been even greater. Unfortunately, this expansion of enrollments has often been achieved at the expense of the quality of education, and high dropout rates.

Despite this rapid expansion in the student population, high population growth rates have meant that the demand for education has still frequently gone unsatisfied and that educational targets have not been met. A good example is the fact that illiteracy, which has fallen in proportionate terms, has risen in absolute numbers. For developing countries as a whole between 1960 and 1970, illiteracy fell from about 50 percent to 40 percent for males over 15 and from almost 70 percent to 60 percent for females. (Annex Table 7.) The absolute number of illiterates, however, rose from 295 million to 306 million males and from 406 million to 450 million females. The costs of illiteracy are to be found not only in the missed opportunities for the affected individuals but in its effects on fertility. For reasons discussed in Chapter 3, the level of a woman's education appears to be an important element determining her fertility. In a sense, therefore, the high fertility-high illiteracy pattern is a self-perpetuating cycle that is being overcome only very slowly.

Another way to illustrate the implications of alternative rates of population growth for educational progress is to estimate the likely savings in expenditure from reduced fertility and a smaller number of children of school age. Under two plausible assumptions about the decline in fertility, the population in ages 6–14 in developing countries in the year 2000 is likely to be between 70 percent and 79 percent of the level it will be if fertility does not decline. (Table 13.) A growth in school enrollment and expenditure that could provide full enrollment of this age group under a low fertility assumption would provide only 89 percent enrollment under moderate fertility assumptions, and 70 percent with no decline in fertility at all.

The available data for 1969–1970 on public expenditure for primary education in developing countries indicate an average annual per pupil

Table 13

Children Ages 6–14 in Developing Countries Under Alternative Fertility Trends

millions

| Year | Population Projection With | | |
	Low [a] fertility	Moderate [a] fertility	Constant fertility
1970	560.7	560.7	560.7
1980	698.1	708.0	712.5
1990	829.6	885.8	971.9
2000	934.9	1,046.7	1,331.0

Likely Savings in Expenditure on Primary Education at Per Pupil Cost of $18.00
Compared with Constant Fertility
(millions of U.S. dollars)

1970–80	1,296	405
1980–90	14,103	8,154
1990–2000	48,456	33,336

[a] Based on U.N. population projection series, moderate fertility implies a drop in fertility of approximately 27 percent between 1970 and 2000. The low fertility series implies a decrease of approximately 37 percent.

Sources: United Nations. 1974. United Nations Population Projections. Unpublished.
United Nations. 1973. *UNESCO Statistical Yearbook: 1972.* Paris: U.N.
United Nations. 1971. *World Economic Survey, 1969–1970; The Developing Countries in the 1960s: The Problem of Appraising Progress.* New York City: U.N.

cost of $18.[5] Inflation has probably raised this figure, and further increases are unavoidable. Even according to this cost figure, a moderate decline in fertility implies savings of the order of about $400 million during 1970–1980, $8 billion during 1980–1990 and $33 billion during 1990–2000 (at constant prices) compared with constant fertility, if full enrollment were achieved throughout each period. With a rapid movement towards low fertility, the savings of course would be much larger.

Employment. Lower infant and child mortality during the late 1940s and 1950s has resulted in significant increases in the growth rates of the working age population during the 1960s. Since the young people who will enter the labor force during the 1970s and the 1980s are already born, continuing rapid growth in the labor force can already be foreseen for the next two decades. Declines in mortality and morbidity also serve to lower the rates of withdrawal from the labor force, and thus slow down the rate of turnover.

Table 14 shows the estimates of the labor force for the developed and developing countries of the world, by sex, for the period 1950–70 with

Table 14

Size of Labor Force in the Developed, Developing, and All Countries of the World, 1950–1970, and Projections Up to 2000

	World labor force (millions)	Developed countries labor force (millions)	Developing countries labor force (millions)
Total			
1950	1,066.8	392.2	674.6
1970	1,500.8	487.8	1,012.9
1990	2,115.0	588.0	1,527.0
2000	2,528.0	627.0	1,901.0
Male			
1950	725.8	249.2	476.6
1970	981.8	301.1	680.6
1990	1,410.0	361.0	1,049.0
2000	1,686.0	380.0	1,306.0
Female			
1950	341.0	143.0	198.0
1970	519.0	186.7	332.3
1990	705.0	227.0	478.0
2000	842.0	247.0	595.0

Source: Annex Table 10.

---

[5] The figure is based on UNESCO data for sixty-six developing countries accounting for about 55 percent of the total population of such countries. The costs in national currencies have been converted into dollars at prevailing exchange rates.

projections up to year 2000. Growth has been, and will continue to be, much faster in developing than developed countries. The estimates are affected by the difficulties of measuring of the labor force, which are particularly acute for females in developing countries. The very large increase in the size of the female labor force in developing countries during the decade 1950–60 is partly due to changes in definition of the labor force used in censuses, but even in the developed countries, the female labor force seems to have grown faster than the male in both the 1950s and 1960s, due to rising female participation rates.

Two questions are of particular interest. The first is the extent to which a structural shift from agricultural to non-agricultural occupations has been occurring. Past experience of the developed countries, where the proportion of food in total consumption and raw materials in total output declined as development progressed, has led many planners in developing countries to expect a decline first in the *proportion* of agricultural workers and then in the *numbers* of agricultural workers. The arithmetic of an absolute decline in agricultural workers under conditions of fast population growth has not always been fully appreciated. In a country where 65 to 70 percent of the workers are engaged in agriculture, and the labor force grows by 2 percent, non-agricultural employment opportunities would have to grow at a rate of about 6 percent to absorb the full growth of the labor force. For densely populated countries, the implications of this are serious: unless non-agricultural employment grows very fast, pressure on land is bound to increase. The second question is related to the first: to what extent has the rapid labor force growth created by conditions of high fertility manifested itself in unemployment or underemployment, and what does this imply for future employment? Despite growing concern over the problem of unemployment, information on its extent remains fragmentary.

In Latin America, the structure of employment shows clear evidence of a decline in the proportion engaged in agriculture from 54.1 percent in 1950 to 46.1 percent in 1965, but a decline in the absolute number of workers in agriculture has not yet occurred. The average annual rates of increase in labor force, employment, and unemployment during 1950–1960 are estimated to have been 2.8, 2.4 and 8.0 percent, respectively. The number of unemployed is estimated to have increased from 2.9 million, or 5.6 percent of the labor force, to 6.3 million or 9.1 percent (Organization of American States 1971). Both unemployment and underemployment have probably increased since 1960. Unemployment rates in some Caribbean islands are very high indeed. The 1971 census for Trinidad and Tobago showed island-wide unemployment for both men and women to be 22 percent of the labor force. In the age group 14–19, 65 percent of boys and 64 percent of girls were out of work.

For those aged 20–24, unemployment was 35 percent and 29 percent respectively.

In South Asia the proportion of workers engaged in agriculture had either increased or changed very little.[6] The rate of growth of non-agricultural employment opportunities appears to have been far too slow to lead to any change in the industrial structure of the labor force.

In Southeast Asia, few countries had significant structural changes in employment patterns in the 1950s. But in the 1960s, five countries— Republic of Korea, Thailand, Taiwan, West Malaysia and the Philippines—had an average employment growth in manufacturing of 5.8 percent per year, and in the service sectors of 4.0 percent, which appears to have been much faster than in agriculture (0.9 percent) (Oshima 1971, p. 68). For most countries in Asia, open unemployment is relatively low, though there are exceptions (Annex Table 9). Underemployment, manifested in occupations that provide only intermittent work and very low incomes, is a more serious problem.

What is the contribution of population growth to the employment problem? Slow employment growth in non-agricultural activities and high levels of unemployment reflect economic policies as well as population growth. In many countries, industrialization and trade policies have combined to favor capital-intensive manufacturing activities to replace imports. The capital-labor ratios of new investment have often been disturbingly high. Agriculture has often been relatively neglected; possibilities for public works have frequently been ignored. Such inaction has contributed to rural poverty and high rates of migration to the city, which have worsened the urban employment situation. In addition, urban unemployment, which often is higher than rural unemployment, is often a consequence of an excessive disparity between incomes earned in rural and urban areas. Appropriate policies might reduce this disparity. For example, some of the open unemployment, especially among the well-educated, appears to reflect a reluctance to accept prevailing wage rates. In some countries, including some of the largest with the most severe underemployment, better economic policies might have increased rates of economic growth and so improved the absorption of labor.

Nevertheless rapid population growth makes an inevitably difficult task much harder. Although their labor force is often growing more than twice as fast, investment per worker in developing countries is often less than a tenth of that in developed countries. Their investable

---

[6] Findings are based on the censuses of 1946–1966 in Sri Lanka, India, Nepal and Pakistan. The extremely slow pace of urbanization in Sri Lanka and Bangladesh provides indirect evidence of the absence of any diversification in employment structure; for India, the evidence is based on the results of successive censuses as well as the 21st Round of the National Sample Survey, 1966–1967.

resources per new member of the labor force may be only 5 percent or less of those in developed countries. Since alternatives to the technology employed in developed countries in many activities, especially in manufacturing, may be very limited, it is not surprising that the growth rates of the labor force offer a challenge that few policymakers have so far successfully met.

Future prospects are not reassuring. Labor force growth rates in developing countries will increase slightly over the remaining decades of the century; in absolute numbers the annual increments to the labor force will rise sharply. By 1990, the annual increase will be more than twice the 16–18 million that have been added to the labor force each year for the past two decades. (Annex Table 10.) It is to be hoped that the greater attention now being paid to the problem will lead to considerable improvement in policies. Nevertheless it is clear that the absolute numbers in agriculture in many countries, including the most densely populated countries, will continue to rise, thus increasing pressures on land and worsening rural underemployment. Problems of urban unemployment are also expected to become more serious.

In most countries, present high levels of unemployment make it difficult to increase the employment of women in the modern sector. Lower growth rates of working age population would increase the opportunities for this. Women with modern sector employment are likely to have lower fertility than they would otherwise have. As in education, there are elements of a self-perpetuating cycle in the relationship between unemployment and high fertility.

A fall in fertility will not solve the employment problem by itself or for a considerable time. Because of the inevitable lag between a reduction in fertility and any impact on the size of the population of working age, present high fertility is apt to appear unconnected to the employment situation, since their relationship falls outside the normal time horizons used by planning ministries. But present trends suggest it is unlikely that the future unemployment problem will be easier to manage unless labor force growth falls considerably.

The Effects of Population Growth on Income Distribution

The effect of population growth on the distribution of income has been studied much less than its effect on the growth of per capita income. Whereas some people regard the effect of reduced fertility on per capita income growth as ambiguous, there appears to be no explicit dissent from the view that lower fertility contributes to greater income equality.[7]

---

[7] It is sometimes argued that a reduction in population growth might be undesirable because it would also reduce pressures for radical social and political

There are several ways in which a rapid growth of population might generate income inequality. The first and most obvious is through the effects of population growth in increasing the supply of labor relative to other factors of production. To what extent this operates by restraining the growth of real wages, perhaps even reducing them, and to what extent by increasing underemployment, varies between countries. Individuals dependent on their own labor alone will generally be the poor; and so lower labor income implies a less equal size distribution of income. Small farmers receive some implicit rental income as well, but the effect of population growth is to increase the fragmentation of holdings and the extent of landlessness in rural areas, which probably also worsens income distribution.

The association of population growth and income inequality is likely to be accentuated by the inverse association between the birth rate and family income, although this is partially offset by differential mortality, especially among infants and young children. The available empirical data on this subject are very limited. The National Sample Survey in India has tabulated some of its data on birth and death rates according to per capita monthly expenditure of the household. The rates are not standardized for differences in sex-age-marital status composition. In addition, the rates are affected by a significant degree of "recall lapse" because the question pertains to births and deaths during the year preceding the date of interview. The recall lapse is known to be higher with respect to deaths than births, and is probably greater among lower economic strata of the community where mortality, particularly among infants, is high. Yet, the data for urban areas of India for the year July 1960-June 1961 do suggest a sharp inverse relationship between birth, death, and natural increase rates, and per capita expenditure which may be accepted as a proxy for income. (India National Sample Survey 1971). Malaysia's 1970 Post Enumeration Survey shows similar results, also not standardized for sex-age-marital status. The average number of children under age 15 was significantly higher in the bottom 40 percent of the poor households than among the non-poor households in the rural areas as well as in the country as a whole. (Anand 1973).

The inverse relation between the rate of natural increase and the level of income is likely to have been accentuated since 1950. In this period, the increase in the rate of population growth has resulted mainly from a decline in death rates. Reflecting both a reduction in major diseases and

---

change; in other words, things have to get worse before they can get better. A discussion of the extent to which revolutions can be shown to have arisen from worsening income distribution would be interesting, but outside the scope of this paper. It is not a population question at all, but a general argument against all policies which reduce poverty without simultaneously upsetting the political and social structure.

improved public health, the decline in death rates is disproportionate in poorer income groups which, of course, had the highest initial death rates. In addition, higher income groups have already taken a lead in lowering their family size.

The results of an international comparative analysis of the relation between the size distribution of income and fertility are given in Appendix A and discussed further in Chapter 3. Findings confirm the theoretical expectation that high fertility countries tend to be those with less equal distributions of income. Correlation does not reveal what is cause and what is effect. Faster population growth makes for greater income inequality, but poverty itself is likely to encourage high fertility. It is therefore likely that the two are mutually supportive. A recent analysis by Ahluwalia (1974), using international cross section data to explain the share of the lowest 40 percent in different countries, confirms that the rate of growth of population is a significant explanatory variable in determining the degree of inequality in the distribution of income.

Not surprisingly, population growth has similar effects on the international distribution of income. The population in poorer countries has been growing faster. Table 15 shows how different income strata of the world population shared total world income in 1960 and 1971.[8] The proportion of world income enjoyed by the poorest 40 percent of the population has declined from 6.9 percent in 1960 to 5.2 percent in 1971.

Table 15

Distribution of World Income, 1960 and 1971, by Quintiles

	Share of income		Cumulative share	
	1960	1970	1960	1970
Poorest 20 percent	3.0	2.1	3.0	2.1
21–40 percent	3.9	3.1	6.9	5.2
41–60 percent	5.2	4.4	12.1	9.6
61–80 percent	16.9	19.1	29.0	28.7
Richest 20 percent	71.0	71.3	100.0	100.0

See notes and sources in Annex Table 11.

POPULATION, LAND, AND NATURAL RESOURCES

The oldest concern over population growth is whether population growth will outstrip the growth in food supplies. The current global food

[8] An exercise of this kind necessarily involves overlooking several elements which reduce comparability of data, including inconsistencies among sources, alternative methods of national accounting, differences in purchasing power not reflected in exchange rate, et cetera. Country populations have been included at their average incomes; in other words, internal income inequality has been ignored.

situation has rekindled these anxieties. Of course, food production is not the only potential resource problem but its overwhelming importance makes it a useful example of the issues involved. For other resources, income levels are a much more important determinant of demand than the number of consumers. For example, energy consumption per person in North America, Western Europe, Japan, South Africa, and Oceania averages eighteen times that in developing countries. Income levels are also an important determinant of demand for food, especially since as incomes rise, people meet a higher proportion of their new food requirements with livestock products, which require a greater use of agricultural resources. Nevertheless, the population growth component is a relatively large determinant of the growth in demand.[9]

For the world as a whole, food production increased from 1950–70 at an average annual rate of nearly 3 percent in total and almost one percent per person. Though the average annual rate of growth of both food and agricultural production in aggregate terms has been higher in developing than in developed countries, higher rates of population growth in developing countries have meant that the rate of growth of per capita food production has been only 0.6 percent per year compared to 1.6 percent in the developed countries. During the 1960s, per capita food production in developing countries barely increased at all (Table 16).

Table 16

Annual Rates of Growth in Aggregate and Per Capita Food Production, 1950–1970

(Percent)

	Food production	
	Aggregate	Per capita
1950–1960		
World	3.27	1.32
Developed countries	3.18	1.80
Developing countries	3.39	1.02
1960–1970		
World	2.66	0.64
Developed countries	2.61	1.53
Developing countries	2.79	0.19

Source: Annex Table 12.

---

[9] The income elasticity of demand for food in the developing countries as a group is estimated to be about 0.4. (The figure for some of the poorest countries, however, is up to about 0.7). The corresponding figures for the developed countries and the centrally planned economies are placed at 0.25 and 0.14 respectively. (Food and Agriculture Organization 1971. pp. 130, 163, 274.)

Table 17

Contribution of Land Area and Yield to Increases in World Grain Production, 1948–1971 and 1960–1971

(percent of total change)

Region	1948–1971		1960–1971	
	Area	Yield	Area	Yield
World	27.6	72.4	20.0	80.0
Western Europe	3.0	97.0	−2.9	102.9
North America	−50.0	150.0	−34.6	134.6
Oceania	73.0	27.0	118.5	−18.5
Latin America	68.6	31.4	57.4	42.6
Far East	50.0	50.0	41.7	58.3
Near East	77.8	22.2	36.4	63.3
Africa	48.3	51.7	43.3	56.7
Eastern Europe and USSR	10.8	89.2	3.3	96.7
China, People's Republic of	28.1	71.9	21.2	78.8

Source: Food and Agriculture Organization. 1972. *The State of Food and Agriculture*. Rome: FAO.

Sharp interregional differences in the rate of growth of food production were apparent. (Annex Table 13.) Relative to the previous decade, the performance of the African and Near East countries appears to have been particularly unsatisfactory during the last decade. They have not been able to maintain earlier rates of growth of food production. With acceleration of population growth, per capita food production has either declined or remained virtually static. As a consequence, imports of cereals, of which more than 75 percent came from developed countries, increased in the developing countries, of which about a third imported food.

The relative contribution of increases in land area under foodgrains production and increased yields per acre is shown in Table 17. For the period 1948–1971, productivity gains have been more important in North America, Western Europe, Eastern Europe, the USSR, and the People's Republic of China, whereas in most developing countries, expansion of acreage was much more important. Since even with considerable investment, additional land is limited in most countries, future increases in output will be dependent largely on increasing productivity. This is likely to involve an increase in costs.[10]

---

[10] Recent events have also renewed interest in the question of the world's carrying capacity. Sooner or later, the finiteness of the earth will make itself increasingly apparent. This may, however, create problems relating to the environment, to the size and density of settlements or to the availability of fossil fuels long before it does to food supply. There is no consensus on the number of people the earth could support, but it is clearly several times the present number. Colin Clark estimates the carrying capacity of the earth to be nearly 47 billion

Although this in itself is a disturbing picture, it does not reflect the fact that in many countries, present food supplies permit only miserable nutritional levels. Data from the Food and Agriculture Organization (FAO) suggest that nearly four out of five persons in developing regions live in countries where the caloric supply was less than the estimated requirements.[11] Further, these estimates do not take account of the prevailing inequalities of income, which cause wide disparities in caloric as well as protein intake.

The global food situation is important because it greatly affects the conditions under which countries can import food, and also determines whether international assistance can be invoked at times of crises. Obviously, however, the main questions are national concerns.[12] Agri-

people with the American-type of food consumption and forest land requirement and about 157 billion people with Japanese standards of food consumption and Asian standards of timber requirements (Clark 1967, p. 153). A more recent estimate, based on the assumption that about 10 percent of the gross cropped area would be used to grow fibers, beverages and other non-cereal products, suggests that the remaining area would be adequate to provide a "minimum subsistence diet" of 2,500 kilocalories per day for 97 billion people, or an "adequate diet" equivalent to 4,000 to 5,000 kilocalories for about 50 to 60 billion people, provided that cultivation was done with technology and sufficient purchased inputs of production, equivalent to those used in Iowa corn farming (Revelle 1973). These large numbers seem less impressive if it is realized that a continuation of the rates of population growth projected for the period 1970–2000 of 1.9 percent, which assume some fertility decline, means that the total world population would reach a level of 47, 97 or 157 billion in about 130, 168, or 193 years, respectively.

[10] The concept of a nutritional "requirement" is a difficult and controversial one and the FAO concepts used here are not universally agreed upon. FAO data, summarized in Annex Table 14, shows that only twenty-five developing countries, representing a mere 14 percent of the population, had a rate of growth of food grain production adequate to match increases in demand resulting from both income gains and population growth. At the other end of the scale, 16 percent lived in countries with wholly inadequate caloric supplies and food production growing more slowly than population. The majority (61%) lived in countries with inadequate caloric levels, where production was growing faster than population but not as fast as estimated demand.

[12] In contrast to its role in 19th century Europe, international migration can obviously be expected to play little role in relieving population pressure in developing countries. At its peak in 1906–1910, the average annual number of emigrants from Europe was 1.44 million, or about 3.2 persons per thousand population (Kirk 1946, p. 279). If the densely populated countries of the Indian subcontinent were to experience emigration at this rate, the annual number of emigrants during 1970–1975 would average about 2.3 million, which would account for a mere 12 percent of their annual natural increase. But the numbers involved over a five year period (11.5 million) would exceed net migration (10.7 million) during 1950–1970 to the two continents that were net recipients of immigrants—North America and Oceania. Quite apart from the numbers involved, the cultural and racial implications of massive permanent migration from developing to developed countries are likely to make it politically unthinkable.

cultural self-sufficiency is not a necessary aim of all countries, but economic viability demands that countries which are not self-sufficient in food must develop export activities to pay for food imports.

National differences in the effects of population growth on food prospects are greater than in other aspects of population growth. An obvious distinction has to be made between the densely populated developing countries, largely in Asia, and more sparsely populated countries elsewhere. (Annex Table 15.) The nature of the problems of the first category can be illustrated by the example of India. With 0.44 hectares of cropland per agricultural population in 1970, and still very low yields per hectare, India's potential for absorbing the inevitable growth in her agricultural populations appears greater than that of several other countries, especially Bangladesh. There can be little doubt, however, that the food problem is the major manifestation of India's population problem.

Recent growth experience may be a better indicator of what can be achieved in Indian agriculture than absolute measures of population density or current yield. The precarious current situation, aggravated by power and weather difficulties, fuel and fertilizer shortages, means that foodgrains output has not repeated its 1970–71 peak. Yet long run trends in performance are moderately encouraging. Agricultural output rose 3.7 percent a year from 1962–63 to 1971–72 compared with 2.8 percent in the preceding ten years. But during the 1960s, this growth resulted from annual increases in yield of 3.0 percent and increases in area of 0.7 percent compared with 1.6 percent in yield and 1.2 percent in area during the 1950s. Some of the costs of population pressure are being felt in activities which tend to lower productive potential. For example, increasing pressure to encroach upon forests to grow foodgrains or to obtain wood for use as fuel is resulting in soil erosion.

A failure of food production to match population growth over the long run carries two major implications. First, since 70 percent of India's population is engaged in agriculture, mostly in food production, and the proportion is not likely to change greatly in the near future, the absence of self-sufficiency implies very considerable rural poverty. This condition is already acute. Rural wages are very low. They have shown no tendency to rise in many areas, and a possible tendency to fall in real terms. Underemployment is serious. Pressure to migrate to urban areas is considerable, even though urban poverty appears to be at least as bad as rural poverty (Dandekar and Rath 1971). Second, a further increase in rural poverty would mean a very severe disruption of the whole development process. Unless and until major structural changes take place in India's economy, the prospect of India's being able to import food on a significant scale without severe detriment to the rest of the economy is remote. Her exports are too small a proportion, about 4 percent, of total output, amounting to only about 10 percent of the value added in agriculture and less than the annual agricultural fluctuations recently experienced, to offer any possibility of being able to pay for massive food imports on commercial terms. Exports have also been growing too slowly—3 percent a year during the 1960s. Recent growth has been greater and no doubt more could have been achieved by wiser export policies. Nevertheless, the balance of payments has also been very stretched at recent inadequate growth rates.

An instructive contrast to India is provided by Mexico. Many of the same symptoms of population pressure are evident in Mexico, although on a regional rather than a national basis. For many decades, the most populated areas in the center of the country have been characterized by considerable population pressure on land with its attendant manifestations—land erosion, fragmentation of holdings, little further irrigation potential, low real wages with little tendency to rise, and high rural-urban migration. Despite these similarities, however, there are two important reasons why the problem of population pressure is significantly less serious in Mexico than in India. First, her uncultivated potential is higher. Thirty years of attempts to develop the tropical river deltas of the Southeast still leave this area relatively unexploited. Second, and far more important, is Mexico's potential for importing food. In spite of the substantial effects of the Green Revolution which had earlier made them both appear agriculturally self-sufficient, both India and Mexico have recently been importing foodgrains as a result of poor harvests. Unlike India, however, Mexico can face the prospect of long-run food importing without undue alarm from the balance of payments point of view. Rapid growth in manufacturing has not only replaced most imports but has led to the development of substantial manufactured exports. Even though exports are only about 8 percent of GNP, these manufactured exports plus Mexico's substantial tourism potential, make export prospects good. There is much less likelihood that population pressure in Mexico will bring other development processes to a virtual halt, as it might in India. Of course, this does not mean that population growth is not a problem for Mexico. As a source of regional inequality, landlessness, and underemployment, its main consequence is its adverse effect on the distribution of income, which is already less equal in Mexico than in many other countries.

The slow growth of food output in Africa in the 1960s is a reminder that it may be difficult for food supplies to keep pace with population even in sparsely populated countries. Many African countries have densely populated regions, and tribal restrictions which limit access to land. In several countries, the problems of population pressure on land are plainly unimportant, both for the country as a whole and for many individual families. Elliot (1973) observes that for subsistence farmers in Zambia, the area of food crops cultivated by a household rises with family size, and especially with the availability of female labor. But even if the subsistence sector is able to absorb growing numbers without serious erosion of income levels, it does not provide the growth in agricultural output needed to feed increasing numbers in urban areas or meet the growth in demand due to rising incomes.

CONCLUSIONS

Population growth interacts with the economic growth process in a great number of ways. It may reduce the level of savings and investment. The investment that does take place must go to educate and equip a growing labor force, at the expense of raising educational standards or productive capacity per worker.

It is often difficult to disentangle the effects of population growth from the many other influences on economic growth. With hindsight, it often appears that wiser policies might have overcome some of the problems which are often attributed to population growth. Nevertheless, population growth has certainly made many problems harder to solve. Though it has sometimes been suggested that population growth imparts a needed pressure for change and a youthful vigor to the population, this hardly seems relevant in the case of such rapid growth in population and very young age structures now common in developing countries.

For many countries population growth appears to affect the rate of growth of average per capita income less than the quality of the development process. Population growth contributes significantly to inequality. It has made social targets, such as universal literacy or full employment, much harder to attain and slowed down improvements in health and nutritional standards. It diminishes an individual's chances for education and, in the competition for entry into the educational system, children from poorer backgrounds do relatively badly. When opportunities for productive employment are limited, again the poor suffer. In many countries, population growth has started to push against the limits to cultivable land, leading to smaller holdings and perpetuating rural poverty and malnutrition. Those who leave rural areas for the cities increasingly find urban underemployment and wholly inadequate shelter and other amenities.

Population growth is an important cause of poverty. Chapter 3 discusses the evidence for believing that population growth is also an outcome of poverty.

Chapter 3

THE EFFECT OF ECONOMIC DEVELOPMENT ON FERTILITY

COUNTRIES AT A LOW LEVEL of economic development have high levels of fertility and mortality. With the process of economic development, countries eventually pass through a stage of low mortality and continued high fertility to low mortality and low fertility. This process is known as the "demographic transition." Developed countries have completed the transition, whereas developing countries are at an earlier stage of the process. In most developing countries, mortality has fallen but fertility has not yet declined significantly. Consequently, population growth rates are high.

A low level of mortality is desired by all societies; significant reductions can be brought about by public action, such as public health programs and improvements in living standards. In contrast, fertility depends on individual decisions. Indeed, in no country of the world does the level of fertility approximate its possible maximum.[1] A fertility decline occurs only when a significant proportion of the adult population reduces its desired family size.

The question of the speed of transition is crucial to the prospects of the developing countries. In the best of circumstances, the adjustment to lower mortality rates and to economic factors affecting family size will be slow. This slow adjustment and resulting increase in numbers of people are compounded by the population growth momentum inherent in the present age structure of the developing countries. Consequently, a principal policy question is to identify the important factors which would help to hasten fertility decline.

THE DEMOGRAPHIC TRANSITION

The theory of demographic transition has attempted to provide a formalized explanation of changes in mortality and fertility experienced by the industrialized countries. A pre-industrial state of high death and high birth rates was virtually stable with very slow population growth. The socio-economic changes concomitant with the Industrial Revolution

---

[1] This maximum is usually inferred from the behavior of high fertility groups such as the Hutterites, a North American sect who scrupulously observe a religious prohibition against the use of contraceptives.

resulted in a mortality decline. One reason why fertility did not decline concurrently was the time lag between the common recognition of lower death rates and the individual family's appreciation of the significance of the lower mortality and changes associated with industrialization and urbanization. Hence, population grew quite rapidly because of the disequilibrium between birth and death rates. Ultimately, however, fertility did decline to the low level of mortality, and a new demographic equilibrium emerged.

To the demographers of the 1930s, the demographic transition theory seemed to describe the available historical data quite well. England, whose modern economic growth dated from about the last quarter of the eighteenth century, saw its fertility start to decline approximately a century later in the 1870s. Fertility in Sweden, Belgium, and Denmark began to fall around the same time, just after the start of sustained economic development. In the United States, the death rate appears to have declined over the period 1775–1855 and then to have levelled out; both the birth rate and other rough measures of fertility fell throughout the nineteenth century. It was recognised, however, that the theory of the demographic transition did not fit the demographic history of all countries; in France, for example, fertility began declining as early as the late eighteenth century, before much economic development occurred. Nevertheless, the theory was generally accepted as an adequate description of broad trends.

Review of the theory during the 1950s criticised the lack of precision in identifying the factors which reestablished the demographic equilibrium. Doubts were raised whether the classical theory was an accurate description of the European experience. More important, it was questioned whether the experience of the industrialized countries was applicable to non-Western countries. Further analysis of the fertility changes in sixteen European countries at the time when their fertility declines began showed that the ubiquity of the fertility decline in Europe and the diversity of conditions under which it occurred was a far more complex phenomenon than conventional statements of transition theory had suggested (van de Walle and Knodel 1967). Very different packages of social and economic factors appeared responsible for the fertility decline in different countries.

The most recent analysis of demographic change suggests that European countries first experienced a spread of delayed marriage, which lowered the proportion of married people; this was followed by a decline in marital fertility. Three preconditions for the decline in family size were "the acceptance of calculated choice as a valid element in marital fertility, the perception of advantages from reduced fertility, and knowledge and mastery of effective techniques of control" (Coale 1973, p. 15).

Correlates of Recent Fertility Levels

Recent refinements and qualifications to any simple theory of the demographic transition have not destroyed the central conclusion: with a sufficiently advanced level of economic development, fertility does fall, restoring relatively low population growth. The basic question for developing countries aiming to bring about this fertility decline earlier in the development process than it might occur spontaneously is to try to identify the threshold levels of the critical variables which trigger this fall in fertility and to see whether they can then be achieved by policy. A recent study observed that from the early 1920s to the late 1940s, no major country entered the transition stage of fertility—but a growing number now appear to be doing so (Kirk 1971). For this analysis, the "transition stage" was defined as the period when birth rates are between 35 and 25; as noted in Chapter 1, once declining birth rates reach 35 per thousand, they appear to fall fairly rapidly. Using data from Latin America, East and South East Asia, and several Islamic countries, the same study found evidence of fertility decline in all regions. The resulting encouraging conclusion was that the average length of time required for a country to pass through this stage of demographic transition had been greatly reduced, from some fifty years for countries entering the transition in 1875–1899 to half that time, or less, for countries entering the transition since 1950.

In an attempt to identify when rapid fertility declines will start to occur in the developing countries of today, Kirk related birth rates to a variety of development indices including income, urbanization, literacy and newspaper circulation, telephone coverage, and health conditions. For Latin America, 90 percent of the variance in birth rates was explained by these variables, but income and urbanization were not as strong predictors of birth rates there as they were in Asia. Except for the Philippines, all Asian countries which had reached a per capita GNP of $200 were experiencing or had experienced a rapid decline in the birth rate by 1960–64. Fertility decline began at a significantly earlier stage of development in most countries of Asia than in Latin America.

Appendix A, a comparative analysis of sixty-four developed and less developed countries, suggests that the fertility rate is negatively correlated with per capita income, life expectancy at birth, population density, effective literacy,[2] and distribution of income. Of particular interest is the relatively low correlation between income distribution and the level of income and social development. As many economists have noted, countries at higher levels of per capita income tend to have somewhat more equal income distributions. But the tendency is rather weak,

---

[2] As measured by newspaper circulation.

and at all income levels there is substantial dispersion in income distribution. However, the intercorrelations among the level of per capita income, the extent of effective literacy, the expectation of life, and other measures of welfare are all quite high. This illustrates the difficulty in disentangling their separate effects on fertility—a difficulty felt equally in cross-section and time-series investigations. Taken together, however, the independent variables are able to explain about eighty percent of inter-country variation in the general fertility rate.[3]

Income distribution is statistically highly significant and contributes substantially to explaining variations in fertility. One calculation, measuring the equality of income distribution by the percentage of total income received by the poorest 40 percent of the population, found that each additional percentage point of total income received by the poorest 40 percent is associated with a reduction of 2.9 points in the general fertility rate. Each additional year of life expectancy at birth is associated with a reduction in the general fertility rate of 1.9 points. It appears that fertility decline is much more sensitive to changes in income at the bottom end of the distribution than to changes in per capita income.[4] At the top end of the distribution, fertility may even be positively related to income. This is consistent with other research findings on the relationship of income to fertility, and implies that the pattern of income distribution is at least as important as the rate of income growth for the decline in fertility.

Consideration of changes or differences in income distribution thus adds considerably to explaining fertility differences at the aggregate level. Birth rates in Latin America, for example, are higher than would be expected from the level of economic development of the region. Explanations of this phenomenon have included cultural factors such as the "machismo" complex, and religious factors such as the dominant Catholicism. Whatever the importance of these factors, at least a partial explanation seems to be that in most countries of Latin America, the distribution of income is very unequal. Thus the large majority live at low absolute levels of consumption, and display fertility behavior consistent with that level of economic development.[5] In Eastern Europe, by

---

[3] The general fertility rate is the annual number of births per thousand women of reproductive age.

[4] The logarithmic model shows that the elasticity of the general fertility rate, with regard to changes in the share of income received by the poorest 40 percent of households, is 0.36; the elasticity of fertility with regard to increases in average income per capita is 0.20, little more than half as great.

[5] The possible importance of cultural and religious factors is not disproved by this finding. Religious factors, however, have never appeared to be strong enough in themselves to prevent a fall in fertility as part of the demographic transition. In Ireland, where there have been religious taboos on the practice of contraception, and sales of contraceptives were illegal until very recently, the demographic

contrast, birth rates have been found to be exceptionally low for countries at their levels of economic development. A partial explanation seems to be that, in countries of Eastern Europe, measured income is distributed relatively evenly and overall fertility is correspondingly lower.

THE PROCESS OF FERTILITY DECLINE

The mechanisms of control over fertility operate both through the regulation of nuptiality—the timing of marriage and the proportion of women who remain unmarried to the end of the reproductive period—and through the limitation of family size by those who marry.

Age and Incidence of Marriage

As seen in Table 5, the mean female age at marriage in many developing countries is low relative to that observed at an earlier stage of development of the now developed countries. But it has tended to rise in developing countries, as it did in the first stage of the European fertility decline. Similar differences are also found in the proportion of women who remain unmarried through the reproductive period. Around 1960, this proportion among females ages 40–44 ranged from 1.9 percent in the eleven Middle Eastern countries and 1.4 percent in fourteen Asian countries, to 6.6 percent in both Eastern Europe and the English-speaking countries of North America and Oceania, and 11.9 percent in twenty Western European countries (Dixon 1974).

Both the rise in the age of marriage in developing countries, and current differences in proportions of women never-married between developed and developing countries, are consistent with the view that better economic circumstances will be associated with lower marriage. This has been formalized into a theoretical model of marriage as an exchange of services according to which better economic opportunities for women reduce the potential "gains from trade" in marriage (Becker 1973). However, the model does not sufficiently explain recent movements in developed countries or differences between them. Cultural and other factors are also obviously important. In addition, marriage rates in developed countries seem to rise and fall with cyclical economic fluctuations (Kirk 1960); a similar response probably exists in traditional societies. In predominantly rural societies, the availability of agricultural land holdings is often the critical determinant of the rate, as well as age, of marriage. In Cental Java, for example, the age at marriage has been

---

transition has meant a fall in fertility through low rates and late ages of marriage. In contrast, most other countries have experienced reduced fertility largely through a drop in marital fertility.

reported to be strongly and inversely related to the amount of land available for the couple (Sinzarinbum and Manning 1973). In such a setting, an improved economic situation might tend to lower the marriage age in the short run, but economic progress involving change in traditional life styles and values, particularly those which alter the roles of women, tends to raise it.

Marital Fertility

Differences in fertility among societies are greater than differences in the incidence of marriage. They reflect differences in desired family size, which in turn are related to social characteristics and circumstances. Cultural factors and individual tastes are also important; there is substantial variation in fertility among societies at roughly similar levels of development. Without some reference to tastes or fashions, it is difficult to explain such recent fertility movements in developed countries as, for example, the rise of U.S. fertility to a peak in about 1957 and its subsequent fall. Nevertheless, the number of desired children has some broad relationship to the level of economic development.

According to over 400 KAP (Knowledge of, Attitude towards, and Practice of Family Planning) surveys, undertaken in sixty-seven countries over the past twenty years, the ideal and desired family size in the developing countries was about four children. This figure is substantially higher than in the developed countries, where it is between two and three (Mauldin, Watson, and Noe 1970). Of course, responses to hypothetical questions, employing concepts which may be strange or ambiguous to the respondent, may consist of the "socially correct" answers rather than the respondents' own views. This may be the case for KAP studies, especially if there has previously been a well publicized attempt to lower fertility. Yet within any cultural group, KAP responses do suggest a consistent pattern of fertility norms, with a plausible relation with behavior. The number of children born in developing countries usually exceeds the number desired, but the number cited as desired probably refers to surviving children, rather than to the actual number of births.

An alternative approach attempts to analyze reproductive behavior in terms of the roles of parents and children. Raising children involves both economic and non-economic costs. Decisions therefore have to be made on how best to maximize the net benefits from having children. In the course of economic development and modernization, the net costs of children tend to increase for a number of reasons. In a traditional society, motherhood raises the status of young women; and children—particularly sons—assure the parents of continuing financial support in old age and of the fulfillment of certain religious rituals. They are preferred as associates or subordinates in the family enterprise. Children are able to contribute, at an earlier age and with lower formal educational qualifications than in developed countries, to the family's agricultural and other enterprises. Direct expenditures for food and clothing are lower, school attendance is less universal and usually brief, housing costs are less, and children require less supervision within the village. Urbanization—and the shift from family enterprises in agriculture and petty trade or industry to wage labor tend to increase the cost of children, and therefore to lower fertility.

In the course of modernization, there is typically a disintegration of the many-generation, extended family and a corresponding strengthening of the nuclear family centering around parents and children. This makes it harder for parents to shift some of the costs of children to other members of a joint family. It also reduces the likelihood that children can be counted on for support and security in later life, when they have become adults and formed nuclear families of their own. Such changes or differences in the expectation of support from grown children have been found to be related to lower family size and desired family size, especially in East Asian populations where the tradition of filial loyalty to parents has been extremely strong in the past.

Equally, or even more, important is the impact of changes in the role and status of women that accompany economic development. As women become better educated and gain opportunities to work in non-traditional jobs outside the household, their aspirations and preferences shift to activities other than the traditional maternal and domestic roles. Education also affects attitudes toward birth control, if only by making the information about contraception more accessible and may increase the efficiency with which contraceptive methods are used.

More generally, education raises the potential direct economic costs and lowers the economic benefits of children to parents. As school attendance becomes at least customary, if not compulsory, and advantageous for later advancement in the non-agricultural labor market, children cannot contribute to household income by staying home to care for younger pre-school siblings while the mother works. Parents have to make a decision on the trade-off between the number of children and the time and money to be spent on their upbringing. Parental aspirations for their children change as they recognize the scope for improving economic and social status through education. Perception of these possibilities is likely to reflect the degree of economic progress that is actually visible at the family level. For this reason one would expect to find fertility falling most rapidly in those societies where gains in economic development are widely shared. In addition and as would be expected, the higher the level of literacy and school enrollments, the lower the fertility.[6]

Effect of Infant and Child Mortality

Despite the rise in life expectancy during the past quarter century, the developing countries have relatively much higher levels of infant and child mortality than the developed countries. The most extreme differentials are for young children from one-to-five years. Even in a comparatively well-developed country like Mexico, death rates at these ages are fourteen times higher than in Sweden. In many of the poorest countries, the rates are probably from thirty to fifty times the rates of developed countries.

To offset child loss in these conditions, couples desiring a given number of surviving children need more than that number of births. Biological factors also contribute to the association between high mortality and high fertility. A high infant mortality implies a shorter average period of lactation and, therefore, a shorter period of post-partum sterility, so that in the absence of contraception, an additional pregnancy is facilitated. Conversely, high levels of fertility usually mean larger and more closely spaced families, which increases the likelihood of maternal and child mortality.

The factors that determine the demand for surviving children are not well understood; the extent to which couples deliberately or consciously decide to replace a dead child is debatable. It has been suggested, however, that parents do replace lost children. In countries with varying socio-economic environments, such as Bangladesh (1951–1961), Puerto Rico (1950–1960), Taiwan (1964–1969), Chile (1960), and the Philippines (1968), both individual and grouped data show a positive and statistically significant relationship between child mortality and subsequent fertility [7] (Schultz 1973). The relationship was stronger when the incidence of child mortality was related to fertility three to five years later, and somewhat higher following the death of a male child than after the death of a female child (Schultz and Da Vanzo 1970).

---

[6] In the 1960s, the correlation between effective literacy, measured by newspaper circulation per thousand population, and the total fertility rate in sixty-four developed and developing countries listed in Appendix A was −0.81, which is statistically significant. Among developing countries, there were significant differences in literacy rates of females ages 15 and over by fertility level. In thirteen countries with a GRR between 2.00 to 2.49, female literacy rate was 40.1 percent. In thirty-eight countries with a GRR between 2.50 and 3.09, it averaged 31.6 percent. In thirty-four countries with a GRR of 3.10 or more, it averaged 29.5 percent. (United Nations 1965).

[7] The effect was not entirely due to the biological factors referred to above because deaths up to age 5 were taken into consideration.

Not all deceased children can be replaced because of the onset of secondary sterility or because the end of the reproductive period is reached. The expenditures on raising children who die increase the average cost of a surviving child. With a fall in mortality, the expected returns from expenditures on raising children would increase; however, they do not appear to lead to a larger desired number of surviving children. Instead, in situations where child mortality is falling, parents tend to devote more resources to the education and training of their children, and have fewer children—a phenomenon described as substituting "quality" for "quantity" of children (Becker 1960).

A separate parental reaction to high level of infant and child mortality is for each set of parents to anticipate and insure against such losses by having more children than the desired number of survivors. Because all families do not experience high child mortality, the aggregate net effect is to "overcompensate" for the mortality that will actually occur. Overcompensation is even more likely during periods of falling mortality, since there is usually a time-lag in parental perception that children are enjoying an increased probability of survival. At some point, however, as the chances that each child born will survive to adulthood improve, the gap between the desired number of children and the number of births will be reduced.

Observed differences in the desired number of children among different socio-economic groups within developing countries and between the developed and developing countries are consistent with the view that a fall in death rate should be followed eventually by an even greater fall in birth rate and a consequent lower natural rate of increase. Yet, despite the declines in infant and child mortality that have occurred in the developing countries since the end of the Second World War, the fall in fertility in most developing countries has not yet compensated for the decline in mortality. As a result, the rate of natural increase has accelerated. It is impossible to foresee the likely duration of the time-lag, but declines in fertility are already evident in several developing countries and suggest that the others will eventually follow a similar course.

CONCLUSION

Past experience suggests that a "demographic transition" from high to low fertility rates accompanies economic development. The timing and pattern of the transition may have been influenced by local cultural and social factors, but eventually it did take place. Some of the important elements that led to a reduction in fertility in developed countries have already become significant in many developing ones. There have been substantial declines in mortality, although infant and child mortality do

53

remain high compared with developed countries. A mortality decline reduces the number of births required to attain a given number of surviving children. Until this is perceived at the family level, however, population may grow at a faster rate before compensating fertility decline takes place.

With economic development, developing countries are also experiencing slow but significant improvements in educational levels. The effective costs and benefits of children change as employment possibilities for children fall and those for women increase. The desired number of children will also fall as individual couples perceive the benefits of development, and raise their aspirations for their children.

It is not possible to identify precisely the threshold levels of infant mortality, literacy, and industrialization or urbanization beyond which fertility would spontaneously decline. There are signs, however, that the speed of transition in those developing countries where fertility began to decline in the 1950s has been faster than it was in Europe. In most of these developing countries, economic development has meant perceptible improvements in living standards among the poor. In all developing countries, policies which succeed in improving the conditions of life for the poor, and in providing education and employment opportunities for women, are likely to help reduce fertility. An improvement in the welfare of the poor appears to be essential before fertility can fall to developed country levels.

Even in those countries where the fall in birth rates has already started, attainment of replacement level fertility will take several decades and population growth will continue well beyond the point where the replacement level is achieved. In a number of other countries, fertility must be expected to begin to fall in the fairly near future. These include several countries in Latin America where economic development has proceeded rapidly for many years with little impact on fertility, apparently at least in part because the benefits from development have been very unequally distributed. Often, present levels of fertility are very high and the age structure consequently very young. No matter how rapid the fall in fertility will be when it does occur, the eventual size of the population will probably be several times its present levels, and even some of the now sparsely populated countries may feel the pressure of high population densities. Meanwhile, population growth creates a large dependency burden and unemployment, and contributes to the forces making for social and economic inequality.

For many countries, including some of the largest and most densely populated ones, the gap is very wide between present fertility levels and the socio-economic levels at which fertility decline has come about spontaneously elsewhere. Several of these countries also have very slow per capita income growth rates, and if left to its own momentum achievement of lower fertility levels might take a very long time, even if every effort is made to have the poor share in the gains from development. For some countries there is even a serious possibility that the mutually reinforcing problems of rapid population growth, slow economic growth, and inequality of income distribution might prevent a significant fall in fertility from ever occurring without deliberate population policies.

If effective, policies which reduce rates of population growth can therefore significantly contribute to the development of all types of developing countries, even those with incipient fertility declines or rapid economic growth. By hastening the decline, population policies can diminish the effects of rapid population growth in retarding development and accentuating inequality, and thereby advance the date at which countries attain the levels of modernization at which a small family is accepted as the norm. How useful direct policies can be depends on how effective they can be made. The remaining chapters of this study consider the question of what can be learnt from recent experience with population policies.

Chapter 4

POLICIES TO REDUCE FERTILITY IN DEVELOPING COUNTRIES

THE REMAINING CHAPTERS deal with government policies which influence fertility, especially those whose explicit objective is to reduce fertility. Policies of this type are considered to be population policies—deliberate attempts by a government to affect the size, structure, or geographic distribution of the population.[1] Such policies can conceptually be distinguished from the demographic consequences of many other national policies that are undertaken primarily to accomplish other objectives. For example, a family planning program with a declared aim of fertility reduction is obviously population policy. A subsidy to public education may also have demographic effects, but since it is usually instituted without reference to its effects on fertility it is not generally regarded as a population policy.

In practice, it is difficult to make a clear-cut distinction between those measures which influence fertility deliberately and those which influence fertility indirectly through their side effects. In addition, the objective of similar measures may differ between countries. For instance, family allowances in France have been intended to encourage childbearing, while in the United Kingdom, they have been regarded simply as a redistributive measure to help equalize income. Contraceptive sales or advertising may be restricted in one country as a pronatalist measure, and in another, on moral grounds. It is also often impossible to ascribe any dominant single objective to policy measures.

By explicitly considering the population impact of many types of policies, a government may often be able to strengthen the factors which would reduce fertility at little or no additional cost and without hampering the primary objective. The discussion of fertility determinants in Chapter 3 makes it clear that policies to lower the cost of bearing and raising children will generally have a pronatalist effect; while policies which reduce child mortality, provide women with alternatives to motherhood through educational and employment opportunities, and

---

[1] Policies affecting mortality and migration can also influence population size, structure, or geographic distribution and are also population policies, but are not discussed in this study. Sometimes, measures designed to reduce the problems *caused* by population growth are also described as population policies.

assure parents of the benefits expected from children—such as care and security in old age or during disability—will have an antinatalist effect. Not all policies can be readily categorized as pro- or antinatalist. Redistributive measures, including nutrition and child health programs and education, can have both an antinatalist effect by raising the probability of child survival and the level of education, as well as a pronatalist effect by lowering the cost of childrearing. In general, however, the net effect of the incentives and disincentives involved in redistributive measures is likely to be antinatalist: a conclusion strengthened by evidence in Chapter 3 that among countries at similar levels of development, those with more equal distributions of income tend to have lower fertility.

DIRECT POLICY MEASURES

Table 18 presents a continuum of policies directly influencing fertility. They are arranged in order of the degree of compulsion. The most restrictive pronatalist measure—*use of contraceptives prohibited*—is at the head of the table. The most restrictive antinatalist policy—*involuntary fertility control*—is at the foot.[2] Neither of these extremes exists currently[3] although restrictions on contraceptive distribution—such as a ban on sales or extremely strict prescription requirements—are still found in a few countries.

The policy positions noted as *official support of voluntary family planning programs* and *official family planning programs* do not generally derive from objectives to reduce the rate of population growth. Rather these programs usually aim to provide family planning services to those who wish to utilize them, perhaps on the grounds that access to family planning is a human right and that family planning is important to the health of mothers and children.

Family planning programs that place emphasis on national demographic targets and stress the economic benefits to family or nation imply a stronger antinatalist approach and such a policy is classified as *official family planning programs including motivation campaigns*. These programs involve a deliberate government effort to persuade people to change their intended behavior. Chapters 5 and 7 discuss programs to implement policies that fall in this category. Policies which entail *official family planning programs with economic incentives and disincentives* to discourage fertility are discussed in Chapter 6.

---

[2] Abortion policies are hard to classify in this framework and are discussed separately in this chapter.

[3] Prohibition of contraceptive use has appeared on statute books, for example, in some states of the United States before such laws were declared unconstitutional.

Table 18

A Continuum of Population Policy Positions Directly Influencing Fertility

PRONATALIST

Use of contraceptives prohibited
Contraceptive sales illegal
Contraceptive sales allowed, advertising illegal
Pronatalist incentives
    Income tax deductions for children
    Maternity benefits
    Child allowances
    Public housing preferences for large families
    Scholarships

LAISSEZ FAIRE

ANTINATALIST

Official support of voluntary family planning programs
    Cash subsidies to private organizations
    Facilities provided free or at subsidized rents

Official family planning program
    Use of public health services to supply family planning services
    Health advantages advertised

Official family planning program including motivation campaign
    Demographic target
    Use of mass communications, group meetings, home visits, postpartum
        program
    Population education

Official family planning program with economic incentives
    Payments for acceptance (immediate or deferred)
    No-birth/no pregnancy bonus schemes
    Dowry for late marriages
    Scholarships for children of small families

Curtailment of rights and privileges with excess children
    Social security benefits conditional on small families
    Discrimination in favor of small families for public housing
    Curtailment of maternity leave for higher parity pregnancies

Restraints on marriage
    High minimum legal age
    Social sanctions, e.g., housing restrictions, scholarships

Restrictions on number of children
    Marketable licenses to have children
    Social sanctions
    Taxes on children

Involuntary fertility control
    Temporary sterilizing agent
    Compulsory sterilizing agent

Curtailment of rights and privileges will seem more restrictive to most people than the offer of rewards to achieve the same ends. This often depends on the way in which the scheme is perceived rather than because of any difference in operation. If certain rights and privileges have in any case to be rationed, it would be possible to make eligibility for them a reward for desirable behavior, or to withhold eligibility as a penalty for undesirable behavior with an otherwise identical scheme. Taxes on large families also appear more coercive than subsidies to small ones, even if the economic costs and benefits to individuals are no different. If it is the poor whose fertility is affected, taxation to discourage fertility will tend to be regressive—that is, it will redistribute income from poor to rich.

A further degree of restriction, involving legal or social *restraints on marriage* or *restrictions on number of children* would be politically unacceptable in most countries. Only the People's Republic of China has introduced such restrictions on marriage or on the number of children that couples may have, although there the sanctions take the form of social pressures rather than legal restrictions. Many countries enforce a legal minimum age at marriage, but this is primarily in pursuit of other social objectives—such as the right of young people to defer decisions until a certain level of maturity is reached, or protection of the potential health and welfare of a mother and child.

The spectre of *involuntary fertility control* has sometimes been raised as an eventual necessity if current levels of fertility in developing countries do not fall far enough, soon enough. Most countries would find such a policy a politically unacceptable violation of human rights.

NATIONAL POLICY POSITIONS

The continuum in Table 18 is intended to classify individual policies, rather than country positions. Tables 19 and 20 a, b, c use the same continuum to classify developed and developing countries, according to the most restrictive measures they have adopted, consistent with the general thrust of the country's population policies and pronouncements. This classification has an obvious limitation because policies of any country often fall into more than one category and may appear inconsistent, especially in large countries with a multiplicity of jurisdictions. Governments have a multitude of objectives. They may be prepared to make contraceptive services available to individuals as an implicit recognition that family planning is a human right while at the same time maintaining the demographic objective of a larger population; this is not uncommon in Latin America. There may be also a divergence between a government's action and its declarations, especially on so sensitive an

Table 19
Distribution of Selected Developed Countries by Government Policies on Population and Family Planning Activities *

Pronatalist			Laissez faire		Antinatalist	
Sales Illegal	Sales allowed; advertising illegal	Pronatalist incentives	Pronatalist	Neutral	Government support of private programs	Official programs
Irish Republic (FPA 1969)[1]	Argentina (FPA 1966)	Bulgaria (No FPA; u)	Israel (2 FPAs: 1932, 1966)	Austria (FPA 1966)	Australia (FPA 1926)	Chile (FPA 1962; 1966)
Spain	Malta	Czechoslovakia	USSR	Greece	Belgium (FPA 1963)	Denmark (FPA 1955; c. 1966)
		France (FPA 1956)		Iceland	Canada (FPA 1963)	Finland (FPA 1941; c. 1951)
		Hungary		Italy (FPA 1968)	German Federal Republic (FPA 1952)	German Dem. Republic (FPA 1964; c. 1965)
		Romania		Switzerland (FPA 1971)	Luxembourg (FPA 1965)	Japan (FPA 1954; 1952)
				Uruguay (FPA 1961)	New Zealand (FPA 1935)	Netherlands (FPA 1881; c. 1968)
					Portugal (FPA 1967)	Norway (FPA 1969; u)
						Poland (FPA 1957; u)
						Sweden (FPA 1934; c. 1938)
						United Kingdom (FPA 1930; 1974)
						United States (FPA 1917; 1965)
						Yugoslavia (FPA 1966; 1969)

* Dates are given for both the founding of the private family planning association (FPA) and the year in which governments began offering family planning services in their health programs, where applicable.
[1] The law prohibiting the import and sale of contraceptives has recently been declared unconstitutional; controversial legislative proposals were introduced in March 1974 to allow sales to married persons.

Sources: International Planned Parenthood Federation. 1973. Family Planning in Five Continents. London: IPPF.
U.S. Agency for International Development. 1972. Population Program Assistance. Washington, D.C.: Government Printing Office.
International Planned Parenthood Federation. 1969–1974. Situation Reports. London: IPPF.
Robert J. McIntyre. 1973. Pronatalist Policies in European Socialist Countries. General Conference, International Union for the Scientific Study of Population, Liège. University Park, Pennsylvania: Pennsylvania State University. Mimeo.
Bernard Berelson, ed. 1974. Population Policy in Developed Countries. New York City: McGraw-Hill.

Table 20a

Distribution of Selected Developing Countries in Africa by Government Policies on Population and Family Planning Activities *

Laissez-faire

Pronatalist	Neutral	Neutral	Antinatalist
Cameroon	Angola	Mozambique	Burundi
Central Af. Repub.	Cape Verde Islands	Niger	Liberia
Gabon	Chad	Portuguese Guinea	(FPA 1956)
Guinea	Congo,	Senegal	Sierra Leone
Libya	People's Rep.	(FPA 1970;	(FPA 1960)
Malagasy Republic	Dahomey	closed 1971)	
(FPA 1967)	(FPA 1972)	Seychelles	
Malawi	Equatorial Guinea	Somali Republic	
Rwanda	Ethiopia	Namibia	
	(FPA 1966)	Spanish Sahara	
	Ivory Coast	Swaziland	
	Lesotho	Tanzania	
	(FPA 1968;	(FPA 1959)	
	closed;	Togo	
	reopened 1971)	Upper Volta	
	Mali	Zambia	
	(FPA 1972)	(FPA 1971)	
	Mauritania		

* Dates are given for both the founding of the private family planning association (FPA) and the year in which governments began offering family planning services in their health programs, where applicable.

Table 20a (Continued)

	Antinatalist		
Government Support of Private Family Planning Program	Official Family Planning Program	Official Family Planning Program Including Motivation Campaign	Official Family Planning Programs and Stronger Measures
Gambia (FPA 1969)	Algeria (1967)	Botswana (1970)	
Nigeria (FPA 1964)	South Africa (FPA 1932; 1966)	Egypt (FPA 1958; 1965)	
Reunion (FPA 1966)	Zaire (1973)	Ghana (FPA 1966; 1969)	
Rhodesia (FPA 1957)		Kenya (FPA 1961; 1966)	
Sudan (FPA 1965)		Mauritius (FPA 1957; 1965)	
Uganda (FPA 1957)		Morocco (FPA 1971; 1965)	
		Tunisia (FPA 1968; 1964)	

Sources: International Planned Parenthood Federation. 1973. *Family Planning in Five Continents.* London: IPPF.

U.S. Agency for International Development, Office of Population. *Population Program Assistance.* 1972. Washington, D.C.: U.S. Government Printing Office.

International Planned Parenthood Federation. 1969–1974. *Situation Reports.* London: IPPF.

U.N. Economic and Social Council. 1969. *World Population Situation.* Geneva: U.N.

Table 20b

Distribution of Selected Developing Countries in Latin America by Government Policies on Population and Family Planning Activities *

Laissez-faire		
Pronatalist	Neutral	Antinatalist
Brazil [1]	Bahamas	
(FPA 1965)	(FPA 1965)	
Guyana	Bolivia	
	Br. Honduras	
	(Belize)	
	Martinique	
	St. Lucia	
	(FPA 1967)	
	Surinam	
	(FPA 1968)	

* Dates are given for both the founding of the private family planning association (FPA) and the year in which governments began offering family planning services in their health programs, where applicable.

[1] Brazil features some government support, by states, to a private family planning agency.

Table 20b (Continued)

Antinatalist			
Government Support of Private Family Planning Program	Official Family Planning Program	Official Family Planning Program Including Motivation Campaign	Official Family Planning Programs and Stronger Measures
Antigua (FPA 1970)	Bermuda (1937)	Colombia (FPA 1965; 1967)	
Barbados (FPA 1955)	Costa Rica (FPA 1966; 1968)	Dominican Republic (FPA 1966; 1968)	
Grenada (FPA 1964)	Cuba (c. 1964)	Haiti (1971)	
Guadeloupe (FPA 1964)	Dominica (FPA 1973; 1973)	Honduras (FPA 1961; 1966)	
Montserrat (FPA 1966)	Ecuador (FPA 1966; 1968)	Jamaica (FPA 1966; 1966)	
Netherlands Antilles (FPA 1965)	El Salvador (FPA 1966; 1968)	Panama (FPA 1965; 1969)	
Peru (FPA 1964)	Guatemala (FPA 1962; 1969)	Trinidad and Tobago (FPA 1961; 1967)	
St. Vincent (FPA 1965)	Mexico (FPA 1965; 1972)		
	Nicaragua (FPA 1970; 1967)		
	Paraguay (FPA 1966; c. 1972)		
	Puerto Rico (FPA 1954; 1967)		
	St. Kitts, Nevis, Anguilla (FPA 1966; 1971)		
	Venezuela (FPA 1966; 1964)		

Sources: As listed in Table 20a.

Table 20c

Distribution of Selected Developing Countries in Asia * and Oceania by Government Policies on Population and Family Planning Activities **

		Laissez-faire	
Region	Pronatalist	Neutral	Antinatalist
ASIA	Malaysia (Sabah) (FPA 1967)	Bahrain Bhutan Brunei Burma (FPA 1960) Khmer Republic (FPA 1973) Kuwait Oman Qatar Saudi Arabia Sikkim Syria United Arab Emirates Yemen, Arab Rep. Yemen, People's Dem. Repub.	Cyprus (FPA 1971) Iraq (FPA 1971)
OCEANIA		Tahiti (2 FPAs: 1968, 1969)	

* No information was available for the Democratic People's Republic of Korea and Mongolia.

Sources: As listed in Table 20a.

Table 20c (Continued)

Antinatalist			
Government Support of Private Family Planning Program	Official Family Planning Program	Official Family Planning Program Including Motivation Campaign	Official Family Planning Programs and Stronger Measures
Afghanistan (FPA 1968)	Vietnam, Republic (FPA 1968; 1967)	Bangladesh (FPA reorganizing; 1965; 1973)	China, People's Rep. (1962; Restrictions on number of children)
Hong Kong (FPA 1936)		China, Rep. of (Taiwan) (2FPAs: 1954, 1963; 1964)	Singapore (FPA 1949; 1965; Curtailment of rights and privileges with excess children)
Jordan (FPA 1963)		Indonesia (FPA 1957; 1968)	India (FPA 1949; 1952; Economic Incentives)
Lebanon (FPA 1969)		Iran (FPA 1958; 1967)	
Malaysia (Sarawak) (FPA 1962)		Korea, Republic (FPA 1961; 1961)	
		Laos (FPA 1969; 1972)	
		Malaysia (W.) (FPA 1958; 1966)	
		Nepal (FPA 1958; 1966)	
		Pakistan (FPA 1953; 1960)	
		Philippines (FPA 1961; 1970)	
		Sri Lanka (FPA 1953; 1965)	
		Thailand (FPA 1970; 1970)	
		Turkey (FPA 1963; 1965)	
		Vietnam, Dem. Republic (1967)	
	Papua and New Guinea (1968)	Fiji (FPA 1963; 1962)	
	Tonga (FPA 1969; 1958)	Gilbert and Ellice Is. (FPA 1969; 1970)	
		Western Samoa (1971)	

** Dates are given for both the founding of the private family planning association (FPA) and the year in which governments began offering family planning services in their health programs, where applicable.

issue as population policy. Many countries are in the *laissez faire* category; they make no effort either to restrict or to promote family planning activities. On the basis of attitudes expressed in official pronouncements, they have been further classified as leaning toward pronatalism or antinatalism.[4] The absence of pronatalist policy headings from Table 20 reflects the fact that no developing country has adopted pronatalist measures.

ABORTION

Although legalization of abortion is often considered a "stronger" population policy than the provision of family planning services, it is not in itself restrictive and does not fit into the continuum. It has, however, been of great importance in Eastern Europe and Japan, which had very rapid falls in fertility. Specific government policies toward abortion are not usually directly related to their overall population policy. (Tables 21 and 22.) Ireland, a country with extreme pronatalist policies,[5] also prohibits abortion (without exception, including possible risk to the life of the mother as a result of pregnancy), but so also do several countries which have official family planning programs including motivation campaigns.

Most countries have specified medical grounds under which the procedure is legal. The countries which also permit abortions for social reasons—which include rape or incest, and economic or psychological conditions certified by doctors or official panels—vary widely in their other population policies. In contrast, elective abortion is more closely associated with other antinatalist policies. But at present, elective abortion is allowed in only a few countries; except for the People's Republic of China, most of these are developed countries and they have permitted it only recently. The USSR first legalized elective abortion in 1920; it was restricted in 1936, but the law was reliberalized in 1955. The People's Republic of China has allowed elective abortion since 1957, provided that the procedure is performed during the first trimester and that no other abortion has been performed during the prior

---

[4] For instance, the government of Cameroon has strongly expressed a wish to increase its population to 15 million from approximately 6 million (1970), but it actually has no pronatalist incentives. In contrast, Iraq currently offers no family planning services, but there are plans to introduce them under the basic health network.

[5] In March 1974, the government of Ireland announced controversial proposals in the legislature to allow the sale of contraceptives to married persons because the current law prohibiting the import and sale of contraceptives had just been declared unconstitutional. There appears to be widespread opposition to this bill, and its future is uncertain.

Table 21

Distribution of Selected Developed Countries by Population Policy and Classification of Induced Abortion Statutes

	Population policy						
	Pronatalist			Laissez faire		Antinatalist	
Classification of induced abortion statute	Sales illegal	Sales allowed; advertising illegal	Pronatalist incentives	Pronatalist	Neutral	Official support of voluntary programs	Official programs
Illegal	Ireland[a]					Belgium Luxembourg Portugal	
Legal							
Medical		Spain	France	Israel	Italy Switzerland	Canada German Fed. Repub. New Zealand	Chile Netherlands
Social							
Medical and social		Argentina	Romania Czechoslovakia Hungary Bulgaria		Greece Iceland Uruguay	Australia	Finland Japan Norway Poland Sweden United Kingdom Yugoslavia
Elective				USSR	Austria		Denmark German Democ. Rep. United States

[a] The law prohibiting the import and sale of contraceptives has recently been declared unconstitutional; controversial legislation proposals were introduced in March 1974 to allow sales to married persons.

Source: Kalis, Mary G. and Henry P. David. Forthcoming 1974. Abortion Legislation: A Summary International Classification. In *Abortion Research Reader.* H. P. David, ed. Lexington, Massachusetts: Lexington Books.

Table 22

Distribution of Selected Developing Countries by Population Policy and Classification of Induced Abortion Statutes

Classification of induced abortion statute	Population policy						
	Laissez faire			Antinatalist			
	Pronatalist	Neutral	Antinatalist	Official support of voluntary program	Official program	Official program including motivation campaign	Official program and stronger measures
Illegal	Guyana	Bolivia		Barbados Hong Kong	Vietnam, Rep. of	Mauritius China, Rep. of (Taiwan) Colombia Dominican Rep. Haiti Jamaica Panama Trinidad & Tobago Indonesia Philippines	

Legal						
Medical	Malaysia-Sabah	Ethiopia Ivory Coast Senegal Br. Honduras Khmer Repub. Kuwait Syria	Burundi Sierra Leone Cyprus Iraq	Nigeria Sudan Uganda Peru Lebanon Malaysia-Sarawak	Algeria S. Africa Costa Rica Guatemala Nicaragua Paraguay Venezuela	Egypt Ghana Kenya Morocco Bangladesh Iran Malaysia (W.) Pakistan
Social				Jordan		
Medical and social	Cameroon Brazil				Cuba Ecuador El Salvador Mexico	Korea, Rep. of Thailand Turkey
Elective					Tunisia Vietnam, Dem. Rep. of	India Singapore China, People's Republic of
Information unavailable	(7)	(37)	(1)	(11)	(7)	(7)

[1] No information available for Democratic People's Republic of Korea, Mongolia, or Albania concerning their population policies or abortion statutes.

Source: Kalis, Mary G. and Henry P. David. Forthcoming 1974. Abortion Legislation: A Summary International Classification. In *Abortion Research Reader.* H. P. David, ed. Lexington, Massachusetts: Lexington Books.

twelve months. Hungary, Bulgaria, and Romania legalized elective abortion in 1956, but each has since restricted the procedure to medical and social indications. No other country appears to have permitted elective abortion before 1970.

Though estimates have been made, no data are available on the absolute number of abortions being performed throughout the world. A survey by International Planned Parenthood Federation (IPPF) estimates that in 1971 more than 55 million women terminated their pregnancies by legal or illegal induced abortion, at a ratio of four abortions for every ten live births or one out of three to four pregnancies. Although these estimates are controversial, there is no doubt that, regardless of population policy, abortion has been and remains a frequently used method of birth prevention and fertility regulation (David 1974). "No developed country has ever had a substantial decline in the birth rate without a marked recourse to abortion and it is unlikely that any developing country will see the demographic changes desired in the coming decades without abortion playing an important role" (Potts 1973). The use of abortion as an aid to lowering rates of fertility in the course of the demographic transition is apparently unaffected by the legal status of the procedure. Japan's legalization of abortion dating from 1948 coincided with the stage in the demographic transition characterized by falling birth rates; in contrast, liberalization of abortion in Great Britain in 1968 came about a century after abortion began to make a significant contribution to the country's demographic transition (van der Tak 1974).

PRESENT DISTRIBUTION OF THE POPULATION
OF THE WORLD BY POLICY TYPE

Over 70 percent of the world's population live in countries which offer family planning in their existing public health services (see Table 23 and Annex Table 16). The proportion of total population in countries with an official family planning program is much higher in the developing world (over 80 percent) than in the developed world. At the other extreme, only 4 percent of the world's people live in countries with pronatalist policies; all are developed nations.

Within the developing world, different policy orientations are emerging on different continents. Latin America shows the least tendency toward official programs: although one-half of its population live in countries which offer family planning in the existing health services, a majority of the remaining half live in countries which maintain a *laissez faire* pronatalist attitude toward family planning. Almost two-thirds of the African population live in countries which either support a private family

Table 23

Distribution of the World's Population by Government Policy on Population and Family Planning Activities

Government position	Total world	Devel-oped coun-tries	Total	Africa	Asia	Latin America	Oceania
			Developing countries				
All positions	100.0	100.0	100.0	100.0	100.0	100.0	100.0
Use of contraceptives prohibited	—	—	—	—	—	—	—
Sales illegal	1.0	3.4	—	—	—	—	—
Sales allowed, advertising illegal	0.7	2.2	—	—	—	—	—
Pronatalist incentives	2.6	8.9	—	—	—	—	—
Laissez faire	17.3	30.1	11.9	37.4	3.6	39.3	7.3
Pronatalist	(10.2)	(22.8)	(4.9)	(8.1)	—	(36.9)	—
Neutral	(6.6)	(7.3)	(6.3)	(27.1)	(3.0)	(2.4)	(7.3)
Antinatalist	(0.5)	—	(0.7)	(2.2)	(0.6)	—	—
Official support of voluntary programs	7.1	10.6	5.6	24.8	1.4	10.3	—
Official program	18.0	44.8	6.7	16.5	0.9	36.1	47.8
Official program including motivation campaign	16.8	—	23.9	21.3	25.6	14.3	44.9
Official program and economic incentives	14.9	—	21.2	—	28.0	—	—
Curtailment of rights and privileges with excess children	0.1	—	0.1	—	0.1	—	—
Restrictions on marriage	—	—	—	—	—	—	—
Restrictions on number of children	21.5	—	30.6	—	40.4	—	—
Involuntary fertility control	—	—	—	—	—	—	—

Note: 1971 estimate; if unavailable, latest available estimate, usually 1970, taken from International Planned Parenthood Federation. 1973. *Family Planning in Five Continents.* London: IPPF.

Sources: Tables 19, 20 and Annex Table 16.

planning program, or at least offer family planning services in their public health program; *laissez faire* policies prevail in the remaining countries. Asia shows the strongest emphasis on official programs: the overwhelming majority of people (94 percent) live in countries where governments have established official programs with the deliberate objective of reducing fertility. Nearly 30 percent live in India, which has added economic incentives to its program; and 40 percent live in China, which seeks to control the number and timing of births.

GROWTH OF ANTINATALIST POLICIES

A decade ago, countries of the world classified on the policy continuum would have been bunched more strikingly to the left. The trend toward antinatalist policies featuring family planning programs can be traced from the year of founding of both private family planning associations and official programs shown in Tables 19 and 20. Private family planning associations have usually preceded the establishment of official programs. Indeed, their own information and education programs, clinical services, and training programs have facilitated the start of official family planning programs by governments.

Tables 24 and 25 show the growth of both private and governmental family planning programs. Few of the developing nations had private family planning associations in 1960, and only four—Bermuda, India, Tonga, and Pakistan—had official government programs. The largest number of private as well as official programs were in Asia and Oceania. By 1965 nearly one-third of the developing nations had family planning associations, and official family planning programs had increased more than three-fold. Latin America showed the largest increases in establishing family planning associations, while Asia and Oceania led in establishing official family planning programs. By 1970, over half of the developing nations had family planning associations, with the largest increases in the Latin American region. Over one-third of the developing countries had established official programs, with large increases both in Latin America and Asia. The pace has slowed since 1970. While over three-fifths of the developing nations now have private family planning associations, the proportion with governments offering programs of offi-

Table 24

Number of Countries with Private Family Planning Associations (FPA) by Region and Selected Years, 1960–1974

	Total no. of countries	Cumulative number of countries with FPAs				Percent of countries with FPAs in 1974
		1960	1965	1970	1974	
Developing Countries						
Africa	53	7	10	18	23	43
Latin America	36	1	13	28	29	81
Asia and Oceania	46	11	17	26	30	65
Total	135	19	40	72	82	61
Developed Countries	36	13	19	26	27	75
Total World	171	32	59	98	109	64

Sources: Tables 19 and 20.

Table 25

Number of Countries with Official Family Planning Programs by Region and Selected Years, 1960–1974

	Total no. of countries	Cumulative number of countries with FP programs				Percent of countries with FP programs in 1974
		1960	1965	1970	1974	
Developing Countries						
Africa	53	0	4	9	10	19
Latin America	36	1	3	15	20	56
Asia and Oceania	46	3	11	21	23	50
Total	135	4	18	45	53	39
Developed Countries	36	3	5	9	12	33
Total World	171	7	23	54	65	38

Sources: Tables 19 and 20.

cial family planning services is still less than 40 percent. Africa has the lowest proportion of countries with family planning associations and official government programs. Many of the African nations maintain a *laissez faire* policy toward population, and a few have pronatalist attitudes.

Beginning with the Netherlands in 1881, private family planning associations were established in some developed nations during their demographic transitions. The majority of these associations, however, are very recent. About a third of the developed countries had such associations in 1960; by 1974, the proportion had risen to three-quarters. The establishment of official family planning programs in the developed countries has been slower; by 1974, only one-third had such programs. In several developed nations, the problem for population policy appears to be less how to reduce fertility than of how to stabilize it at roughly replacement level. In some countries, where the right of individuals to use artificial means of birth control encounters strong opposition on religious grounds, the ease of access to family planning services remains an issue.

As population problems become more apparent, countries can be expected to adopt increasingly stronger antinatalist measures. These shifts are likely to be gradual because the subject is politically sensitive; abrupt changes can arouse emotions, while a series of small steps may be quite acceptable. But at the present time there appears to be relatively little political support for measures stronger than motivation campaigns. Even India, which has offered economic incentives for some years, recently withdrew a program offering relatively very large incentives for sterilization. See Chapter 6.

International Policies

The idea that fertility could be influenced through policy measures has long historical roots. Until 1950, policies designed to influence fertility were virtually all pronatalist, with no apparent significant effect. In addition, most of the discussion of population and economic development was concerned with how to mitigate the effects of population growth rather than how best to reduce its rate.

A number of factors combined during the 1960s to change very strikingly the international climate of opinion about what could and what should be done. The seriousness of the problem was increasingly appreciated. Population projections prepared by the Population Division of the United Nations and training programs, seminars and conferences sponsored by the United Nations, other international agencies, and private foundations widened awareness of the long-term implications of a continuation of the fertility rates of developing countries. This awareness was reinforced by the censuses taken about 1960; they showed that the population of several developing countries was greater than was earlier projected. The growing dependence of several developing countries on a few developed countries for meeting the food needs of their increasing populations was highlighted during the poor harvests in India and elsewhere during 1966 to 1968. Together with increases in unemployment resulting from the growing number of new entrants into the labor force, the food shortage emphasized the development implications of rapid population growth.

Reflecting this increase in concern were the frequent discussions and other activities in the United Nations and its specialized agencies which served to legitimize and reinforce the possibility of using deliberate government policies to reduce fertility. The General Assembly of the United Nations first considered the issue of population growth in relation to economic development in 1962, when it attempted to ascertain the role which the U.N. should play in assisting governments to implement programs which would moderate population growth. The resulting resolution highlighted the relationship of the health and welfare of the family to economic and social progress, and noted that nations must formulate their own policies. Over the years, the deliberations and resolutions of the General Assembly and the Economic and Social Council have increased awareness of the relationship between population policy issues and social and economic development; increasingly, member nations have accepted the concept that family planning is a human right.

In the face of considerable and remaining skepticism, a belief finally grew that something could be achieved by deliberate policies. This was

Table 26

Assistance to Population Activities by Selected Major Donors, 1960–1972

(thousands of U.S. dollars)

Year	Governments	Multilateral organizations	Private organizations	Net total [a]
1972	160,130	55,027	53,327	182,695
1970	87,187	18,750	56,012	126,663
1968	37,806	4,667	26,523	58,038
1966	5,256	—	39,043	34,311
1963	241	—	11,688	10,722
1960	91	—	3,107	2,148

[a] Excludes double counting of funds from governments to multilateral and private organizations.

Source: Annex Tables 18, 19, 20.

influenced by several related events. These included improvements in contraceptive technology; increasing knowledge, derived from surveys in developing countries, of a widespread desire for family planning information and services; and the course of the demographic transition in some developing countries, which suggested that a more rapid fertility decline could be brought about through policy measures (U.N. Economic and Social Council 1969).

Growth in international concern and the increasing number of official family planning programs have been reflected in a growth of bilateral and eventually multilateral assistance. Private assistance has also grown. The amount of international assistance for various kinds of population programs increased from $2 million in 1960 to $183 million in 1972 [6] (Table 26). Most international assistance (72 percent in 1972) has been for the provision of family planning services. Demographic activities, including research and training programs oriented towards ascertaining population growth trends and their causes, are also important (Table 27).

In 1972, nearly one-fifth of assistance went to biomedical activities—that is, for research and training programs in reproductive biology and contraceptive development.[7] This assistance is of particular interest, since the donor governments finance a much greater share of the amounts

[6] This excludes assistance from a number of smaller private agencies.

[7] Amounts classified as assistance for population programs are substantially less than donors spend on reproductive biology and contraceptive research and development. Annex Table 21 presents an attempt at a comprehensive estimate of total expenditures.

Table 27

Assistance to Population Programs by Region and Type of Activity, 1972

(thousands of U.S. dollars)

Activity	South Asia	East Asia	Africa	Oceania	Latin America	Inter-regional [a]	International assistance net total
Demographic	2,023	127	3,069	0	1,476	10,471	17,166
Biomedical research	5,076	424	4,624	93	5,354	19,109	34,680
Family planning	67,896	3,036	11,019	311	21,736	26,851	130,849
Total	74,995	3,587	18,712	404	28,566	56,431	182,695
Administration costs, excluded from total							15,744

[a] Under this heading is classified assistance given for general purposes (such as international conferences, seminars, publications, and films), and funds allocated by governments to enable special institutions in the donor countries to develop expertise and undertake research in the population field.

Source: Annex Table 17.

involved in this type of program than in other activities. In addition, in contrast to other activities, financial support in this field is declining. Although, as shown in Annex Table 21, expenditures for research and training by governments and private foundations reached $61 million in 1972, compared to only $15 million five years earlier, there was no increase in 1973 and none is planned for 1974 despite substantial cost increases. This declining government support comes at a time when research and development activities in this field by pharmaceutical companies appear also to be declining. The current fall in research support comes at a level well below what many authorities have recommended in the light of current research leads, gaps in basic knowledge of reproductive biology, the importance of the subject, and the amounts spent on other kinds of medical research.[8] Both United States and World Health Organization studies have recommended amounts in the order of $200–$250 million.

---

[8] The role that improved contraceptive technology might contribute to the success of family planning programs is controversial and difficult to assess. The demographic transition in developed countries was completed with contraceptive technology that was much less sophisticated than today. But, as observed in Chapter 5, high discontinuation rates among acceptors of family planning methods are an indication of the unsatisfactory nature of present technology.

WORLDWIDE PRACTICE AND EXPENDITURE PATTERNS

To sum up the current situation, it is useful to look at the worldwide picture. Comprehensive estimates, based on a survey of over 200 countries, have been attempted by the International Planned Parenthood Federation for 1971. Because of difficulties in obtaining data, especially for some large countries, the data can only be very approximate. The results are summarized in Tables 28 and 29.

In 1971, 70 percent of the world's women at risk of pregnancy were not practicing a contraceptive method. While 56 percent of all the women practicing contraception live in the developed nations, only 28 percent of the women at risk of pregnancy in the world live in these nations. In developed countries, three-fifths of the women at risk are using a contraceptive method; only one-fifth of the women in the developing world have adopted one. However, about two-thirds of those practicing contraception in developing countries were using one of the most effective methods—the pill, IUD or sterilization—about twice the proportion of women using these methods in developed countries.

A total of $3,000 million was spent worldwide for fertility control services in 1971. The services include not only official family planning programs, but also family planning services provided through private channels such as private clinics and commercial marketing of contraceptives. (Table 29.) More than three-fifths of the expenditures for fertility control came from individuals who paid for their own services in doctor

Table 28

Estimated Number of Women at Risk of Unwanted Pregnancy and Number Practicing Contraception, by Methods Used in Both Developing and Developed Countries

	At risk (millions)	Practicing contraception (millions)	Distribution of contraceptors by method used		
			Pill/IUD	Sterilization	Other and unknown
All countries (N=208)	496	153	46	24	81
Developed countries (N=44)	141	85	22	4	59
Developing countries (N=164)	355	68	26	20	22
China, People's Rep.	112	39	13	13	13
Developing countries other than PRC	243	29	13	7	9

Source: Robbins, John. 1973. Unmet Needs in Family Planning: A World Survey. *Family Planning Perspectives.* 5:1, 234.

Table 29

Estimated Worldwide Expenditures for Fertility Control Services, by Source of Funds and Development Status, 1971

(millions of U.S. dollars)

Sources of funds, by development status	Type		
	All services	Contraception	Abortion
Total World	*2,981*	*1,496*	*1,485*
Developed nations	*2,122*	*1,031*	*1,091*
Private individuals	1,273	825	448
International donors	27	27	–0–
National governments and private contributors	822	179	643
Developing nations	*859*	*465*	*394*
Developing nations excluding China	740	400	340
Private individuals	472	132	340
International donors	71	71	–0–
National governments and private contributors	197	197	–0–

Sources: John Robbins. 1973. Unmet Needs in Family Planning: A World Survey. *Family Planning Perspectives.* 5:4. Table 3, p. 236. Annex Table 17.

and clinic fees and for supplies bought commercially; national governments contributed 34 percent of the total expenditures.

In both developing countries, excluding the People's Republic of China, and developed countries, about 60 percent of funds spent on fertility control came from individuals paying for their own services. The remaining 40 percent came from national governments, private contributions, or international donors. Of the $740 million spent for fertility control in the developing world, excluding the People's Republic of China, an estimated 54 percent was spent on contraception and 46 percent on abortion.[9] Most abortions in these countries were illegal, so that individuals had to pay for their own abortions. Also financed by individuals in the developing world was about one-third of the expenditure for contraception.

The major international donors contributed over $70 million to fertility control programs in developing countries, excluding the People's

[9] This does not take into account the expense of dealing with medical complications due to poorly performed illegal abortions, estimated to be more than $300 million in Latin America alone.

Republic of China, in 1971—roughly one-tenth of the total cost of fertility control. This assistance, however, amounted to over one-quarter of expenditures by both governments and private organizations in contraceptive programs. Efforts by national governments have often been very small. The IPPF survey found that although many developing nations had affirmed that population growth posed a danger to their prosperity and stability, in 1971 fewer than 10 percent of developing country governments had assigned a high enough priority to family planning to put more than $1 million of their own funds into official programs.

Table 30 relates the per capita annual family planning budget in selected countries, classified by continent, according to population policy type.[10] As would be expected, countries which have established an official family planning program that includes motivation or economic incentives have allocated a larger amount per capita to family planning in their national budgets than countries which offer the service in their existing health networks or support a private program. The largest per capita allocation was made by Mauritius, which spent $1.07 per person from all sources, with 81¢ per person coming from the national government.

CONCLUSION

The past decade has witnessed a very marked growth in antinatalist policies in developing countries, especially in the number of official family planning programs. Countries which offer family planning services in their health services now account for over 80 percent of the population of the developing countries, but the proportion of women who are exposed to the risk of pregnancy and use a method of contraception is less than 20 percent. Future progress obviously depends mainly on more countries moving further on the spectrum of antinatalist policies and on increasing the effectiveness of existing family planning programs.

In formulating development or social policies it is important for the population impact of these policies to be considered explicitly. The factors which would reduce fertility may be strengthened at little or no additional cost and without hampering the primary objectives.

Most of the costs of contraception in developing countries are provided by government services, to which international donors contribute very

---

[10] The table must be interpreted with caution. It is difficult to assign a true value to the purchasing power of budget allocations within each country without knowing more about the cost of personnel, equipment, facilities, and related services in each of the nations.

Table 30

Annual Family Planning Budget Per Capita for Selected Countries, by Official Population Policy

Official population policy type, continent/country, and fiscal year	Annual family planning budget per capita (U.S. cents)	
	Government	All sources, including government
Official program & economic incentives		
India. 1972	15.3	u
Official program & motivation campaign		
Asia		
Korea, Rep. of. 1972	10.4	16.7
W. Malaysia. 1973	11.1	u
Thailand. 1973	4.8	14.0
Indonesia. 1972	4.6	7.9
Pakistan. 1965–1970	u	11.8
Iran. 1972	29.0	35.0
China, Rep. of. 1974	7.1	8.5
Turkey. 1972	u	4.8
Philippines. 1972	3.4	15.6
Nepal. 1970	0.8	3.5
Bangladesh. 1972	4.0	5.0
Laos. 1972	u	17.0
Africa		
Tunisia. 1973	5.2	30.0
Morocco. 1972	2.2	u
Ghana. 1972	4.0	7.0
Mauritius. 1972	81.0	107.0
Latin America		
Dominican Republic. 1972	1.9	4.1
Jamaica. 1971	56.0	u
Oceania		
Fiji. 1971	29.0	29.0
Official program		
Guatemala. 1973	0.6	12.0
Official support of private programs		
Africa		
Rhodesia. 1973	u	14.0
Uganda. 1972	1.2	u
Asia		
Hong Kong. 1972	6.0	11.1

Source: Nortman, Dorothy. 1973. Population and Family Planning Programs: A Factbook. In *Reports on Population/Family Planning.* No. 2. Fifth Edition. Table 17. pp. 89–91. New York: The Population Council.

significantly. Expenditures on abortion, however, which amount to about half of the cost of fertility control, are not publicly financed. In a great many countries, access to abortion procedures is very restricted. As a result, fertility control efforts are less effective than they might be, and unregulated illegal abortion continues to be very costly in health terms.

Official expenditures on family planning in developing countries still remain a small proportion of national budgets. Given the high economic benefits from a reduction in fertility, constraints on program expansion should not be budgetary. National governments and donor agencies must consider both how to raise additional resources for expanding national programs and how to utilize them most effectively. Support for contraceptive research and development appears to be both inadequate and declining.

The implications of recent experience with family planning programs for the prospects of their successful performance in the future are discussed in Chapters 5 and 7.

Chapter 5

PERFORMANCE OF
FAMILY PLANNING PROGRAMS

IN CHAPTER 3, it was argued that high levels of fertility in developing countries are to a large extent the product of socio-economic circumstances and high levels of mortality. These conditions set an upper limit on the demand for the services of family planning programs. Because these conditions vary a great deal among developing countries, the potential for increasing contraceptive use through family planning programs also varies. For instance, it should be easier to reduce fertility in Hong Kong, Singapore, Taiwan, and the Republic of Korea, where socio-economic development is higher and mortality lower than in Pakistan, India, Bangladesh or Indonesia. An increase in contraceptive practice from 15 to 25 percent in some circumstances may represent a greater achievement than an increase from 35 to 65 percent elsewhere.

Nevertheless there is enough evidence that few if any programs are yet at the point where a lack of demand for family planning services is likely to be a constraint on progress. Even at low levels of socio-economic development, experimental family planning schemes have sometimes obtained much greater declines in birth rates than regular programs. During the course of one such program in a poor rural area of South India, where infant mortality was still well above 100 per thousand births, the birth rate among a population of about 100,000 was brought down in a few years from above 40 to below 30 per thousand persons. Administrative reasons may make it difficult to replicate such experiments nationally. But they establish that socio-economic or mortality factors are not yet an irreducible constraint on family planning practice even in circumstances which seem unpropitious for fertility declines. The ubiquity of induced abortion is further evidence that an unmet demand for family planning services exists everywhere. Not all unwanted conceptions end in abortions, and the number of children whose births were unwanted by their parents is probably very large indeed. These parents at least are a potential market for family planning services.

MEASURES OF PROGRAM PERFORMANCE

A reduction in fertility is not the only objective of a family planning program. For those programs which governments have established with a demographic purpose, however, this reduction is the most important aim. Conceptually, the best measure of accomplishment of a family planning program would be the difference between the reduction in fertility produced by the program and what theoretically could be achieved in given socio-economic conditions. This is, however, impossible to estimate at present. Program achievement must therefore be judged in terms of the effect on fertility or—since as discussed in this section, this is also difficult to measure—in terms of such intermediate outputs as acceptance rates or contraceptive practice.

Fertility reduction, acceptance and contraceptive use are all measures of output, rather than performance. The ideal program must not only achieve high levels of output but must also perform efficiently; that is, the level of output should be obtained with the minimum use of scarce resources. For this reason, cost-effectiveness and administrative efficiency should be among the indicators of program performance. The discussion in Chapter 7 of alternative ways of providing family planning services suggests that the appropriate approach will vary in different cultural contexts and states of development. Cost-effectiveness, therefore, can only be discussed in relation to national circumstances. It is also not possible to try to evaluate the administrative efficiency of about twenty official national programs analyzed below. Program cost data discussed in Chapter 7 provide some indication of possible economies of scale. This suggests that programs which achieve a high measure of output are also likely to be relatively cost-effective.

Impact on Fertility

It is difficult to estimate the impact of a program on fertility. One problem is the fact that most programs are very new. It takes considerable time to set up a program organization, train staff, and acquire experience; there is a further lag between family planning acceptance and its effect on fertility. This makes it difficult to trace the link between program expenditures, acceptance, and fertility trends. In addition, data gathering and evaluation units in many programs were established some time after the program got going. Even today the evaluation effort remains seriously inadequate in many programs. The most serious difficulty, however, is in identifying the net impact of a family planning program and isolating the extent to which program acceptance serves as a substitute for other contraceptive practice. Attempts to calculate the effects of program acceptance on the birth rate usually have been unable to take into account the fact that, in the absence of the official program, some of the acceptors would have obtained supplies privately or utilized other means of fertility regulation. For instance, estimates that the Tunisian birth rate was 4 percent lower in 1968 as a result of the family planning program (Lapham 1970), and that the Indian birth rate was reduced by 8 to 9 percent in 1969–70 (Simmons 1971) are likely to overestimate program impact.

An offsetting factor is that calculations based on official program acceptors do not reflect the impact of educational and other activities of the program supplied by non-program sources which may lead to increases in contraceptive practice. In a number of countries, private doctors and organizations are a very important source of contraceptive supplies. (Table 31.)

Attempts to overcome these difficulties include observations of the behavior of matched groups of acceptors and non-acceptors and of the relative fertility of acceptors before and after acceptance (Ross and Forrest 1971). Both approaches face the problem that the very fact of acceptance implies that acceptors are atypical to some extent; in the absence of the program they might have found other means for fertility control. Where data permit, a comparison of fertility movements in different geographical areas where the program has had different local characteristics or levels of activities is perhaps the most promising approach. Taiwan has good information for a large number of small areal units, and has been the focus of several studies which suggest that the official family planning program has indeed made a significant contribution to the reduction in birth rates. One estimate of the effect of family planning inputs on the 1966 fertility level found that the official program accounted for a 6 to 8 percent reduction in the birth rate (Schultz 1969). Estimation of the effect of *increases* in family planning inputs on the mean decline in the fertility rate over the period 1964–1969 showed that program expansion accounted for about 15 percent of the observed fertility decline. By contrast, changes in socio-economic conditions entered into the model accounted for about 42

Table 31

Users of Contraceptives as a Percentage of Married Women Ages 15–44 by Source of Supplies for Selected Countries, 1973

Country	Official program supplies and service	Private sector supplies	Total
Taiwan	27.0	30.0	57.0
Hong Kong	27.1[a]	25.2	52.3[a]
Korea, Rep. of (1972)	24.0	6.0	30.0
Thailand	17.7	8.0	25.7
Egypt	15.8	4.9	20.7

[a] Sterilization acceptors are not considered program acceptors.

Source: Annex Table 22.

percent of the observed decline. Acceptances, however, were significantly associated with fertility declines only in areas where fertility had been relatively high at the beginning. In these areas, the possibility that program acceptance was substituted for other contraceptive practice was presumably very small. In other areas, where fertility was already low, widespread program acceptance of IUDs was not related with fertility declines, possibly because the official program was substituting for private contraceptive practice (Hermalin 1972).

In Indonesia, acceptance was higher in areas with relatively low fertility, which indicates the probability of substantial substitution effects (Repetto, Reese, and Haryono 1973). An analysis of the determinants of acceptance rates also indicates that perhaps half of the variation among areas, and over time, can be attributed to variations in socio-economic factors, and about half to differences in program inputs.

These results indicate that unless the substitution between program and nonprogram mechanisms of fertility control is taken into account, program impact on fertility is likely to be overstated. But this should not obscure the fact that official programs have had a significant effect on fertility in a variety of socio-economic circumstances. In some instances, the effect may have appeared small because the program studied had been operational for only a short time.

Users versus Acceptors

Two other ways of assessing program performance are measures of contraceptive use and of acceptance of family planning methods under program auspices. Both are less satisfactory than estimates of the impact on fertility, but both are easier to obtain. User data are, however, normally provided by limited surveys and often do not provide reliable national figures. Because of reluctance of some women to admit to contraceptive use, surveys are thought to underestimate family planning practice. Nevertheless, they suggest considerable variation among developing countries. (Table 32 and Annex Table 23.) Only in countries of East Asia are a substantial fraction of fertile women—say, more than 25 percent—current users of official program contraceptives.

Data on contraceptive use more closely approximate information on fertility and, for most purposes, would be preferable to data on family planning acceptance. Available acceptance data, however, are usually much more complete and so are more commonly used. A program acceptor is usually defined as a person, not previously practicing contraception, who decides to begin practice with a given method under program auspices. In reality, however, data on acceptors may include persons who have changed from one method to another, who have

Table 32

Percentage of Married Women Ages 15–44 Using Contraceptives in January of Each Year

Country	Year		
	1969	1971	1973
Taiwan	32.0	44.0	57.0
Hong Kong	42.0	51.0	52.3
Korea, Rep. of	25.0	42.0	—
Fiji	—	—	33.4
Thailand	7.4	9.6	25.7
Singapore	37.0	25.0 p	—
Mauritius	—	25.0	—
Egypt	10.0	9.0	20.7
India	8.0	—	13.6 p
Philippines	—	—	11.0
Malaysia (West)	6.0	8.0	9.3 p
Tunisia	8.2	12.0	6.4 p
Morocco	1.0	3.0	5.6

p Program only.

Source: Annex Table 23.

moved from one program to another, and who had temporarily stopped practice.

For comparing relative achievements of different programs, divergence between statistics on rates of use and acceptance is not too great but it is systematic, reflecting to a large extent the time the program has been in existence (Table 33). Five countries—Morocco, Pakistan, Fiji, Hong Kong, and India—show relatively higher user rates than acceptance rates. These countries have had family planning programs for a sufficiently long time to accumulate users, but are not doing as well at present. Most countries with relatively better acceptor than user rates are those with recent programs. Although they have not had enough time to accumulate users, their acceptor rates have grown fast in recent years. Indonesia, Iran, and the Philippines are in this category. The Dominican Republic and Jamaica, however, cannot be explained in these terms.

To assess the role and relative importance of program inputs and the level of socio-economic development in explaining variations in acceptor rates and the program user rates, a statistical analysis of family planning performance as related to the socio-economic environment and official efforts was made for sixteen states of India and for nineteen

Table 33

Classification of Countries by User Rates and Acceptor Rates per Thousand Married Women Ages 15–44 *

	Users		
New acceptors	Low Less than 40	Medium 40–120	High More than 120
Low Less than 30	Ghana Guatemala Nepal Turkey Uganda	Morocco Pakistan	
Medium 30 to 59	Dom. Republic Indonesia	Malaysia (West) Tunisia	Fiji Hong Kong India
High More than 60		Iran Jamaica Philippines	Korea, Rep. of Mauritius Taiwan Thailand

* Data on users are for 1973 except for 1970 for Ghana; 1971 for Nepal, Indonesia, Pakistan and Iran; 1972 for Republic of Korea and Mauritius. Data on acceptors are for 1971 for Iran and Mauritius, and 1970 for Nepal.

Sources: Annex Tables 23 and 25.

countries including India.[1] A third measure was the total user rate, including nonprogram use for the inter-country analysis and birth rates for India. Both socio-economic development and program inputs explain a significant part of the variation in output measures. In some cases, four input and four socio-economic variables together explained more than 90 percent of the total variance.[2] Inter-country differences

[1] Program inputs consist of service points, personnel, expenditure, etcetera. Socio-economic variables include per capita income, literacy, mortality level, urbanization, and several other variables. A complete list of variables and further details are in Appendix B.

[2] A stepwise regression procedure was used to select variables according to successive maximal explanatory power, that is in order of the proportion of variance they could explain. The variables explaining the variations in different output measures were not necessarily the same. Given the high intercorrelations among different variables, the particular indices of program inputs or socio-economic development are less important than their effects as a group. The analysis does not attempt to identify a precise cause-and-effect relationship between particular socio-economic variables on program inputs and reasons of output. Given the limitations of data and small number of observations, this was not possible.

The proportions of variations in output measures, explained separately by

in acceptor rates, however, were not well explained by either socio-economic or program input variables, primarily because of differences in the length of time over which different country programs have been in existence. This factor is less important in the Indian case, and variance in acceptor rates is much better explained. As a result of greater uniformity in data, concepts, and a similarity of program approach, on the whole, relationships between outputs on the one side and inputs and socio-economic variables on the other appear to be better defined in the Indian than in the international case.

PROGRAM ACCEPTORS

Quantity

Annex Tables 24 and 25 show the number of acceptors during 1968–1972 in countries with significant official programs, and the rate per 1,000 married women ages 15–44. A wide variation in acceptance rates is evident from Table 34. Examination of changes over time reveals that programs can be arranged in two distinct groups, according to whether the acceptance rate is increasing or declining. The group of countries with programs that have growing acceptance rates can be subdivided according to whether they have ever reached an annual rate of sixty or more acceptors. Several countries which have never reached a rate of sixty have relatively old programs, which either took some years to become effective, or exhibit very slow growth. Those that have reached a rate of sixty and are still growing reasonably fast are relatively new programs, started in 1967 or later.

The second group includes countries where the acceptance rate is decreasing. All the countries in this group began an official program during or before 1968; all, except the programs in West Malaysia and Turkey, are regarded as successful because they have reached annual ac-

---

four selected socio-economic variables (SEV), four selected program input variables (PIV), and all eight variables jointly, were as follows:

	Indian states			International		
	Proportion of variance explained (R^2) by			Proportion of variance explained (R^2) by		
Dependent variable	4SEV	4PIV	4SEV + 4PIV	4SEV	4PIV	4SEV + 4PIV
Acceptor rate	0.76	0.94	0.97	0.29[a]	0.53	0.38[b]
User rate, program	0.79	0.84	0.98	0.54	0.74	0.93
User rate, total	—	—	—	0.63	0.54	0.85
Birth rate	0.80	0.65	0.88	—	—	—

[a] This value is not statistically significant at 5 percent level.

[b] Obtained with only one SEV and one PIV; additional variables increased R^2 but made it insignificant at 5 percent level.

Table 34

Acceptance Rate in Both Official and Private Programs in Year Program Becomes Official and in Following Years, According to Recent Trends

(per thousand married women ages 15–44)

Country	Year program becomes official	Years							
		1965	1966	1967	1968	1969	1970	1971	1972
COUNTRIES WHERE THE ACCEPTANCE RATE WAS OVER 60 BUT IS NOW DECLINING									
Korea, Rep. of [a]	1961	119	153	129	121	169	187	159	153
Singapore	1965	47	144	144	158	161	103	82	86
Mauritius	1965	30	67	114	81	72	90	85	67
Trinidad and Tobago	1967	—	—	u	72	94	62	49	u
Chile	1966	—	42	97	73	64	47	59	42
Jamaica	1966	—	4	4	10	122	76	84	105
Taiwan	1968	—	—	—	73	68	87	94	86
Hong Kong	1956	80	50	40	51	56	56	56	61
COUNTRIES WHERE THE ACCEPTANCE RATE WAS OVER 60 AND IS STILL INCREASING									
Philippines	1970	—	—	—	—	—	40	78	118
Iran	1967	—	—	2	29	54	70	88	u
Costa Rica	1968	—	—	—	59	74	71	97	118
Thailand	1970	—	—	—	—	—	45	76	81
COUNTRIES WHERE THE ACCEPTANCE RATE HAS NOT BEEN OVER 60 AND IS ALREADY DECLINING									
Malaysia (West)	1966	—	u	16	55	50	43	45	43
Turkey	1965	1	7	9	13	15	12	9	7
COUNTRIES WHERE THE ACCEPTANCE RATE HAS NOT BEEN OVER 60 BUT IS STILL INCREASING									
India	1952	3[a]	19[a]	31	32	35	38	50	56
Indonesia	1968	—	—	—	1	2	8	20	40
Venezuela	1968	—	—	—	6	18	25	32	49
Egypt	1965	u	40	31	30	31	43	48	48
Sri Lanka	1965	u	9	23	26	32	31	31	37
Dominican Republic	1968	—	—	—	8	27	29	33	33
Ghana	1969	—	—	—	—	2	5	14	18
Ecuador	1968	—	—	—	5	4	9	19	19

[a] Does not include all methods.

u Unavailable

Sources: Nortman, Dorothy. 1969, 1971, 1972, 1973. Population and Family Planning Programs: A Factbook. In *Reports on Population/Family Planning.* No. 2. Table 4, 1969; Table 4, 1971; Table 4, 1972; Tables 4 & 13, 1973. New York: The Population Council.

R. T. Ravenholt; James W. Brackett; and John Chao. 1973. Family Planning Programs and Fertility Patterns. *Family Planning Programs.* Series J, No. 1.

ceptance rates of fifty or more. After a period of fast growth, these programs experienced a decline in acceptance rates, perhaps due to a saturation of the market as the initial reservoir of easily accessible potential acceptors dried up. In some cases, health resources or manpower which may have been temporarily stretched to accommodate the initial program have gradually returned to their original activities.

Table 34 indicates that for at least half the programs, the rate of acceptance more than doubles in the first two years after a private program becomes official. This means that the higher the initial rate, the higher the absolute increase in acceptance during these two years. Almost without exception, countries with a high initial rate of acceptance have had a relatively successful experience with private, non-official family planning services for several years before. When the official program begins, some degree of awareness and motivation for family planning already exists, along with a core of trained personnel, established training procedures, communications, and other aspects of the delivery system. Even after the adoption of an official program, private organizations usually continue to conduct a wide range of family planning activities, although sometimes their efforts become concentrated in specific areas such as communications or educational programs.

Characteristics

From the point of view of demographic effect, family planning acceptance may be of varying quality—determined by parity, age, method and probability of continuation.

Age and Parity.[3] In the few countries for which some time trends can be inferred, data show that the initial acceptors of a program consist primarily of women who have already reached their desired family size and who are, therefore, likely to be older and of higher parity. (Annex Table 26). Age and parity vary also according to contraceptive method. As the program continues, however, the tendency is toward an increase in the proportion of acceptors recruited from the pool of younger women beginning to lower their desired family size and/or seeking to space births.

Contraceptive method. Accepted methods vary both between and within countries. Choice may be determined by local constraints, methods offered by the program, and the preferences of physicians or clients. All these factors interact to a great degree. For example, in many situations, the client has little choice since the program decides which method it will offer. Generally, however, programs offer a variety of methods but emphasize a particular one. In India, sterilization and IUDs are the predominant methods both offered and advocated. In the

---

[3] Parity is the number of children ever born alive to a woman.

Republic of Korea and in Taiwan, the IUD is the main method; in Thailand and Iran, the pill is preferred. The distribution of acceptors by method for several countries is given in Annex Table 27.

Differences in methods cannot be ascribed to anything more systematic than the attitudes of the program administration. These differences are important, however, since contraceptive methods differ considerably in both their clinical- and use-effectiveness. In comparing data on acceptors, differences in the use-effectiveness of methods are more important than clinical effectiveness. For sterilization, the two concepts are identical. Pills have a clinical-effectiveness almost equal to sterilization, but a much lower use-effectiveness since they require considerable motivation and care to use regularly. Irregular use merges into discontinuance. The data in Table 35, based on sample surveys, indicate that the relative efficiency of programs in adding acceptors must be weighted by the method used. The first year continuation rate for pills is generally between 50 and 60 percent, with a rather wide variance; the rate for IUDs is between 60 and 80 percent, with a smaller variance.

Follow-up surveys of acceptors to determine the underlying reasons for discontinuance show that for the IUD, removal is generally much more important than expulsion, and pregnancy is the least important reason of all. For example, a 1967 follow-up survey in the Republic of Korea reported a pregnancy rate of 2.9 percent, an expulsion rate of 12.4 percent, and a removal rate of 28.2 percent at twelve months (Kim 1970). In a 1966 Taiwan survey, the rates were 6.1, 8.5, and

Table 35

Continuation Rates Twelve Months after Acceptance for Selected Countries from Sample Data

(percent)

Country	Method	
	IUD	Orals
Colombia [a]	75	56
Hong Kong [a]	64	38
India	78[b]	53
Korea	53	—
Philippines [a]	82	56
Singapore	68[b]	—
Taiwan	60	42
Trinidad and Tobago	57	91
Turkey [a]	67	38

[a] First-method continuation rates for total program.
[b] With reinsertion.
Source: Annex Table 28.

23.1 percent, respectively (Chow 1970). Several surveys have found that IUD continuation rates increase with age and parity and, surprisingly, have some negative correlation with education. Less information appears to be available about pill discontinuance.

It is unlikely that many persons who discontinue methods joined the program with the intention of practicing for only a few months and then becoming pregnant. Instead, high dropout rates imply that many acceptors find present contraceptive methods highly unsatisfactory. Of course, not all who discontinue one method cease to practice contraception. In Taiwan, for example, a survey found that thirty or more months after the first IUD insertion, 49 percent of the women who had discontinued use of the IUD had been sterilized or were practicing another method of contraception (Freedman et al 1969). Nevertheless, high dropout rates are an indication of user dissatisfaction or inaccessibility of contraceptive supplies.[4]

One important task for program management is to develop systems for following up acceptors and encouraging initial acceptors to remain users. Variations between programs in continuation rates for the same method may be an indication of management effectiveness. Variations in continuation rates between methods reflect not only the technical characteristics of the methods themselves but also differences in characteristics of acceptors of different methods. Terminal methods such as sterilization usually attract older couples with a lower average fertility potential than do IUDs or pills. As a result, the demographic effectiveness measured by births prevented of an average year of contraceptive practice due to sterilization tends to be somewhat lower than that of a year of IUD use. On the other hand, methods used for spacing pregnancies seem to have relatively lower use-effectiveness than sterilization because they are adopted by the relatively young who, until they achieve their desired family size, may be less careful in contraceptive practice and less likely to seek an abortion in case of contraceptive failure.

---

[4] Apart from causing discontinuation, technical imperfections of existing methods lead to many unwanted pregnancies. One would expect this to be less true in developed countries, where the regular practice of contraception has become a way of life for most adults. Nevertheless, during the first two years of New York State's liberalized abortion law, the number of legal abortions performed equaled 10 percent of the annual number of births for the country as a whole. Over 80 percent of the women concerned were using a contraceptive method at the time of the unwanted conception (Segal 1973). This is not surprising, since it has been estimated that among 100 couples marrying in their early twenties, over 80 will have unplanned pregnancies after the last desired conception during their remaining twelve to fifteen years of fertile marriage if they consistently use a 95 percent effective method, and about 30 will experience unplanned pregnancies while using 99 percent effective methods, such as the pill (Hulka 1969, pp. 443–447).

It is difficult to devise universally valid weights for alternative methods according to their presumed demographic effectiveness. The average ages of acceptors, as well as such socio-cultural factors as the duration of breastfeeding which seem to affect fecundability, are subject to important international and interregional variation. Nevertheless, some attempts have been made to calculate the relative impact of different methods on fertility. One study of cost-effectiveness of family planning was based on the premise that, given the typical age composition of acceptors of different methods, the demographic effect of a sterilization is about three times that of an IUD insertion (Robinson 1969). For India, it has been estimated that a sterilization prevented 2.4 births, while an IUD insertion prevented only 0.7 births (Jain 1969). Because of lower continuation rates, the births prevented by pill acceptance are not as many as those averted by an IUD insertion. However, age differentials between the acceptors of the two methods partly compensate for differences in continuation rates. A best guess is that the births prevented by the acceptance of IUDs and pills are approximately in the ratio of three-to-two. Other methods may be assumed to avert only about one-third as many births as the pill. If these assumptions are accepted, a sterilization would produce about 13.5 times the effects produced by an acceptance of condoms, rhythm, or other methods except the IUD and the pill. After some years, the difference in predominant methods in different programs shows up in a divergence of relative country ranking in acceptance and use. For example, in Table 33, India, where sterilizations have accounted for a relatively high proportion of acceptors, shows a better relative performance in use than in acceptance.

Two conclusions can be drawn from the deficiencies of current methods. First, despite very significant improvements in contraceptive technology over the past fifteen years, further advances can play a substantial part in increasing the effectiveness of family planning programs. The declining financial support for contraceptive research noted in Chapter 4 is, therefore, most unfortunate, especially since none of the several new developments in the pipeline appears to overcome all the drawbacks of current technology (Segal 1973). Given the high demographic effectiveness of sterilization, but its drawback as a terminal method, reversible sterilization appears to be an important potential area in which to seek technological advances.

The second conclusion is that a strong practical case can be made for providing abortion as a back-up to family planning services in countries which can afford the trained manpower and facilities required by abortion procedures. At present, many unwanted pregnancies end in abortion. Some of these abortions are legal and safe; most are illegal, and these usually entail much higher degrees of risk. Considerable evidence that pregnancy resulting from contraceptive failure or dropout often ends in abortion appears in the Worldwide Follow-Up Survey of the International Postpartum Program. Among women who accepted contraception under this program, the proportion of pregnancies ending in live births was 68 percent during the three years after acceptance compared with 87 percent before acceptance (Ross et al 1972). Abortion by itself is an inefficient method of birth control. Used alone, one hundred abortions will avert, demographically, only thirty to forty-three unwanted births.[5] If adopted as a backstop method when contraceptives fail, one hundred abortions will prevent up to eighty-nine unwanted births (van der Tak 1974).

CONCLUSION

While it is not possible in most cases to disentangle fully the effects on fertility of family planning programs and changes in socio-economic conditions, the available evidence indicates that family planning programs have substantially increased the use of contraception and contributed to declines in fertility.

The extent to which family planning programs can have an impact on fertility depends on many factors, including the initial fertility level, socio-economic environment, degree of official support, size and intensity of the program, the type of contraceptive methods offered, and management effectiveness.

Although there is ample evidence—for example, the worldwide prevalence of abortions—that the desired number of children is lower than the number of live births, some family planning programs reach a plateau of acceptors fairly quickly, while covering only a small proportion of potentially fertile women. Among the many potential reasons for this leveling off of new acceptance is the management and operation of the program itself. Yet, evaluation units generally still are in their infancy and inter-country performance norms, such as those suggested by the discussion in this chapter, are rarely used even as a point of departure for considering how this problem might be overcome.

There are major differences in effectiveness of alternative contraceptive methods. Sterilization has by far the greatest impact on births pre-

---

[5] This may seem puzzling and, of course, is true only in a special sense. Although, by definition, an abortion prevents a birth, it also has the effect of returning a woman to the fertile population and future risk of pregnancy. While the abortion ends the pregnancy, the woman is exposed to the risk of another pregnancy sooner than if she had delivered a child and gone through the period of postpartum amenorrhea and subfecundity due to breastfeeding. Therefore, for a large number of women, more pregnancies may occur as a result of ending some pregnancies in abortion than if all came to term. For this reason, one abortion does not have the demographic effect of preventing one birth (Potter 1972, pp. 53–59).

vented, followed by the IUD and the pill, but the present irreversibility of sterilization limits its potential market. Yet even allowing for the varying cultural acceptability of different devices, the methods offered by family planning programs do not seem to be based on a systematic evaluation of the differences in their effectiveness. Even in programs which offer a full array of services, there is an obvious choice to be made by program managers as to the priority to be given to the promotion of different methods.

The deficiencies of the current technologies suggest that increased support for research is important. Until improved techniques of conception control can be developed, there is much to be said for offering abortion as a backup to contraceptive failure as part of a complete program aimed at control of unwanted fertility.

The growth of many of the family planning programs has tapered off. It is, therefore, essential that the causes be better understood and consideration be given to how motivation to use the services can be increased. One aspect of this problem—the use of incentives and disincentives to increase demand for family planning services—is discussed in Chapter 6.

Chapter 6

INCENTIVES AND DISINCENTIVES
FOR FERTILITY REDUCTION

THE SLOW GROWTH of family planning acceptance in several programs, and its tendency in some of the more successful programs to level off and even fall when national fertility levels are still far above replacement, has led to growing interest in the possibility of using economic incentives or disincentives to strengthen antinatalist policies. Few countries have yet utilized such schemes in national programs. See Chapter 4. A small number have reached the experimental stage, and a larger number have been proposed.

For the purpose of this discussion, incentives are payments to acceptors of family planning services or to persons who limit family size. In a few schemes, payments are made to those who delay marriage or postpone first births. Disincentives are the withholding of social benefits from those whose family size exceeds a desired norm. If successful, such schemes will increase the demand for family planning services. This chapter is concerned with policies which aim to strengthen the "demand side" of programs, in contrast to the next chapter which is concerned with strengthening the "supply side"—that is, the provision of information and the delivery of services. The incentive schemes discussed here should be distinguished from payments to family planning field workers or others for persuading other individuals to accept family planning methods, which are discussed as a part of the supply side.

INCENTIVES TO REDUCE MARITAL FERTILITY

Incentives can attempt to do either or both of two things. First, incentives designed to give a push to hesitant potential acceptors could help close the considerable gap between what is actually achieved by most family planning programs and what could be achieved at a given level of socio-economic development. Parents sometimes do not practice contraception even after achieving their desired family size whether through ignorance, because of discomfort, or because acceptance involves some time or out-of-pocket costs they cannot afford. In such cases, incentives are a way of calling attention to family planning; of making individuals consider it more seriously; of overcoming conservatism, fear and procrastination; and of compensating costs.

Second, incentives can try to change desired family size by affecting the costs and benefits of children to their parents. In the circumstances of poverty in developing countries, parents may desire large families. Since this is not in the interest of society as a whole, society is likely to benefit more by providing incentives to limit the number of children than by bearing the social costs of raising them and having them compete later for scarce resources such as land and employment opportunities. Private and social returns from children may differ in other ways. For instance, in the absence of other means of insuring against disability or providing for old age, children are often regarded as insurance. From a social point of view, it is inefficient for parents individually to provide themselves with protection against disability when only a small proportion will become disabled. Old age is more universal, but it is possible to establish reliable savings institutions which, if safeguards against inflation are included, would provide a better long-run return than children.

Economic motivations are not the only reason why parents have large families, but economic factors are among the important determinants of fertility. By offering alternative ways to ensure benefits which children otherwise provide, several incentive proposals try to address various motivations for having children. For example, annuities schemes for couples with smaller families are more likely to be successful as incentives if support in old age plays some role in parental decisions about fertility. It is not, however, a necessary condition for the success of such schemes that the incentives actually replace benefits from children. All that is needed is for parents to value what is offered as an incentive and to compare it with whatever benefits, economic or otherwise, they receive from children.

If the problem is simply one of parents needing some stimulus to get them to act in their own interest, then the form of incentive payment may not be very important. For several years, India has used relatively small cash payments, especially for sterilization, in its regular program.[1] The incentives are officially described as compensation for the time lost from work; in most states, compensation payments for vasectomy are a few days' wages. By definition incentives to overcome an initial hesitation should be required only once. These one-time payments are

---

[1] These small payments are not to be confused with much larger incentives given at mass camps during the period 1970–1973 but subsequently abandoned. The official rationale for the incentives in these mass camps was much the same, but the incentives were usually so much larger (one month's wages compared to a week or less) than those of the regular program that they constitute a different approach. They are therefore discussed later in this chapter with other attempts to increase the level of demand for family planning services significantly by reducing desired family size.

likely to be effective for sterilization programs. For other methods, the administrative complexities of avoiding duplicate or repeat payments become overwhelming.

If the objective of an incentive scheme is to align more closely the values on which decisions on family size are based with social benefits, the incentives must be large enough to cause fundamental changes in traditional values. The financial commitment per couple for such a scheme will, therefore, have to be substantial and may have to extend over a long period of time—though for sterilization it would also be possible to make only a one-time payment. Two schemes are being tried on an experimental basis. One offers deferred incentives to limit births among residents of tea estates in South India. The other offers payment of educational expenses to small families in Taiwan. Other schemes have been proposed in varying degrees of detail. Although Table 36 is not comprehensive, especially with respect to variations to a basic scheme, it summarizes the principal proposals.

Economic Considerations

From a national accounting point of view, incentives are transfer payments and in themselves do not use up resources. Their economic impact depends on the savings and consumption patterns of those who are taxed and those who receive payments. Insofar as such schemes successfully redistribute income from the rich to the poor, their impact will be similar to other successful redistributive schemes. The principal questions are likely to be the fiscal constraint and the need to choose between incentives and other possible items of government expenditure, rather than the cost in terms of long-run total investment and growth.[2] If some of the proposals were implemented and were successful, the amounts to be transferred might be large and would pose important

---

[2] This cost, however, may not always be negligible. The capacity of different developing economies to raise additional very large revenues, without significantly affecting the willingness of people to work or to take risks, varies a great deal. Adequate discussion is beyond the scope of this chapter. It is clear that many governments of developing countries find themselves prevented from investing, or lending to the private sector, as much as would be ideally required in current circumstances. This stems from an unwillingness or political or economic inability to use fiscal measures to reduce current consumption and so to free resources for investment. In these circumstances, more consumption is not as socially valuable as more investment. The costs of an incentive scheme should, therefore, include the difference between the social present value of investment and that of consumption. Though there is not yet an agreed way of arriving at this, the main questions which must be considered are fairly clear (Little and Mirrlees 1969). In many circumstances, incentive payments will be far from socially costless, though not as costly as a financially equivalent public expenditure which, in itself, uses up productive resources.

Table 36

Some Proposed Incentive Schemes

Author	Column A Immediate payments		Author	Column B Deferred payments *	
	How checked	Amount (U.S. dollars)		Deferred until	How checked
			NON-PREGNANCY		
1. Sirageldin & Hopkins (1972)	4 mos. exam	Graduated with length of enrollment up to $U.S. 11 per year	1. Enke (1960)	Economic value of averted birth accumulated	4 mos. pregnancy check
			2. Ridker (1971)[d]	Women's age 45	3 mos. check
			3. Ridker & Muscat (1973)	Age 50	6 mos. check
			NON-BIRTHS		
2. Simon (1969)	Birth registration, local knowledge	25-50 percent annual per capita income	4. Balfour (1962)	3 years or later	Certification by local authority
			5. Chow (1971)	3 years or later	Annual inquiry
			6. Finnegan (1972)	Not specified [a]	Affidavit and birth registration
			7. Finnegan & Sun (1972)[d]	10–14 yrs.[b]	Affidavit and birth registration
			8. Chow & Sirageldin (1972)	One year or later	Annual visit to a clinic
			9. Ridker & Muscat (1973)	Age 50	Annual visit to a clinic
			10. Kavalsky (1973)	Age 50	Registered participation, school records

STERILIZATION

11. Ridker (1969)

		Proof of number of children at time of acceptance and payment
3. Enke (1960)	Graduated up to Rs 700 ($U.S.147)	20 years [c]
4. Tata scheme [d]	Rs 200 ($U.S.27)	
5. India mass vasectomy camps [d] (1970–1973)	Rs 60–100 ($U.S.8–$U.S.13)	

* The method of payments is a lump sum deposit in an interest-earning savings account, except where noted.
[a] Scholarship certificate.
[b] Voucher for educational expenses.
[c] Alternatives include lump sum payment, old age pension, life insurance.
[d] Schemes which are being or have been put into operation.
Note: Citations are documented in the section on References.

choices among priorities. For example, suppose that an incentive scheme in India were to pay each couple about $10 per year for the greater part of their reproductive life. (Table 36, scheme A1.) India at present has about 100 million couples in the reproductive age group. Half of these couples participating in the scheme at any one time would represent a bill of about $500 million per year—more than six times the amount currently spent by the government on family planning and about 5 percent of the 1973–74 central government expenditure on both current and capital accounts.

The social cost of incentive payments depends on their timing. The economy reaps the benefits of lower fertility over time. The main benefits from an averted birth come when the child would have become an adult, competing for resources and employment and having further children. Deferred incentives are economically more desirable than immediate ones. Deferred incentives can therefore be a good deal larger in real terms. In some proposals, returns on the waiting period have been made to compare very favorably with those obtainable in local savings institutions. Most of the schemes involving deferment for only a short period suggest that, after the minimum period, a significant rate of interest should be paid on the cash balance not withdrawn by the individual.

Administrative Considerations

Relying exclusively on deferral schemes may be impractical since most people in developing countries are not in the habit of thinking about or planning for the distant future. A number of the deferral schemes, therefore, include an immediate bonus. If repeated visits for supplies are required, as is necessary for schemes that reward nonpregnancy, regular payments will undoubtedly assist regular participation (Sirageldin and Hopkins 1972). To minimize the possibility of rewarding childspacing that might have occurred anyway, or of merely lengthening it slightly with little effect on eventual family size, a number of schemes have proposed short periods of deferment, such as three years.

Two opposite practical arguments, however, have been used in favor of deferring incentives, especially for sterilization. The first is that if there is an immediate cash payment, an individual may ask to be sterilized under conditions of personal financial stress and later regret the move. This would be unfortunate not only for the individual, but also because too many such people would promote an antisterilization backlash. Even with a short deferment, immediate pressures will be relatively less important compared with long-run needs. The second argument is that a system which requires a large number of cash payments to be made by low-level officials in many scattered locations offers considerable potential for corruption.

Other than the issue of deferment, the main practical question is how to devise a system which can check the eligibility of individuals and monitor their reproductive history. In countries with a stable household structure, checking eligibility should not, in principle, be very difficult. But in the absence of any system of vital registration or any network of health centers, physicians, or paramedical personnel, major problems are posed by the need for periodic checks and for avoiding enrollment in two different locations. In its use of personnel and facilities, and its need for record-keeping, a nonpregnancy scheme is more demanding than a non-birth scheme. But if a way can be found to enforce regular attendance at check-up points at least every four months and ensure identification, a non-pregnancy plan is feasible. A pregnancy examination can be kept superficial, does not require much training, and can be given almost anywhere. However, keeping track of all births in circumstances where parents may wish to conceal them, would imply a more effective administrative performance than many developing countries can muster. The scheme offering educational incentives in Taiwan is based on the assumption that the household registration system plus an annual affidavit of family size should be enough to deter extensive fraud, but this is not a general situation. (Table 36, B6). The problem can be mitigated if operations can be decentralized and local leadership involved effectively, particularly in rural areas. Since the possibility of contraceptive failure is substantial, a fair incentive scheme should be accompanied by at least a "no objection" policy with respect to abortion, and preferably its subsidization. Otherwise, incentive programs are likely to lead to increased demand for illegal and unsafe abortions.

Few if any of the proposed incentive schemes seem fully practicable for rural situations in most developing countries. The need for regular attendance by up to a fifth of the population—if all those eligible enrolled—and the requirement of accurate records pose problems for countries with an inadequate network of educational and health facilities and personnel. Where the level of female illiteracy is high, it may be difficult to find a way to enforce attendance at four-month intervals without penalties for non-attendance so harsh, that they threaten the success of the scheme. However, the difficulties do not seem insurmountable in some rural areas of even relatively poor countries. For example, in India, the network of health centers and primary schools is now fairly good and there are increasing numbers of secondary school graduates who might operate the scheme. In more affluent countries like Malaysia, for which a very plausible scheme has been prepared, the administrative problems seem less severe, and it might be possible to convert the regular visit into a periodic health check-up. (Table 36, B9.)

Amounts and Conditions of Payment

Cash incentives. Table 36 shows the suggested cash incentives for the immediate payment schemes. With the exception of A1, all were designed explicitly with India in mind. It is interesting to see that there is considerable variation in the amounts proposed. Most of the schemes that are or have been in operation have had relatively low, flat-rate payments—though some Indian firms have provided graduated payments (Pohlman 1971)—compared with the much higher hypothetical proposals graduated either by the age and parity of the acceptor (Table 36, A3), or length of time enrolled in the program (A1). The hypothetical proposals are based on what society could afford to pay, derived from an estimate of the social value of an averted birth. There is no agreed way of calculating this value, but it is generally accepted to be very large.[3] The very large cash incentives—in one proposal these exceed substantially one year's per capita income—are not likely to be regarded by finance ministries as seriously practicable, from a fiscal viewpoint.

Deferred schemes. Deferred incentive schemes usually vary the incentive inversely with the size of family, at least above three children, providing for the possibility of cancellation with too many live births/pregnancies/survivors. Under the scheme by Ridker and Muscat for Malaysia, women who joined the scheme at age 20, and had children at three- or four-year intervals from age 19 on, would get, at age 50, nothing with five children, M$179 with four children, M$1,250 with three and M$2,679 with one or none. (Table 36, B9.[4]) This last figure is larger than three years' annual income for the poorest 64 percent of the population and larger than six years' annual income for the poorest 36 percent. Yet the authors estimate that the savings on public expenditure alone would permit even greater amounts, if necessary.

An alternative to cash disbursements is the present experiment in Taiwan which releases the blocked account for educational expenditures. It proposes a figure that reaches U.S.$385 after fourteen years of participation and no more than three children (A7). This is not a high figure for a country where incomes are well above those of the poorest Asian countries and are growing very fast. Linking the blocked savings account to education may make the incentive more attractive in a society

---

[3] For example, estimates of the value of a birth averted in India at 1960–1961 prices come to Rs. 712 (Simon 1969), Rs. 1,500 (Repetto 1971), and Rs. 4,600 (Simmons 1971). These figures are much higher than the per capita income of the bottom 40 percent of the population, which was below Rs. 200 a year during 1960–1961.

[4] US$1=M$2.4

which values education highly, but it is not essential to the basic concept. Any scheme which places the differential burden on children rather than on the parents is inherently less attractive.

Experience

The experience of incentives schemes is limited as they have been in operation for relatively short periods. Evaluation lags still further behind. The main schemes involving cash payment are in India, where a number of firms have adopted incentives schemes to promote sterilization. A study of the Tata scheme (A4) concluded that the incentives had been effective in Tata operations in Eastern India but not in Western India (Research and Marketing Services. 1970).

Several studies have been made of some of the mass sterilization camps in India, particularly that at Ernakulam in Kerala. This program began with two camps. The first in November-December 1970 had some 15,000 acceptors; the second in July 1971 had 63,000. The idea became much more widely adopted throughout the following eighteen months. The State of Gujarat had two state-wide campaigns. The first, for six weeks in late 1971, performed 220,000 vasectomy operations, but a similar program a year later attracted only about a fifth of this number. Other states adopted differing patterns, some offering little or no increase in incentives over regular levels—normally about Rs. 20–30 per acceptor.

Apart from the incentives, the main difference between the camps and the regular program was the organization of recruiting in which a large part of the local government apparatus was involved. No study has been able to disentangle the effects of additional incentives from this change in organization. In total, however, there is no doubt at all that, compared with the rest of the program, the camps were effective in recruiting acceptors. In districts where the camps were held, the camps increased considerably the total number of sterilizations performed. They reversed a downward trend in the nationwide number of sterilizations, bringing them up to record levels. However, there was always some danger that the very high incentives would encourage fraud, and at least one study in one state did find considerable evidence of this.

Two experimental schemes entailing deferred incentives are being tried, but it is too soon to draw any conclusions. One of these is a non-pregnancy scheme being tried out on tea estates in South India (B2). The scheme has now been extended to an area with a population of about 900,000. At first it appeared that the effects of the incentives would be difficult to separate from the effect of other changes which accompanied the scheme, such as the provision of more medical attention and family planning information. In addition, several other schemes for family welfare were introduced at the same time on the estates involved. Now, however, attempts are being made to introduce control groups to permit evaluation.

The other experimental incentive scheme currently being tried is the educational incentive scheme in Taiwan described above. The control group here will be a matching group found by utilizing the results of a KAP (knowledge-attitude-practice of family planning) survey.

Both these schemes are being tried in environments atypical of most developing countries. The clients are relatively more likely to reduce their fertility with or without incentive programs. The Taiwan experiment is likely to appeal to parents with educational ambitions for their children, and these parents are likely to be relatively "modern" in outlook. Even without the scheme, the social security system on the tea estates in India is immeasurably superior to that available to most Indians, rural or urban. This does not, of course, argue against testing these proposals more fully and implementing them wherever they may be effective.

INCENTIVES FOR OTHER PURPOSES

To avoid the practical problems associated with incentives to reduce family size, other simpler incentives to raise the age of marriage and to postpone first births have been suggested (Mueller 1967).

Provided that proof of age can be satisfactorily established—which may not be easy in countries where registration of births is not universally carried out—governments can provide inducements to late marriage in the form of dowries, free ceremonies, etcetera. There is no certainty that marriages delayed in this way will lead to a smaller eventual completed fertility of the couple—though there is a probability that some will—but a lengthening of generation is itself valuable, and will reduce both the rate of population growth and the dependency burden. Some sort of screening for absence of prior births is necessary; otherwise, couples might simply cohabit first and marry later.

A variant of these schemes, which goes more directly to the heart of the issue, is a scheme to postpone first births. Suggested for India, this scheme set a minimum age of marriage at 18, and proposed a bonus of, for example, $133 if there was no pregnancy for at least three years after marriage (Mueller 1967).

DISINCENTIVES

The most usual types of disincentive proposals which have been formulated are directed to the withdrawal of specific benefits and tax concessions, which otherwise might be pronatalist in effect. They may imply a narrowing of social or economic opportunities by retracting certain normally available rights or privileges if couples exhibit undesirable fertility behavior. Thus they contrast with incentives, which are designed to offer a widening of social or economic opportunity by granting benefits to couples exhibiting desirable fertility behavior. They may, however, merely be a rationing device for privileges which otherwise have to be rationed in some other way, such as by price. In terms of what actually happens, these disincentives may be operationally no different from a system which utilizes the same benefits as rewards for socially desirable behavior, but their psychological and political effects may be considerably different.

In practice, Singapore is the only country to have attempted use of such disincentives on a national scale. Singapore's disincentives now include limitation of income tax relief to the first three children, restriction of paid maternity leave to the first two pregnancies, an increase in childbirth costs after the first two deliveries, and priority to small families in the allocation of public housing. It is too early to evaluate fully the results of Singapore's disincentive scheme, although it appears that family planning acceptor rates have risen following its inception. The effects are being studied carefully at present.

Elsewhere, some Indian state governments, especially Maharashtra, have proposed restrictions on certain benefits, such as maternity leave, to government employees who have more than three children, but it is not known to what extent these disincentives are implemented. The President of Indonesia has also proposed restrictions on benefits available to government employees who have more than three children in the future.

The obstacles to the wider use of disincentives in most developing countries are very considerable. The ethical objection that such disincentives may adversely affect children has been often discussed (Callahan 1971). Obviously, the welfare of children cannot be completely separated from that of their parents, but it is preferable that penalties or discrimination resulting from undesirable demographic behaviour be borne by the responsible parties—that is, the parents—rather than their children. Pronatalist incentives are often pronatalist precisely because they are directed at the child's welfare. For example, adequate maternity leave benefits the health of the child. But discrimination in educational benefits against later children in large families adds to other disadvantages, including poorer health, that these children often incur anyway (Wray 1971).

Another obstacle to disincentives is the political difficulties faced by any government trying to limit access to privileges that are regarded as a general right. In most developing countries the greatest difficulty is that the potential for utilizing disincentives is limited because the benefits most poor families receive from the government are small or non-existent. Curtailment of income tax concessions given for children is of no interest to those who pay no income tax. Restrictions on maternity or other social security benefits are irrelevant to those who have no access to these benefits. Singapore is quite exceptional in having public housing within reach of the poor.

This is not intended to condemn all attempts made or proposed to utilize disincentives, but merely to point out that such measures are likely to make only a limited contribution to the reduction of the growth rate among the poorest and most fertile populations.

CONCLUSION

The potentially most important approaches to incentive and disincentive schemes are those that offer substantial, deferred incentives. The economic case for them is very strong, if they work. If they do not work, they will have cost nothing beyond their administrative costs. The danger of backlash appears minimal.

If the potential importance of incentives is to be tested adequately, it is important to do this in a variety of circumstances. The present experiments, as noted, deal with groups in above-average socio-economic situations. Even if successful, the lessons would be of limited applicability. It would be highly desirable to test incentives in selected rural areas in India, Indonesia, or Bangladesh, and in different low-income urban settings. The administrative problems would be formidable, but not necessarily insurmountable. The world's major population problems lie in these countries, and it is here that the other forces which might lead to a reduction in fertility are weakest. It would be well worth finding out whether economic incentives can really bring about a significant change in desired family size in these situations.

Problems of obtaining adequate controls to test the effects of incentives—preferably with variations in methods and amounts—separately from complementary inputs, as well as together with them, are always likely to be serious with experimental approaches, unless the experiment is carried out on a large-enough scale. The benefits of experiments can be fully obtained only if they are supported by surveys designed to assess differences between households as well as between groups.

Chapter 7

THE FAMILY PLANNING DELIVERY SYSTEM

PRESENT EVIDENCE of substantial unwanted fertility makes it clear that the first essential requirement of any effective policy to reduce fertility is an efficient system for providing information about family planning, recruiting acceptors, and delivering services. No matter how marked the effect of a reduction of poverty or the use of economic incentives on desired family size, a good family planning program can be a most important link between changes in individual norms and an actual fall in fertility.

In its broadest sense, the family planning delivery system comprises an extensive set of activities. Where the government has a clearly defined objective of reducing fertility, these major activities usually comprise an official family planning program. The main focus of this chapter is on the various components of such a program—its recruiting activities, delivery of services and tasks of program management, and the relationship between a family planning program and health services. In most countries, official programs will be supplemented by important private activities. These may include a voluntary family planning association, for which the operational issues are much the same as for an official program. There is also likely to be a commercial sector with a quite different delivery network, which can be a valuable supplement to the official program.

PROVIDING INFORMATION AND RECRUITING ACCEPTORS

A large number of activities, from the production of simple posters to regular and frequent home visits by program personnel, are involved in providing information and recruiting acceptors. Usually, information activities are intended to promote immediate acceptance. However, information activities could, and probably should, include education in schools about population problems and their solutions.[1] The important operational distinctions are between those information and recruitment activities which involve the use of mass media, those which use informal person-to-person contacts, and those which depend on the regular field staff of the program.

---

[1] Population education, although potentially important, is not yet widespread and is not discussed here.

Mass Media

A recent review of family planning research concluded that mass media were an important source of family planning awareness; that a concentrated public information campaign can increase knowledge of contraceptive methods; and that mass media can have a direct effect on acceptance (Ross et al 1972). In the early stages of a family planning program, personal contact with the target population may be the most acceptable method of information. Indeed, the use of mass media at this stage could produce embarrassment, or even hostility toward the program. As family planning becomes a more acceptable topic for discussion, however, the mass media prove to be a very cost-effective method of providing information, and can help make the subject more respectable and openly discussed.

All countries with family planning programs have used mass communications to some extent. As shown in Annex Table 29, the coverage and the relative availability of different media vary widely between countries and at least some countries do not have adequate mass communications for influencing a large segment of the population except by posters and leaflets. Although all media have been used, radio is especially common because it can reach illiterate persons and frequently has the widest coverage. The Republic of Korea has used the radio continuously since 1962. Analyses of radio campaigns in Colombia and Iran have reported that messages have reached the intended audiences. In general, television, used by some programs, is less promising; production and transmission costs are very high and in addition, it usually reaches only a small, affluent class in bigger cities. In a special family planning month each November, Taiwan has put great emphasis on mass communication and obtained excellent coverage with it (Yen 1972).

Informal Personal Contact

One of the longest and most careful studies of the impact of media, carried out in Taichung, showed that the effect of mass media can be greatly increased when combined with personal contact. Four different communications strategies were conducted over a thirty-month period in different neighborhoods, and acceptance rates among women in ages 20–39 were compared. One strategy involved only posters and meetings by family planning workers with local leaders. When supplemented by group visits and direct mailing, there was little observable difference in acceptance rates. The addition of personal visits to the wife led to a substantial improvement. Visiting both husband and wife yielded little further increase in acceptance. In general, mass media are found to be best suited for providing information about family planning once the subject has gained some legitimacy, and face to face contact is best for persuading individuals to become acceptors.

Personal contact, even if informal, can be very effective by itself. In Thailand, where a program in one rural district preceded the nation-wide official program, a large number of women from surrounding villages came for services, although the work of field workers and midwives was restricted to the district. The Chulalongkorn Medical School Hospital in Bangkok has had IUD acceptors from sixty-six out of seventy-one provinces of Thailand without any public information activities conducted outside the hospital (Rosenfield et al 1973). Obviously, clients in both instances were motivated by and received information from other persons; they did not depend on direct official contacts but on informal word-of-mouth communication.

Informal communication can at times have adverse effects on a program. News and rumors about individuals with adverse experiences of IUD use spread in India very quickly. As a result, the device became unpopular and in recent years, IUD acceptance has been only about one-half of the level reached in the early years after its introduction.

Some programs have tried to utilize informal personal contact to spread information and increase motivation. In Thailand, an experiment to encourage IUD acceptors to find at least one other woman to accept was apparently successful. Sometimes incentives, and occasionally training, have been given to persons not on the program staff. Unofficial vasectomy recruiters received some commission from doctors and clients in Bangladesh; eventually they received official incentives. Pakistan also used village midwives with minimal family planning training to recruit acceptors. During 1960–1963, Madras State in India had a system of vasectomy canvassers, who were vasectomized themselves, and who could employ other agents to recruit acceptors. Paid according to results, the canvassers were successful. Criticism of this approach led to the ending of the program, but the very large drop in vasectomies led to its restoration in a modified form in 1964. Vasectomy acceptance rose again (Repetto 1968). Other parts of the Indian program also pay fees to the motivator who brings an eligible acceptor. The Republic of Korea and Taiwan have also had favorable experiences with schemes using lightly trained local agents who are paid according to results (Kwon 1971; Chow and Gillespie 1966).

There is little doubt that information and motivation from peers will be more effective than abstract propaganda from remote authorities. Because of the possibilities of fraud and corruption, or coercion of potential acceptors, however, it is difficult to utilize an extensive net-work of untrained people without considerable supervision.

Program Field Staff

As used in Table 37, the task of a field worker is to make systematic contact with married couples of reproductive age, informing them about family planning, trying to persuade them to adopt it, and sometimes also distributing contraceptives. Thus, the mainstay of an Indian IUD program—the auxiliary nurse-midwife—is classed as a field worker in the Table even though she has paramedical training. Sometimes, however, the term is confined to persons with limited academic background and a short training.

In a majority of the countries covered in Table 37 field workers have much less training than paramedicals. For many countries, there is probably little choice in the short run; a sufficiently large cadre of paramedicals simply does not exist. Experience in various countries suggests that the more closely field workers possess the personal and economic characteristics typical of the community in which they work, the better their performance. This hypothesis is confirmed by preliminary results of research in Indonesia. In terms of number of monthly visits, number of acceptor referral cards distributed, and number of new acceptors recruited, married field workers performed better than unmarried ones. Older people performed better than younger; and those with primary school or less education performed better than the more educated. (Repetto and Suyatne private communication). Women also performed better than men. These effects were more or less additive, so that a married woman older than 27 with less than a primary school education, would on the average be able to recruit 50 percent more new acceptors per month than an unmarried man younger than 27, with more than a primary school education. This difference was statistically significant. Research in Taiwan, where the field workers are typically married, have children, and use IUDs, also shows a correlation between the performance of field workers and their resemblance to the acceptors in age and marital status.

An important issue discussed later in this chapter is the extent to which field staff should have responsibilities for preventive or maternal and child health services. Provision of such health care may largely determine the size of population a field worker can cover. The population assigned to each field worker varies considerably from country to country as shown in Table 37. Some of the differences may be due to differences in assigned duties, density of the population, and transport logistics. The Indian auxiliary nurse-midwife who also has maternal and child health responsibilities, and who usually prefers not to ride a bicycle, is thought to be able to cover thoroughly a population of 3,000 to 5,000—about half of the usually assigned number. In contrast, the pre-pregnancy health worker in Taiwan, whose duties are simple, appears to cover adequately a population of some ten times that size, partly because cultural practices do not inhibit the use of motorized bicycles. Programs are too new and careful studies too few to permit dogmatic statements about what works best in different cultural settings at different levels of development. In summary, however, it does seem clear that in most developing countries relatively lightly trained field workers are likely to be the single most promising means of providing information and recruiting acceptors, especially where trained paramedicals are very scarce. Their work can be usefully supplemented by mass media.

THE DELIVERY OF SERVICES

The actual delivery of services requires a trained staff of physicians or paramedicals and a network of places at which services are provided.

Physicians and Paramedicals

In most countries of the world, only physicians are allowed to prescribe pills, insert IUDs, or perform sterilizations. Available data on physicians involved in family planning are given in Table 38. These data do not show the amount of the physician's time actually spent on family planning and may exaggerate their involvement significantly.[2]

In most developing countries, physicians are extremely scarce. Often there is not even one doctor per 10,000 people. (Annex Table 30.) Doctors are heavily concentrated in private practice in urban areas, and their cost to the program is relatively high. In a number of countries a viable solution has been found in the use of paramedical personnel, especially nurses and midwives, to carry out some of the responsibilities generally reserved for physicians. In the Republic of Korea and Barbados, the use of paramedicals to insert IUDs has led to a substantial expansion of the program. In Thailand, auxiliary midwives were trained to perform gynecological examinations and to prescribe oral contraceptives. A similar program is being conducted in West Malaysia, where more than half of the acceptors of oral contraceptives receive their prescriptions from nurses and authorized non-medical personnel.

Opposition to such programs has been based on two arguments. First,

---

[2] Physicians listed in the sources as part-time have been included as equivalent to half a full-time doctor, which probably exaggerates their family planning activity. In some cases, however, the data do not distinguish part-time from full-time work. These tendencies to exaggerate the work of physicians may be offset by the likelihood that the data for some countries do not include the work of physicians in public maternal and child health care programs or in private practice who assist the official family planning program. The data for Taiwan and the Republic of Korea include private collaborating physicians who work on a fee-per-case basis.

Table 37

Family Planning Field Workers

Country	Title	Sex	Terms	Duties	Age	Users
Taiwan [1]	Prepregnancy health workers (PPH)	F	Full time	Recruit acceptors & push FP	25+	Yes
Pakistan [2]	Dais (Midwives)	F	Part time	Refer clients to clinics	35+	
Korea (Seoul) [3]	Agents	M, F	Part time	Refer clients to clinics	30+	Some
Morocco [4]	Family planning workers	M, F	Full time	Inform & motivate population to use contraception	16–29	
Indonesia [5]	Family planning field worker	M, F	Full time non-medical	Spread family planning knowledge	26–45	Some
Korea, Rep. of (National Program) [6]	Senior field workers & assistant field workers	89% F 11% M	Full time	Refer clients to clinics & distribute contraceptives	30+	60% are users
India [8]	Auxiliary nurse-midwife	F	Full time	Attend deliveries other maternal & child health	18+	Usually not
India [8]	Family planning health assistant	M	Full time	Motivate potential clients and follow up acceptors	18+	Some
Iran [9]	Field worker	F	Full time	Motivate population by home visits	25+	N.A.

[1] Cernada, George. 1968. Taiwan: Training for Family Planning. *Studies in Family Planning.* 1:36, 1–60.

[2] Ahmad, Wajihuddin. 1971. Field Structures in Family Planning. *Studies in Family Planning.* 2:1, 6–13.

[3] Kwon, E. 1971. Use on the Agent System in Seoul. *Studies in Family Planning.* 2:11, 237–240.

[4] Garnier, Jean-Claude. 1969. Morocco: Training and Utilization of Family Planning Field Workers. *Studies in Family Planning.* 1:47, 1–5.

[5] World Bank data.

Table 37 (Continued)

Population Covered	Salary	Education	Training
A town of about 40,000, of whom 5,000 are women in childbearing age	U.S.$25/month plus bonuses	Junior high school	Two weeks
4 or 5 villages with a target area of 500 fertile married women. Dais could contact all directly or indirectly.	Rs 15/mo. (U.S.$3) salary, Rs 2.5 (U.S.$.50) per IUD acceptor, 80% of contraceptive sales	Very little	"The training they received never went beyond what a middle-aged illiterate woman on a small income could or would acquire." [2]
N. A.	30–50 won (11–19U.S.¢) per acceptor	Agents recruited from various sectors of community. Includes housewives, druggists, Ban Chiefs, etc.	Very limited
30 field workers were divided and assigned to 5 "cities"	N. A.	Junior high school	14 week course
Target is one field worker/10,000 population	Rp 2,500/month (U.S. $7.50) salary, plus Rp 100–200/acceptor	Considerable variation but junior high school preferred	3 weeks
Target is one fieldworker for each township	8,000 won (U.S.$30) per month	Junior high school	(1963)—4-day introduction to their jobs, followed by 2 weeks of on-the-job training. Later, a 20-day, refresher course is given.[7]
Target is one per 10,000 people	Rs 150/month (U.S.$20) salary and small payment per case	8–12th grade	2 years in Nursing and Family Planning
Target is one per 20,000 people	Rs 150/month (U.S.$20) salary and small payment per case	10–12th grade	1 month
N.A.	N.A.	N.A.	2 weeks of lectures, 4 weeks training in the field.

[6] Kim, T. I. and D. W. Han. 1969. *Summary Report: A Study on Administrative Status and Working Conditions of Personnel at Various Levels of the National Family Planning Program.* Seoul: Planned Parenthood Federation of Korea for the Ministry of Health.

[7] Kim, T. I.; J. A. Ross and G. Worth. 1972. *The Korean National Family Planning Program.* New York: The Population Council.

[8] World Bank Data.

[9] Freisen, John K. 1969. Iran. *Country Profiles.* New York City: The Population Council and the International Institute for the Study of Human Reproduction, Columbia University.

Table 38

Number of Married Women Ages 15–44 per Medical Resource Devoted to Family Planning Programs, for Selected Countries, 1972–1973

(thousands)

	Physicians	Other health personnel	Field workers	Service points	Mobile units
Bangladesh	15.0	3.4	1.4	33.0	—
Chile	4.2	2.6	—	—	—
Colombia	7.3	2.3	1.2	4.7	—
Egypt	1.3	0.8	2.7	1.5	—
Fiji	2.7	0.7	—	0.6	6.1
Hong Kong	83.3	3.1	9.6	8.8	—
India	20.0	2.9	13.9	2.6	119.3
Indonesia	32.0	9.8	6.9	12.6	—
Iran	4.3	3.7	2.7	4.9	11.9
Kenya	36.7	73.3	—	8.8	183.3
Korea, Rep. of	2.5	4.5	2.8	2.2	410.0
Malaysia (West)	—	5.6	—	2.8	—
Mexico	—	—	—	62.5	—
Morocco	8.2	0.6	62.9	26.3	—
Nepal	236.3	39.4	—	30.2	1300.0
Pakistan	8.8	19.2	2.1	12.5	—
Philippines	2.6	1.2	—	3.3	625.0
Singapore	35.0	5.6	140.0	5.3	—
Sri Lanka	475.0	475.0	—	3.9	—
Taiwan	2.4	2.6	4.3	1.9	200.0
Thailand	8.3	0.7	55.6	1.0	1,250.0
Tunisia	26.9	12.6	13.0	1.9	46.7
Turkey	5.1	1.6	—	10.5	1,200.0

Source: Nortman, Dorothy. 1973. Population and Family Planning Programs. In *Reports on Population/Family Planning*. No. 2, Fifth Edition. New York: Population Council. Tables 7 and 4. Also Annex Table 31.

the use of non-physicians might lower the quality of service and increase the risk of complications. Second, potential acceptors might resist the non-physicians, and program performance would be lower. Successful results in some countries, however, discount the latter contention. Follow-up studies of the performance of paramedicals indicate no significant drop in quality, as indicated by continuation rates, side effects, and complications. Studies in India and Pakistan find that acceptors who had IUDs inserted by non-physicians compared favorably with those in which physicians performed the insertions. In Nigeria, there was no significant difference between the two groups in the rate of first expulsion and removal (Hartfield 1971). In Barbados, there was a slightly higher incidence of pregnancy and IUD expulsion among women who had insertions by nurse-midwives, but the difference was not statistically significant. In general, there appears to be no consistent difference between the two groups.

Two factors seem to explain the good performance of the non-physician. First, non-physicians are often given thorough training, and have to meet rigorous standards before being allowed to insert IUDs or prescribe orals. This training may exceed that given to physicians in this specific area. Second, non-physicians may be more cautious in selecting acceptors than physicians. In Thailand, for example, midwives were more conscientious in performing a pelvic examination before prescribing orals than the average busy physician (Rosenfield 1971, p. 1036). If and when, however, the IUDs or the orals lead to any complications or side-effects, physicians would probably be more effective.

In most countries where abortion is legal, the law requires that the procedure be certified and performed by trained physicians; it appears increasingly likely, however, that paramedicals, including midwives, may eventually be trained and allowed to perform vacuum aspiration for early abortion, since technical improvements, such as the development of the flexible cannula used in the suction procedure, are decreasing the likelihood of complications. In the People's Republic of China, some paramedicals already receive training in abortion.

Even if paramedicals were less efficient in many activities than physicians, their use may be clearly preferable to not providing services at all. Any health risks from paramedical services have to be weighed against the risks from either childbearing or illegal abortions. (See Annex Table 32 for an estimate of the comparative risks from child birth, abortion, and various contraceptives.)

Facilities

Other than sterilization and abortion procedures, delivery of family planning services requires few physical facilities beyond running water and a room with a table and some privacy. Even the sterilization of males does not need an elaborately equipped operating theatre. The possible demographic impact of legalized abortion does appear limited, however, by lack of facilities, equipment, and physicians that are usually thought to be needed for abortions.

The number of service points or facilities is of considerable importance, especially in rural areas without transport facilities. Table 38 shows the number of married women of reproductive age per service point in several countries. The appropriate number of women depends on the population density, transport facilities, cultural factors and other variables. Health centers in several parts of the developing world over-

119

whelmingly cater to clients living within about a three mile radius—roughly thirty square miles. In rural areas, at a density of about 200 persons per square mile, this would mean one service point for every 6,000 people or roughly one clinic per 780 women needing family planning. It can readily be seen how far countries are from achieving such coverage. Of course, in large urban areas, coverage can be much greater.

In rural areas, mobile units may have considerable potential. Although expensive, they can supply rural communities with services, including a physician, that are otherwise out of reach. The mobile teams may be single-purpose, as in India where they are almost entirely devoted to family planning. In 1972, India had 855 units in operation, of which 399 performed sterilization; the remainder were IUD units.[3] Alternatively, family planning may merely be one of the services offered by a multipurpose team, as in Iran.

Data on performance by mobile teams are limited. In the Republic of Korea, ten teams utilizing only forty people, including the drivers, accounted for about 5 percent of the IUD insertions in the country (Ross et al 1972). They provided IUD and vasectomy services, trained local physicians in family planning methods, and undertook information and education activities. During 1966–1969, they performed an average of 1,400 IUD insertions and 90 vasectomies per month. The cost per acceptor at US $10 was somewhat—but not prohibitively—higher than in other delivery systems. This experience and evidence from other countries implies that these teams have significant potential for family planning programs, especially in medium-income to relatively high-income countries where the population is scattered.

MANAGEMENT OF FAMILY PLANNING PROGRAMS

Characteristics of Management

The critical characteristics of good program management are difficult to outline. A recent World Bank paper contrasts an entrepreneur, possessing "raw energy, imagination, drive, the ability to overcome bureaucratic obstacles without forfeiting credibility" with a trained manager possessing "technical knowledge about sound operating procedures and methods, and the concern for comparing results" (World Bank 1974). Leadership and drive of the chief executive are undoubtedly indispensable, but it is no substitute for organization in a large program. In a small scale effort, the chief executive can personally direct a high proportion of the program's activities, but a regular national program

---

[3] Although the number of mobile units was less than three per district of 1 to 2 million people, they can cover different areas each week. With a limited clientele, mobile units can meet needs as they arise.

has to devise adequately decentralized procedures. The first priority in a new program is to get things going, emphasizing effectiveness rather than efficiency. Eventually, however, a serious budget constraint will be encountered and the two issues amount to much the same concern. Table 39 shows the average cost per acceptor of family planning in selected countries during the past several years. The costs per acceptor fluctuate from year to year in several countries, but Figure 2, based on the data for 1971, shows that the average cost tends to be lower in countries with large numbers of acceptors. This suggestion that economies of scale may exist in this field should encourage managers to try to expand new programs rapidly.

Once a program has been launched satisfactorily, much management expertise will be needed to maintain momentum and avoid the slowdown or even stagnation suffered by a number of programs. For this purpose, a continuous process of evaluation and diagnosis is extremely important. Family planning programs which make serious attempts to influence individual fertility behavior involve an undertaking that is totally without precedent. No other government program aims to affect directly such extremely sensitive and personal individual decisions. It is not surprising that the task has so far proved very difficult. Program managers may learn something from the experience of programs in other countries. But their chances of overcoming local problems are much greater if they establish a good system of evaluating their own performance and use the results to improve program procedures.

Table 39

Cost per Acceptor of Family Planning Programs in Selected Countries, 1971

(U.S. dollars)

Country	Cost	Country	Cost
Fiji	49	Dominican Republic	14
Jamaica	49	Malaysia (West) [b]	14
Ghana	44	Hong Kong	13
Tunisia	33	Morocco	11
Mauritius	28	Korea, Rep. of	9
Turkey	25	Thailand	9
Iran	18	Philippines	7
India	17	Taiwan	5
Indonesia	14		

[a] Information unavailable on precisely what costs include; figures may not be strictly comparable between countries.

[b] 1970.

Source: Annex Table 33.

121

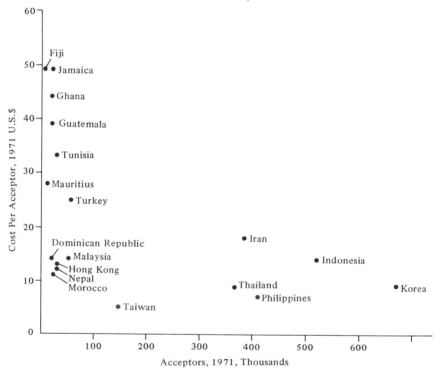

Figure 2

Acceptors and Average Cost per Acceptor of Contraceptives in Selected Countries, 1971 ^{a/}

a India and Pakistan not included: India with 5 million acceptors and an average cost of U.S. $17 in 1971: Pakistan with 1.2 million acceptors and a cost of U.S. $19 in 1969.

Source: Nortman, Dorothy. 1973. Population and Family Planning Programs: A Factbook. *Reports on Population/Family Planning.* No. 2. New York: The Population Council.

Program Evaluation

A mechanism for collecting and processing data must be at the heart of the evaluation system. Much of the data will be service statistics. Also important is an ability to do follow-up and other types of periodic surveys, and to appraise the performance of program personnel. In addition to judging past experience, the evaluation system must propose and assess experiments to improve the different elements of the program.

The administrative location of the evaluation unit is an important decision. Autonomy from the program itself can ensure a high degree of objectivity, but possibly at the expense of influencing management decisions or of direct operational relevance. Integrating the evaluation unit with the program may mean that reporting of program deficiencies—which would imply criticism of friends and colleagues—will be minimized. Furthermore, the implicit assumptions made by program personnel may be too readily accepted by the unit without careful testing. On balance, a unit such as the Taiwan Population Center, which is very close to the program but does not administratively belong to it, might be the best solution.

FAMILY PLANNING AND HEALTH SERVICES

The proper relationship between the delivery of family planning services and basic health services is controversial. This controversy centers on two issues: the location of the management of the program, and the nature and duties of lower-level personnel. Another important question is the extent to which an institutional postpartum program should be developed.

The Location of Central Decisionmaking

In some countries, the family planning program is located within the health ministry. Elsewhere, it is an independent agency—perhaps, as in Indonesia, one that serves all ministries. The question of which base is preferable cannot be answered in the abstract or by comparing the performance of different programs because the number of programs is too small, with too many variations, to permit comparisons. In a paper comparing Pakistan's family planning program during the 1960s with that of India in the same period, Finkle argued that the relative status of the two was critical (Finkle 1971). Because of the commitment and the great personal interest of the president of Pakistan, the family planning program in that country was largely independent of the health ministry, and also free of many civil service and financial regulations. The program was able to exhibit greater single-mindedness and enjoyed higher status than in India. It is difficult to evaluate the success of the Pakistan program in this period because of considerable doubt about the validity of the service statistics. There is little doubt, however, that the program made substantial progress during 1965–1968. But the very autonomy from the other departments of the government and identification of the program with the President meant that its political fortunes suffered with him, and the program has not recovered satisfactorily since he left office.

In India, by contrast, the program has been firmly placed within the Ministry of Health, where it shares the Minister and a Secretary (the top rank of civil servant) with the health services. The staff then divides, although the field staff have both health and family planning responsibilities. Many administrative problems in the Indian program reflect the difficulties of a centrally-financed scheme operated by state governments. In addition no Indian leader has had the degree of personal concern with the program that once existed in Pakistan. Although in general, health ministries have a poor reputation for management, it is not clear that the program in India would have performed better if it had been lodged in a separate agency.

The issue basic to the success of an official family planning program is national commitment, and the amount of resources that a program receives, rather than where the program is located. In many countries, a program within a health ministry may have little autonomy, and be regarded as merely one facet of maternal and child health care. This is often the only feasible way to start a program. But in such cases there is probably also no commitment by the government to making a significant demographic impact through the program.

Health Role of Field Staff

Where health resources permit, the case for integrating family planning and health work at the field level is strong. First, family planning advice from personnel who provide health services which are greatly valued will usually be more acceptable than from other individuals.[4] Second, the combination of maternal and child health care and family planning ser-

---

[4] In Taiwan, village health-education nurses who had some health duties and responsibilities, were gradually displaced by the pre-pregnancy health workers who had only a short training. A controversial study of the different communities in Taiwan suggested that the productivity of the village health nurse in recruiting acceptors was higher than that of the pre-pregnancy health worker and, therefore, the displacement of the former was a mistake (Schultz 1969). On the other hand, the Indian IUD program depends on a trained paramedical—the auxiliary nurse-midwife (ANM)—and the program has been much less successful than in Taiwan. There are several possible reasons for this. One is the fact that the ANM has different characteristics than her clients. She has an above-average education and training, is often young and is likely to be single. This difference appears to outweigh the advantages of her health role. The question is of great importance to programs and needs further research.

vices is logistically attractive because of a common clientele and the fact that the postpartum period is a good time in which to encourage acceptance. Furthermore, a suitable network of health centers would be appropriate for locating service points and basing field workers. It is sometimes argued that doctors and health facilities are associated with illness, while family planning is for the healthy, so the two might best be kept apart. The practical merits of this argument are unknown, but the advantages of integration with health are obvious. In addition, health workers should not be associated with illness exclusively. There is little dispute that the main activities of basic health services in most developing countries ought to be preventive rather than curative.

The main obstacle to integrating health and family planning services is that many of the poorest countries—with a per capita GNP of up to $150—have an extremely limited network of health facilities; with present shortages of health manpower, there is little prospect of improvement. Annex Table 31 summarizes health care indicators in a number of countries. Countries with a GNP in the range of $150–$450 are somewhat better provided with resources or manpower; their current levels of budgetary resources and educated manpower permit the establishment of a national network of health centers that can rely largely on paramedical staff and which can be linked with a corps of field workers, with both health and family planning responsibilities.

Potentially, the most workable organization would be based on a field worker in each community performing a range of preventive health duties and family planning tasks. The area of operation would be limited, and the field workers would become familiar with a larger proportion of potential clients than single-purpose family planning or health workers covering a larger area. Some of the advantages of specialization may be lost but that does not seem a serious obstacle, though the training period might have to be longer than for a single-purpose worker. The main problem might be that if there were an insufficient number of field workers who were then overloaded, their family planning work might be the first to suffer. In addition, individuals who are most effective at providing advice about family planning—that is, married female users—may be less suitable for vaccinating, DDT-spraying, and other preventive health work. The opportunities and drawbacks need further investigation.

As a rule, if a network of basic health services exists, it should be used for providing family planning services. More difficult questions arise when there is no health infrastructure. It has been suggested that the advantages of combining family planning with maternal and child health are great enough to justify setting up such services, despite the great cost (Taylor and Berelson 1971). Apart from its intrinsic health value, reducing infant and child mortality probably has a long-term effect on fertility, as discussed in Chapter 3. But the cost effectiveness of maternal and child health services in reducing infant and child mortality in societies where malnutrition is widespread and contributes to the "pneumonia-diarrhea complex"—the major cause of death in early childhood—has not yet been established.

The costs of this approach, summarized in Table 40, are very high, compared with the health budget. Six carefully monitored experiments are being tried in Indonesia, Turkey, the Philippines, Egypt, Brazil, and Bangladesh under the auspices of the Population Council (Taylor and Lapham 1974). These projects offer an opportunity to test whether this approach is too expensive and cost-ineffective to be applicable in all but the comparatively high-income developing countries.

Table 40

Estimated Per Capita Cost of a Program of Family Planning Combined with Maternal and Child Health and Per Capita Health Budget in Selected Countries

(Figures in U.S. dollars)

Region/Country	Annual per capita costs	
	Program	Budget
Asia		
Philippines [1]	0.60	0.53
Thailand	0.38	1.10
Indonesia [2]	0.41	0.06
Punjab, India [3]	0.32	1.07
Orissa, India [3]	0.36	0.87
Middle East		
Iran	0.92	4.83
Turkey	0.55	2.80
Africa		
Kenya	1.65	1.68
Ghana	0.93	3.66
Latin America		
Colombia	0.36	1.20

[1] The figures for the Philippines represent about 26 percent of the population, in nine provinces selected to reflect the geographical distribution of the country.

[2] The figures for Indonesia represent about 13 percent of the population, in three areas. The areas are not a true sample of the country because the districts included are rather more favored.

[3] The Punjab and Orissa are two states of India.

Source: Taylor, Howard C. and Bernard Berelson. 1971. Comprehensive Family Planning Based on Maternal Child Health Services: A Feasibility Study for a World Program. In *Studies in Family Planning.* 2: 2. p. 39.

Whatever the result of these experiments, the virtual absence of a basic health network places such an approach clearly beyond the reach of many countries, especially those in sub-Saharan Africa. In this region, it would be undesirable to wait for a health network before starting an official family planning program. The extent to which a program should try to develop a corps of full-time, single-purpose family planning workers or rely on part-time input from other government employees with other duties—such as in agricultural extension—is not a question that can readily be answered in the abstract. No good examples exist because most of the countries in this category have not attempted much family planning activity. Obviously, full-time workers would be better if they could be organized properly. If any non-conventional contraceptives are distributed, all will need some supportive facilities. It has been suggested that contraceptive pills might be usefully distributed in such circumstances without additional screening (Speidel, Ravenholt, and Irvine 1974). Subsidized commercial distribution of condoms is also a promising approach.

The Postpartum Approach

One approach which has had considerable success, but which is normally very demanding of facilities, is the institutional postpartum family planning program. Since 1966, the Population Council has organized a carefully monitored international postpartum program in developing countries. By 1972, 114 hospitals in the developing world were in the scheme; seven were in Africa, fifty-three in Asia, and fifty-four in Latin America. More than one million new acceptors had been recruited. The IUD, orals, and sterilizations accounted for 48, 35, and 9 percent of the total, respectively. Of the new acceptors, 60 percent were in Asia and 31 percent in Latin America.

A postpartum approach to family planning has many advantages. The women contacted are of proven fecundity, and are contacted before they become pregnant again. Motivation to accept family planning appears to be at its highest soon after delivery. An offsetting factor is that postpartum amenorrhea causes a lag between acceptance and the time of exposure to risk of pregnancy; during this time, some women may drop out of the program. In addition, insertions of IUDs soon after childbirth lead to higher rates of expulsion.

The postpartum approach is most appropriate for women whose delivery is institutionalized. According to the International Postpartum Program, postpartum acceptors tend to be younger and have fewer living children than other acceptors. Despite their relative youth, low parity, and higher expulsion rates for IUDs, their continuation rates were higher than for those accepting in the general national programs. Direct costs per acceptor were low; the average for the participating developing countries was $3.14. It is difficult, however, to compare the results of this program with other results. In developing countries, women having institutional deliveries are generally not typical of the population. Like other hospitals, maternity facilities are usually found only in urban areas, particularly in larger cities, although the clients may reside beyond city limits.

The marginal costs of providing postpartum family planning services are small if deliveries are institutionalized but the opposite is true if maternity facilities have to be constructed. The benefits from such an effort are probably great enough to justify substantial construction expenditures if additional family planning acceptors can be obtained in no other way. But, prima facie, this appears to be far from cost-effective until other avenues for increasing acceptance have been exhausted. Resources for the health sector are extremely scarce in many developing countries. Some of the poorest have health budgets of less than $1 a year per person. (Table 40 and Annex Table 31.) Institutionalizing deliveries is not a pressing health priority. Many of the advantages of postpartum family planning programs can be obtained, however, without institutionalized deliveries if field workers systematically contact women soon after the birth of each child. Where birth registration is complete, field workers can plan home visits on the basis of recent deliveries. Where registration data are poor, field workers may be able to utilize other sources of information on births in each community and an attempt should be made to keep track of the demographic history of most households in an area. If, as in India, the field staff has maternal and child health responsibilities as well, the opportunity for postpartum work is considerable.

COMMERCIAL DISTRIBUTION OF CONTRACEPTIVES

The literature is replete with discussions of government and non-profit programs in family planning. Yet until recently, little attention has been given to the role of the commercial sector in the distribution and promotion of contraceptives. Commercial firms have played a major role in contraceptive distribution throughout the world. Virtually all contraceptive supplies in the developed countries are provided by such outlets as pharmacies, stores, and other private profit-motivated enterprises. Even in the developing countries approximately 40 percent of the contraceptive supplies are still routed through this channel despite expanding official programs.

The primary advantage of the commercial sector lies in a distribution network which is independent of medical services and reaches a large proportion of the population. The distribution of contraceptives through family planning clinics has a severely limited potential. In many developing countries, a majority of the population live in small towns or rural communities far away from family planning clinics. The commercial distribution network, however, has often penetrated to the village level. For many products, the commercial sector has demonstrated the ability not merely to distribute them, but also to develop a demand among a large number of potential consumers.

The use of the commercial sector for distributing contraceptives is limited to orals and condoms. The demand for other conventional contraceptives, such as foams, jellies, etcetera, which can also be made available through commercial outlets, seems to be small. In Japan, advertising campaigns by the private sector have succeeded in improving the image of the condom as a contraceptive, rather than a device associated with illicit sex relations and venereal disease. During 1950–1970 the proportion of Japanese married couples using condoms doubled to 68 percent.[5] Condoms are readily available in local pharmacies and some larger supermarkets, from vending machines, and through saleswomen who contact wives at home (Matsumoto, Koizumi and Nohara 1972). Although the situation in developing countries is significantly different from Japan, there is substantial scope for a greater involvement of their commercial sector in promoting family planning.

For oral contraceptives, the requirement of prescriptions by doctors steers the poor away from the commercial sector and to the family planning clinic; here a woman can obtain the necessary examination, prescription, and supplies. In some countries—for example, in Colombia—the requirement of a prescription is largely ignored, but in many countries the regulations may be more strictly enforced. However, the demand for oral contraceptives has been dampened by their widely publicized side-effects.

The major disadvantage of the commercial sector is the requirement that prices be high enough to yield profits. High retail prices primarily reflect high promotion costs for pills and high wholesale and retail margins for condoms. Promotional and distributive margins for birth control pills and condoms may be from two-and-one-half to four times the factory cost. In many countries, the growth in demand for contraceptives may have been limited because promotion has been oriented towards physicians and pharmacists, rather than to other retail outlets and potential customers.

In addition to the price factor, several government restrictions hinder

---

[5] Emphasis in advertising campaigns has now shifted to pleasure aspects of the condom. According to one report, the future prospects include "ingenious innovations and improvements" in certain features of condoms and also in dispensing and disposal methods.

the commercial distribution of contraceptives in developing countries. Contraceptives are often imported from the few countries which manufacture a major portion of the world supply. Imports often involve duties, taxes, special banking charges, and the requirement of an import license, which increases costs and complicates the transactions needed to obtain supplies. In Colombia, most condoms destined for the commercial market are smuggled into the country because of the cost and trouble of meeting legal requirements for their import (Arthur D. Little Inc. 1972).

Close coordination between the commercial sector and government programs is possible. The most ambitious example of this approach is the Nirodh program in India where condoms are sold through commercial outlets at prices subsidized by the national program. The family planning program not only subsidizes the cost of contraceptives, but also handles many of the promotional and logistic problems. Preliminary results of this nationwide program appear to be highly successful. Between 1969–1970 and 1972–1973, the commercial sales of condoms rose from 30 million to about 67 million. A similar program, tried on a smaller scale in Pakistan, has also produced encouraging results.

CONCLUSIONS

The family planning delivery system is the major link between a government population policy and the individuals whose behavior determines whether the policy will succeed or fail. To be effective, a family planning program must have a system for motivating and recruiting acceptors. Mass media play a valuable role in spreading information, but personal contact and direct individual communication appear to be the best methods for motivating individual couples to adopt and continue contraception. Family planning workers with characteristics similar to their potential clients, but with little professional training, appear more readily accepted than more highly trained personnel from different socioeconomic strata.

Programs are often constrained by the limited number of physicians and other trained health personnel, but there is evidence that many services can be rendered as effectively by staff with minimal technical training. Some tasks obviously require a high level of skills, but qualifications for other tasks are often set too high, reserving for physicians the work that could be handled as well by paramedicals. Greater use of semi-skilled personnel would permit faster growth of family planning programs in many countries where health staff is scarce.

The appropriate relationship between family planning and other health services is a thorny issue. There is no conclusive evidence as to the most suitable relationship of the family planning program, either to general health services or to such special services as maternity and child care. Any of these existing services that has sufficient coverage, however, would provide an excellent framework for the delivery and enhanced acceptability of family planning services. Where the basic health network does not exist or is inadequate, alternative channels must be developed. The proper balance between health and non-health channels depends on the country situation. The urgency of the population problem and the cost of constructing basic health service networks, however, suggest that it would be unwise to make the growth of the family planning program dependent on the expansion of general health services.

A major family planning effort is always expensive, and must compete with other budgetary priorities. Evidence suggests that there are economies of scale in operation and that starting a program in too small a way is likely to be wasteful rather than prudent. Budgetary competition will, nonetheless, place a premium on cost effectiveness. To assure the most effective use of resources requires competent and innovative management. It also requires constant evaluation of approaches and procedures since these must be developed to suit local socio-cultural conditions.

Since the official family planning programs are rarely wholly adequate, it is desirable to use other existing distribution systems where feasible. The commercial sector has a ready-made distribution system which extends to virtually every village. It can provide a valuable supplement to official programs, particularly if well supported by publicity. The costs of commercial distribution may put the product out of reach of potential users, but this can be circumvented by subsidies or other government intervention.

Chapter 8

CONCLUSIONS: THE DESIGN OF POPULATION POLICIES

MANY DEVELOPING COUNTRIES have adopted population policies during the last decade that are antinatalist. Other countries, particularly in Latin America and Africa, have not yet formulated population policies. Even in countries which have an official family planning program, population questions seldom receive adequate consideration by planners and policymakers. There are two important reasons for this neglect.

First, even though population growth is fundamental in terms of long-term consequences to society, policymakers are preoccupied with more immediate issues. The planning and policy process in most developing countries has a rather short time horizon—generally up to five years—whereas population policies are likely to produce a marked economic impact only after one or two decades. Therefore, policymakers often do not fully recognize how their immediate concerns—food deficits, slow economic growth rates, poverty, unemployment—have been accentuated by past population growth and how the continuation of the present population trends will compound development problems in the future. Second, the population question is a sensitive issue, and the discussion has become unduly politicized. Frequently, participants in the debate adopt highly exaggerated positions. To justify family planning programs, some advocates have attributed most economic difficulties to population pressures. In reaction, others argue that economic development alone can solve the population problem and that such direct measures as family planning programs are ineffective. This polarization has obscured the basic interrelationship between development and population growth and impeded the formulation of antinatalist programs.

The central conclusion of this paper is that direct population policies and general development policies reinforce each other in raising per capita incomes, especially among the poor, and in reducing fertility. Neither can adequately address the problem of rapid population growth alone. Direct population programs can accomplish much in most developing countries, but even the most elaborate programs will not reduce fertility sufficiently unless standards of living of poverty groups are significantly improved. It is therefore essential that population programs be integrated with overall development strategies, and that the design of

133

social and economic policies whose major objective is not demographic take explicit account of how they affect fertility. The findings of this paper can be summarized best by discussing three questions:

- What considerations are relevant in determining national population growth objectives?
- How effective are available policies and programs for reducing fertility?
- What new emphases in population programs and projects appear worthwhile?

POPULATION GROWTH OBJECTIVES

Sharply declining death rates but continued high birth rates have meant that population in most developing countries has been growing at a much faster pace than ever before and much faster than the growth experienced by the now industrialized countries at a comparable stage in their history. Because of past high birth rates and low infant and child mortality rates, a very large part of the total population of developing countries is under 15 years of age. This young age structure embodies a considerable growth momentum since, inevitably, increasing numbers of women now under 15 will enter their reproductive period.

Some large, poor countries are already feeling pressures of population size on arable land that show up as food scarcity, land exhaustion, deforestation, and land fragmentation. At existing levels of technology and on the basis of known natural resources, such countries are already overpopulated. Given uncertain prospects for discovery of new resources or technological breakthroughs, the imperfections of policy, the magnitude of current socio-economic difficulties, and the inevitability of continued population increases, these countries need to pursue a vigorous program to reduce fertility as quickly as possible. Yet, because of the growth momentum built into the age structure, the best that can be hoped for in the near future is a slow down in the rate of natural increase.

In developing countries where population does not yet press against resources, the need to lower fertility may not be obvious. Some governments may even wish, for political and cultural reasons, to expand population size substantially. It is important that such countries recognize that, in virtually all cases, the combination of present high fertility and the momentum of population growth will carry them inexorably to their demographic targets. Indeed, unless policies to reduce fertility are implemented soon, population in most such countries will increase far beyond the intended size.

Whether or not their countries are currently experiencing acute population pressures, planners should recognize the implications of alternative rates of population growth. High population growth rates impose a cost on society by slowing down the growth of per capita income and especially by impeding efforts to improve income distribution. There is a conflict between raising the living standards of the existing population, particularly those of the poorest 40 percent, and accommodating new entrants to the population. The implications of alternative rates of population growth have to be assessed at the national level; the right answers will not emerge by adding up private fertility decisions of individual households.

High fertility, combined with falling infant and child mortality, increases the dependency burden on the economy. Parents have to feed, clothe, and house more children than would otherwise be the case. The government, in turn, has to spread education and health expenditures more thinly over growing numbers or restrict the coverage of these services. The increased dependency burden makes it difficult to raise standards of nutrition, schooling, and health from the very unsatisfactory prevailing levels, and thus impedes the formation of human capital essential for raising productivity. In the intense competition for public services, it is the poorest who lose.

Accelerated population growth also means a faster expansion of the labor force than would otherwise occur. Given the backlog of underemployment and unemployment in most developing countries, new workers face grim prospects in the market for jobs. The economy can spread the available capital among the expanding work force (capital-widening), or use available funds for increasing capital per worker among those who are already employed (capital-deepening), or employ some combination of these two approaches. Capital-widening would absorb a substantial proportion of total available investment and would limit the growth of productivity. Capital-deepening in the organized modern sector of the economy will accentuate the gap between that sector and traditional activities and aggravate underemployment and thereby worsen the distribution of income. The pressure of labor force growth on wages, land fragmentation, and growing landlessness are other ways in which rapid population growth intensifies the problem of poverty.

EFFECTIVENESS OF POLICY INSTRUMENTS

General development policies are of fundamental importance in dealing with population. The relation between fertility and socio-economic development runs both ways. High fertility impedes development, and poverty generates high fertility. The demographic transition of Western Europe and North America, from high to low fertility, accompanied the process of socio-economic development over half-a-century. The transition may not take quite as long in those developing countries which are growing economically much more rapidly than 19th century Europe. The speed of fertility decline will depend as much or more on the quality and pattern of economic growth as on its overall rate. Some of the determinants of fertility cannot be manipulated directly but will respond to the overall pattern of development. Strategies for investment which focus narrowly on the modern industrial sector, or on enclave-type plantations and mines, are not likely to have as great an impact on fertility as policies which bring the benefits of development to the bulk of the population occupied in traditional activities.

Two important determinants of fertility rates are age at marriage and incidence of marriage. Marriage is more nearly universal and occurs much earlier among women in developing countries than in the industrialized Western world. As educational levels of women rise and their economic opportunities expand, they tend to marry later or not at all. Undoubtedly, marriage patterns are also influenced by sociological and cultural factors about which little is known. Population policies cannot easily affect marriage patterns directly. Attempts to legislate the minimum age of marriage have proved to be ineffective. Monetary incentives for delaying marriage have been proposed but not yet tried. Special programs of employment for women are difficult to institute in conditions of high general unemployment. If, however, the general development effort is sufficiently broad-based so that women, particularly those in poor households, share in the benefits of development, their fertility will decline over time.

A third determinant of fertility is desired family size, which tends to be considerably higher in developing countries compared to norms in the industrialized world. The strong demand for children in traditional societies is related to sociological or cultural patterns as well as economic considerations. Parents do not expect to incur large additional costs for child-rearing but, instead, expect children to contribute labor in the home and on the farm and to look after them when they are old or disabled. Such expectations change with the spread of education, the breakdown of the extended family, increasing urbanization, and the establishment of social security systems. The small family ideal reflects a new life-style.

It is probable that development brings changes in values affecting family size only after a significant time lag. In addition to reducing unwanted fertility through the provision of services, family planning programs may be able to accelerate a change in desired family size through information and motivation activities. These activities aim at convincing target groups that a) fertility can be controlled through a variety of techniques and, therefore, family size can be a subject of calculated choice rather than a matter of chance; b) the advantages of

small families increase as socio-economic development takes place, and
c) fewer births serve to secure the desired family size as infant and child
mortality have diminished. Such information activities have met with
some success when they have combined the use of mass media with personal contact by motivators drawn from the peer group of the target
population and from regular field staff.

Population policy can also try to influence desired family size through
a system of economic incentives or disincentives. The latter approach
is being tried in Singapore but may not be feasible elsewhere. Significant cash incentives for sterilization, combined with a special recruitment
effort, have been tried in India; the result was a reversal of a national
downward trend in the number of sterilizations.

Past experience demonstrates that fertility behavior can be affected
significantly by family planning programs. Careful attempts to disentangle the impact of these programs from that of changes in socio-
economic conditions in several countries suggest that family planning
programs have made a sizable contribution to the observed decline in
fertility. Although the level of socio-economic development and mortality conditions set an upper limit on the demand for family planning
services, virtually no program is hitting against that ceiling now. Considerable scope remains for exploiting the existing potential for fertility
reduction. Induced abortion is universal and not all unwanted conceptions are aborted. The number of children whose births are not desired
by their parents must be very large indeed. Meanwhile, the general thrust
of economic and social progress will raise further the demand for family
planning services, particularly if the development strategy improves the
distribution of income.

East Asia is the only part of the developing world in which a substantial proportion of married women—more than 25 percent—use contraceptives. The proportion is much lower in other countries which also
have family planning programs. Although demand for services is not
yet a constraint on these programs, supply bottlenecks impede their
effectiveness. Programs have to contend with the shortage of trained
manpower, particularly of physicians but also of paramedical personnel,
and facilities that are too dispersed. The potential of the commercial
distribution network has often been neglected. High dropout rates among
those who adopt contraception reflect dissatisfaction with existing family
planning services or available contraceptive technology.

To some extent, these shortages are the result of inadequate funding,
indicating that few governments have translated their commitment to
population policies into budget priorities. Together, governments of
developing countries spent $300 million on these programs in 1971,
which is a minute proportion of their total budgets. Inadequacies in the

programs also reflect physical bottlenecks, such as the unavailability of trained manpower, which are difficult to deal with immediately since the number of fully trained professional personnel cannot be increased quickly. But there is evidence that some programs are insisting on unnecessarily high standards. For instance, evidence suggests that many program functions that are reserved for physicians could be performed adequately by paramedical personnel. Any health risks involved in using paramedical personnel have to be weighed against the generally much larger risks of childbearing and illegal abortion. The shortage of paramedicals faced by most developing countries can itself be relieved by a greater use of personnel with very limited training.

New Programs and Projects

It is essential that managers of family planning programs establish a continuous evaluation system so they can feed into the programs the lessons of experience. They should also consider possible new approaches to formulating projects and programs. The analysis of this paper indicates four areas that should be considered: a) stronger emphasis on voluntary sterilization; b) legalized elective abortion, which can strengthen greatly an effective family planning package; c) proposals for stimulating demand through monetary incentives which should be tested out in realistic field conditions; and d) more broadly based information and education programs to create a favorable climate of public opinion for reducing fertility.

The demographic effectiveness of contraceptive methods currently in use varies enormously. Past experience suggests that the demographic impact of sterilization is usually several times greater than that of the intrauterine device, which, in turn, is more effective than the pill. Condoms, rhythm, and other contraceptive methods are still less effective. Despite its high effectiveness, sterilization does not figure prominently in most family planning programs and there are many programs which do not offer this method at all. Considering its advantages, especially to men—a simple once-for-all, inexpensive operation with no need for medical aftercare or acceptor discipline—a case exists for placing stronger emphasis on voluntary sterilization. If sterilization remains a terminal method, however, it will not appeal to persons desiring additional children or wishing to remain capable of replacing a child in the event of death. To enhance the attractiveness of sterilization as a contraceptive measure, it is important for research to try to perfect a reversible procedure.

The argument is also strong for providing facilities for elective abortion as a back-up to contraceptive use. The number of pregnancies is large among individuals practicing family planning, reflecting technical imperfections of contraceptives and lapses on the part of users. When pregnancy is due to shortcomings in the contraceptive method, the demoralization of present and potential users of contraception is serious. At present, many of these unwanted pregnancies are aborted illegally under very unsafe conditions, and can do major damage to the mother's health. The inclusion of elective abortion services within family planning programs promises to become more feasible as recent improvements in techniques may make it possible for abortion to be performed by para-medical staff instead of physicians.

The information and recruitment activities of programs should be reinforced by more powerful incentives than have been tested until now. Underlying most existing schemes is the premise that although family planning is in the interest of parents, its practice encounters obstacles of various kinds such as ignorance, discomfort, procrastination, and out-of-pocket expenses. Many households, however, do not perceive the small family as in their interest. A number of proposals described in Chapter 7 rest on the assumption that economic incentives can reduce the gap between the private and social benefits of children. These schemes aim at modifying basic fertility behavior through financial compensation. Such schemes would be considerably more expensive for government budgets, and would require a more elaborate administrative mecha-nism than incentives tried so far. Their success remains to be demon-strated, but conducting a few experiments in representative low-income areas would be very worthwhile.

Rethinking the strategy for communication, information, and educa-tion may result in programs that exploit the full potential for fertility reduction at any level of socio-economic development. In many coun-tries the target group for such a strategy is confined to fertile women and their husbands, that is, individuals who might immediately practice contraception. This is a worthwhile focus in the early phase of a program, but a more broad-based approach should be considered, particularly in situations where family planning practice is growing only slowly. In many developing countries, attitudes to the desired number and sex of children evolve from a complicated interaction between potential acceptors, their extended families, and the village or urban communities in which they live. Parental concepts of what constitutes an ideal family may be critically influenced by persons and groups other than potential users of contraception. A motivation campaign directed at the community could ameliorate the problem of individuals who at present lose face or encounter group hostility when they adopt family planning methods. Such a campaign could be supplemented by introducing population ma-terials in school curricula; many of the values bearing on demographic behavior are formed in these early years.

Implementing the suggestions made in this study will require an effort to mobilize public opinion that is larger and more sustained than most countries have yet attempted. Unless a vocal constituency on behalf of population programs is deliberately built up and kept informed, it may be difficult for policies to secure the political backing and resources that a solution to the population problem requires.

Essentially the problem of population growth in developing countries has to be defined in those countries themselves. Policies and programs to deal with the problem have to be designed as well as executed in these countries and will depend primarily on national efforts. Nevertheless, the close connection between fertility decline and the eradication of poverty should be considered by donors as well as by national governments. Foreign aid agencies can play an important supportive role in helping reduce fertility, not only by assisting family planning and allied population programs, but also through overall development assistance efforts. The current world economic situation has thrown in doubt the ability to maintain even the present low rates of economic growth, particularly for the poorer countries. Unless resources can be found to maintain their development programs, the support for family planning programs may not help much.

Appendix A[1]

THE RELATIONSHIP OF THE SIZE DISTRIBUTION OF INCOME TO FERTILITY, AND THE IMPLICATIONS FOR DEVELOPMENT POLICY

THE PRELIMINARY FINDING, based on a sample of sixty-four developed and developing countries for which comparable data on income distribution are available, is that more equitable income distribution is strongly associated with lower fertility. This is independent of the association of more equitable income distribution with the broader distribution of social welfare, as indicated by such factors as literacy, increased life expectancy, and so on.

The importance of the distribution of income for fertility is in accordance with expectations. The typical size distribution of income provides the richest 15 percent of households, for which fertility is relatively low, with 50 percent or more of total available income. This leaves the remaining half for the poorer 85 percent of the population, who are usually responsible for a disproportionately high share of population growth. To the extent that income affects vital rates, the 50 percent of income that goes to the richest 15 percent of households cannot be as important in influencing overall population growth as the 50 percent of income received by the poorer 85 percent of households.

Several authors have postulated a link between income distribution and aggregate fertility (Rich 1973; Kocher 1973). However, until now, there have been few if any quantitative studies explicitly exploring the relationship between these two factors. Data on income distribution have been difficult to obtain, especially for countries with low income and high fertility. Also, available data have not been readily comparable either over time or from country to country. For the economically more advanced countries for which data are more easily obtainable, income distributions over time have tended to be relatively stable, so that attention has been diverted away from distribution as a factor in explaining fertility change. Considerably more attention has been given to the impact of changes in the level of income.

Models of household behavior based on utility maximization suggest that desired fertility should be positively related to "pure" income

---

[1] This appendix was written by Professor Robert Repetto.

changes; that is, changes which hold constant the relative opportunity costs of children, consumption of goods and services, and what is unfortunately termed the "quality" of children. However, most changes in household income are not of this pure type, since most raise the opportunity cost of time spent by the parents in child care, which tends to be relatively time-intensive, and create a substitution effect against large families. This effect, combined with changes in values, aspirations, knowledge of contraceptive possibilities, and other aspects of modernization associated with rising income, leads to the typical findings that the *total* impact of increases in the level of household income is a reduction in fertility.

This finding from research on household behavior is reflected in the negative simple correlation between income and fertility at the more aggregate level, including the comparison across countries at different levels of development. At this level, however, attempts to probe more deeply into the relationship have encountered many pitfalls. Depending on the sample of countries and the other socio-economic variables considered in multivariate analysis, the relationship between per capita income and fertility may be either positive, negative, or non-existent.

Undoubtedly, a good part of this difficulty results from inattention to the distribution of income within the individual countries. The relevance of the distribution of income can readily be demonstrated. The overall birth rate in any population is the weighted average of birth rates for all subgroups in the population, the weights being the shares of each group in the total population. If, among other influences, changes in income within each group affect the fertility of that group, then overall birth rate changes will be a weighted sum of these income effects, with the weights given by the shares of the sub-groups in the total *population.* The overall rate of income growth, by contrast, is the weighted sum of the rates of change of income in each sub-group, with the weights given by the shares of each sub-group in total *income.* There is substantial concentration of income in most countries, such that the richest 10 percent may receive 40 percent of total available income, while the poorest 40 percent may receive only 10 percent of total income. Therefore, the two weighting systems will lead to quite different patterns of change unless income growth is proportionate for all sub-groups. Differences in *average* per capita income are not sufficient measures of income differences relevant to population processes.

If the response of population to income changes were constant and identical at all levels of income, income distribution would be irrelevant. However, it is clearly not. For example, mortality rates at lower levels of income fall more quickly than do fertility rates, so that even the sign of the response may change at different income levels.

Consideration of changes or differences in income distribution adds considerably to the explanation of fertility differences at the aggregate level. Based on the level of economic development of Latin America, birth rates in the region are higher than would be expected. An explanation seems to be that in most countries of Latin America, the distribution of income is very unequal. The large majority of the population live at low absolute levels of consumption, and display fertility behaviour normal for that level of development. Birth rates in Eastern Europe, by contrast, have been found to be exceptionally low for countries at those levels of economic development. Explanations have touched on shortages of housing and political factors. A partial explanation seems to be that in the countries of Eastern Europe, income is distributed relatively evenly and overall fertility is correspondingly lower.

Measurement of the size distribution of income involves many choices of income concept, unit of analysis, data sources, period, coverage, etcetera. It is extremely difficult to achieve comparability in measurement either over time or across populations. In this preliminary investigation, there has been little attempt to refine the data available. The data are given in Table A1.

Data on income distribution for a sample of sixty-four countries were taken from Jain and Tiemann (1973). The authors of that paper compiled available data from a number of sources and, for many countries, presented alternative estimates of the size distribution, along with the sources, bases, coverage and reference periods for each. Whenever choices were made among alternative estimates for a single country, the criteria used were 1) national coverage, if possible; 2) use of households as the income-receiving unit, if possible; 3) reference date within the period 1960–65; and 4) quality of sources and agreement with other estimates, if further choice remained. Two measures of income distribution were used: the share of total income received by the lowest 40 percent of the population and the Gini coefficient. These are correlated across the sample at the 0.95 level, and little is altered by the use of one or the other.

Other data were taken from Harbison et al (1970). This is a relatively large and careful compilation of social and economic data for a large sample of countries, with reference to the early and mid-1960s. The measure of fertility used was a close approximation to the general fertility rate; that is, the number of births divided by one-half the population in the age group 15–64. It will differ from the general fertility rate among countries in accordance with variations in the percentage of the population aged 50–64, and in the sex ratio of the population in the age group 15–64. The approximation should be quite close to the ranking of countries by fertility level.

Table A1

Demographic and Socio-Economic Indices for Selected Countries

Country	Fertility index *	Life expect-ancy	Persons per Km²	Per capita income	Percentage share GNP to poorest 40%	Gini co-efficient	Newspaper circulation per 1000 population
Argentina	72	68	8	745	17.3	0.4220	128
Brazil	141	61	10	226	9.8	0.5578	34
Bulgaria	44	70	75	596	26.8	0.2058	190
Burma	128	48	38	60	16.5	0.3720	9
Canada	69	72	2	2,070	20.0	0.3171	212
Chad	172	33	3	63	18.0	0.3545	0.4
Chile	118	62	12	490	13.0	0.4868	118
Colombia	176	62	17	267	8.6	0.5733	53
Costa Rica	178	65	31	370	13.8	0.5064	59
Czechoslovakia	49	71	112	964	27.6	0.1831	283
Dahomey	199	33	22	73	15.5	0.4370	1
Denmark	56	72	112	1,749	15.8	0.3714	354
Dominican Republic	189	59	80	240	13.0	0.4710	27
Ecuador	186	56	19	187	10.0	0.6008	44
El Salvador	183	56	147	256	10.5	0.5210	47
Finland	52	69	14	1,526	11.1	0.4546	359
France	54	71	91	1,658	9.5	0.4984	248
Gabon	117	45	2	380	6.0	0.6505	150a
Germany, Fed. Rep.	55	71	233	1,629	15.4	0.4534	328
Greece	55	69	66	630	21.0	0.3653	121
Guyana	152	65	3	285	14.0	0.4028	191
Honduras	218	50	22	209	7.3	0.6063	19
Hungary	42	70	110	765	24.0	0.2377	197
India	146	45	156	86	18.6	0.3731	13
Iran	201	51a	16	232	12.5	0.4728	15
Iraq	178	54	19	240	6.8	0.6068	12
Israel	84	72	129	1,111	16.0	0.2830	188
Ivory Coast	206	35	12	233	17.5	0.4325	3
Jamaica	147	69	171	437	8.2	0.5581	69
Japan	56	71	270	826	15.3	0.3966	465
Korea, Rep. of	188	58	302	139	23.0	0.2640	51
Lebanon	124	60	242	455	13.0	0.5175	77
Libya	144	57a	1	614	23.5	0.2575	5
Malaysia (West)	149	61	65	269	17.7	0.3633	64
Mexico	170	63	23	443	10.5	0.5208	116
Netherlands	61	74	375	1,348	14.0	0.4246	301
New Zealand	74	71	48	1,836	22.0	0.2957	380
Nigeria	178	41a	67	78	18.0	0.3570	7
Norway	57	73	12	1,635	16.6	0.3478	382
Pakistan	183	45	113	85	17.5	0.3713	18
Panama	155	65	18	488	14.5	0.4815	78
Peru	162	59	10	307	8.6	0.6204	47
Philippines	175	55	116	151	11.8	0.4891	27
Poland	54	68	102	640	23.5	0.2519	189
Puerto Rico	108	72	303	1,064	13.7	0.4367	102

Table A1 (Continued)

Country	Fertility index *	Life expect- ancy	Persons per Km²	Per capita income	Percentage share GNP to poorest 40%	Gini co- efficient	Newspaper circulation per 1000 population
Rhodesia, Southern	181	52	12	209	8.2	0.6239	15
Senegal	182	38	19	204	10.0	0.5640	6
Sierra Leone	155	48 ª	34	139	10.0	0.6025	10
South Africa	146	55	15	530	6.2	0.5602	57
Spain	65	70	64	614	17.0	0.3754	159
Sri Lanka	120	62	179	147	13.7	0.4543	44
Sudan	206	40	6	94	14.2	0.4279	5
Sweden	48	74	17	2,169	14.0	0.3900	514
Taiwan	131	68	365	219	20.4	0.3180	64
Tanzania	176	41	13	71	14.0	0.4815	3
Thailand	176	68	64	125	12.9	0.4964	22
Tunisia	173	53	28	194	10.5	0.4975	27
Uganda	153	44	34	96	17.1	0.3817	8
United Kingdom	56	71	226	1,549	18.0	0.3353	488
United States	63	71	21	3,357	16.0	0.3705	309
Uruguay	68	69	15	547	14.3	0.4809	314
Venezuela	167	68	10	817	9.7	0.5240	68
Yugoslavia	63	65	78	488	19.0	0.3304	80
Zambia	205	43	5	177	14.6	0.4881	8

* For units of measurement of indices, see text.
ª Estimated data.
Source: Harbison, F. G. et al. 1970. *Quantitative Analyses of Modernization and Development.* Princeton: Princeton University Industrial Relations Center. Appendix VII.
Jain, S. and A. E. Tiemann. 1973. *Size Distribution of Income: Compilation of Data.* World Bank. Discussion Paper No. 4. Washington, D.C.: World Bank.

Table A2 presents the matrix of simple correlations among the variables used in the study. Life expectancy is a measure of the level of mortality, and is expected to be negatively related to fertility, in accordance with the generally supported hypothesis that households adjust fertility rates to survival probabilities. Newspaper circulation is taken as a measure of effective literacy of the population, and is expected to be negatively related to fertility. Per capita income is a total rather than a pure income measure, and includes substitution effects, and is expected to be negatively related to fertility. The share of the bottom 40 percent of households in total income is an indicator of the extent to which the income weights discussed in the preceding section approximate population weights, and is expected to be negatively related to fertility. In the simple correlations, all of these expectations are fulfilled.

Means of the variables reflect the fact that the sample includes both developed and developing countries. The sample has not been divided

Table A2

Matrix of Simple Correlations Among Dependent and Independent Variables

	Means	1	2	3	4	5	6
1. Income per capita	623	1.00	0.65	0.11	0.80	0.24	−.72
2. Life expectancy	59.6		1.00	0.36	0.70	0.21	−.78
3. Population density	77.2			1.00	0.24	0.14	−.32
4. Newspaper circulation	125				1.00	0.28	−.82
5. Income distribution	0.146					1.00	−.47
6. Fertility rate	128.8						1.00

into subsamples for developing and developed countries, because this would eliminate much of the systematic variance in fertility. For developing countries with birth rates distributed around 40 per thousand, much of the variance has to be considered as a probable measurement error. The confidence limits around parameter estimates of the systematic components of the relationship of fertility to socio-economic variables would be quite wide. The variance in fertility between developing and developed countries is not primarily due to measurement error, but to systematic differences in socio-economic structure, so that estimation of the parameter values of the systematic component can be accomplished with less error.

Of interest is the relatively low correlation between the distribution of income and the level of income and social development. As many economists have noted, there is some tendency for countries at higher levels of per capita income to have somewhat more equal income distributions, but the tendency is rather weak and there is substantial dispersion in the income distribution at all income levels. The intercorrelations among the level of per capita income, the extent of effective literacy, the expectation of life, and other measures of welfare are, however, all quite high. This illustrates the difficulty in disentangling their separate effects on fertility, a difficulty felt equally in cross-section and time series investigations.

In view of this problem of multicollinearity, a step-wise multiple regression procedure was used. Explanatory variables were entered in order of their partial correlations with fertility until no variables remained with a partial correlation of 0.05 or more. Both linear and logarithmic linear models were used, as were measures of income distribution. Final regressions for all variants are given in Table A3, along with the t-statistics, standardized beta coefficients, and corrected multiple correlation coefficients.

The results of the regression analysis show a strong and stable rela-

Table A3

Final Stepwise Multiple Regressions of Fertility on Income Distribution, Income Per Capita, and Other Socio-Economic Variables

	Income per capita	Life expectancy	Persons per Km²	Newspaper 1,000 pop.	Distribution of income
I. INCOME DISTRIBUTION MEASURED BY THE SHARE OF THE BOTTOM 40 PERCENT OF HOUSEHOLDS IN TOTAL INCOME *					
A. *Linear model*					
Coefficients		−1.86		−0.19	−290
t-statistics		(5.05)		(6.00)	(4.45)
Beta-coefficients		−0.40		−0.47	−0.26
Corrected R²: .81					
B. *Logarithmic model*					
Coefficients	−0.20			−0.12	−0.36
t-statistics	(3.68)			(3.76)	(6.10)
Beta-coefficients	−0.40			−0.40	−0.36
Corrected R²: .79					
II. INCOME DISTRIBUTION MEASURED BY THE GINI COEFFICIENT					
A. *Linear model*					
Coefficients		−1.85		−0.18	125.0
t-statistics		(4.85)		(5.40)	(3.81)
Beta-coefficients		−0.39		−0.45	−0.24
Corrected R²: .75					
B. *Logarithmic model*					
Coefficients	−0.18			−0.12	0.76
t-statistics	(3.42)			(3.69)	(6.63)
Beta-coefficients	−0.36			−0.39	0.39
Corrected R²: .80					

* Column 5 in Table A1 divided by 100.

tionship between the distribution of income and fertility. The coefficient of the measure of income distribution has the expected sign in each equation, is statistically highly significant, and contributes substantially to the explanation of variations in fertility over the sample. The high degree of intercorrelation among the other variables leads to substitutions in the stepwise regression procedure when the functional form of the equation is altered. Nevertheless, the relationship between income distribution and fertility is unaffected. Together, average per capita income, life expectancy, effective literacy, and the distribution of income are capable of explaining approximately 80 percent of intercountry variation in the fertility index.

In the linear model using the percentage of total income distributed to the poorest 40 percent of the population as the measure of distribution, equation I.A. states that each additional percentage point of total income received by the poorest 40 percent reduces the fertility index by 2.9 points. By contrast, each additional year of life expectancy at birth reduces the fertility index by 1.86 points. In the logarithmic model, the elasticity of the fertility index with regard to changes in the share of income received by the poorest 40 percent of households is 0.36; the elasticity of fertility with regard to increases in average per capita income is 0.20, little more than half as great. These coefficients suggest that fertility decline is much more sensitive to changes in income at the bottom end of the distribution.

Appendix B

THE RELATIONSHIP BETWEEN PROGRAM INPUTS, SOCIO-ECONOMIC LEVELS, AND FAMILY PLANNING PERFORMANCE: A REGRESSION ANALYSIS

THIS APPENDIX DISCUSSES the results of a statistical analysis assessing the relative importance of family planning program inputs and levels of socio-economic development in explaining variations in family planning performance. The analysis relates to 1) sixteen states of India, and 2) nineteen countries, including India, for which the relevant data are available.

METHOD

The analysis attempts to ascertain the extent and direction of association between the output of family planning programs on the one side and socio-economic and program input variables on the other. It does not seek to find structural relationships or to identify cause-effect linkages; the available data do not permit consideration of all the independent variables that need to be included to formulate a structural model. First, important variables, such as the quality of management, cannot even be measured. Second, it is impossible to make allowance for the likely time-lags in the effect of several independent variables on the performance of family planning programs. Third, the high intercorrelations between indicators of socio-economic development and between program inputs mean that the effects of different indicators cannot be distinguished from each other, given the scarcity of data. For example, the particular socio-economic independent variables, such as mileage of surfaced roads, need not have a direct effect on program performance; they are only an indicator of the level of development. The possible causal implications of the program inputs are, of course, much clearer, but these are too closely connected with each other to let one input be singled out as more important than others.[1]

With states or countries as the units of analysis, regression methods are used to estimate the amount of inter-state or inter-country variation in selected measures of family planning program output, explained

---

[1] Moreover, a cross-section areal analysis of data for one year is not adequate to evaluate the stability of the observed relationships.

by selected socio-economic variables (SEV) and program input variables (PIV). For each output variable, the number of independent variables selected from each group (SEV and PIV) has been successively increased until additional variables could not increase significantly the proportion of variance explained. The selection of variables within each group is accomplished on the basis of their successive optimal explanatory power.

To assess the relative importance of SEV and PIV, the total explained variation (R^2), corresponding to each set of socio-economic variables and program input variables is decomposed into three parts—R_s^2 the part of the variations explained exclusively by the SEV; R_I^2 that explained exclusively by the PIV; and R_{IS}^2 that explained by an interaction between the two sets of variables.[2]

This interaction (R_{IS}^2) is an indicator of the interdependence between socio-economic variables and program input variables which is evaluated also on the basis of: 1) the zero-order correlations between pairs of variables (one from each group); and 2) multiple correlation of selected program input variables individually regressed on the socio-economic variables through a stepwise regression procedure.

ANALYSIS OF FAMILY PLANNING PERFORMANCE IN SIXTEEN STATES IN INDIA [3]

Table B1 [4] lists the various dependent (output) and independent (input and socio-economic) variables. The two measures of program performance are the acceptor rate and the user rate [5] which represent

---

[2] If R is the multiple correlation coefficient between output variables and the total set of socio-economic (SEV) and program input variables (PIV), R_1 is the multiple correlation coefficient with the set of SEV alone and R_2 with the set of program input variables (PIV),

1) the part of the total variation explained exclusively by SEV is given by $R_S^2 = R^2 - R_2^2$

2) the part of the total variation explained exclusively by PIV is given by $R_I^2 = R^2 - R_1^2$; and

3) the part of the variation explained by the interaction between SEV and PIV is given by $R_{IS}^2 = R_1^2 + R_2^2 - R^2 = R^2 - R_1^2 - R_S^2$.

[3] The sixteen states are: Andhra Pradesh; Assam; Bihar; Gujarat; Haryana; Jammu and Kashmir; Kerala; Madhya Pradesh; Maharashtra; Mysore; Orissa; Punjab; Rajasthan; Tamil Nadu; Uttar Pradesh; and West Bengal.

Several studies have attempted to analyze the inter-state variation in family planning performance in India (e.g., Jain 1971; Agarwala 1972; Misra 1973; Srikantan 1974; Jain and Sarma 1974).

[4] Data on the family planning program in India are available in published and unpublished documents of the Ministry of Health and Family Planning, Government of India. Figures on the socio-economic indicators (per capita electricity consumption, surfaced road per km^2, etcetera) have been obtained from Misra (1973). Estimates of female enrollments have been taken from World Bank reports.

[5] User rates are calculated by cumulating acceptors of different methods over

Table B1
Variables Used in Regression Analysis

Indian analysis	Inter-country analysis [1]

DEPENDENT VARIABLES (PROGRAM OUTPUTS)

1. Acceptor rate, 1971–72.	1. Acceptor rate.
2. User rate, 1971–72.	2. User rate—program.
3. Estimated birth rate, 1970.	3. User rate—total.

INDEPENDENT VARIABLES: SOCIO-ECONOMIC

4. Electricity consumption per capita, 1964–1965.	4. Per capita GNP.
5. Death rate, 1971.	5. Female secondary school
6. Hospital beds per 1000 population, 1967–1968.	enrollment.
7. Female secondary school enrollment rate, 1971.	6. Death rate.
8. Proportion of population living in districts at higher level of development.	7. Proportion of population in urban areas.
9. Proportion of population living in urban areas, 1971.	8. Newspaper circulation per 1,000 persons.
10. Per capita income, 1964–1965.	9. Density of population per km².
11. Literacy rate, 1971.	
12. Surfaced road per 100 km ², 1967–1968.	

INDEPENDENT VARIABLES: PROGRAM INPUTS [2]

13. Locally run urban service points, 1971–1972.	10. Service points.
14. Rural field workers, 1971–1972.	11. Personnel.
15. Rural physicians, 1971–1972.	12. Physicians.
16. State urban service points, 1971–1972.	13. Funds expended or allocated for family planning program.
17. Urban field workers, 1971–1972.	
18. Program expenditures excluding compensation, 1971–1972.	
19. Rural program service points, 1971–1972.	
20. Cumulative service point years, 1965–1972.	
21. Cumulative expenditure (including compensation), 1966–1971.	

[1] The latest available data pertaining to one of the years during 1970–73 have been taken into account.

[2] Program input variables are all expressed as rates for 1,000 married women in reproductive ages.

the current and cumulated output, respectively. Estimated birth rates are taken as another dependent variable indicating the overall impact of programs and related activities on fertility. Nine socio-economic and nine program input variables have been selected on the basis of some initial scrutiny and their likely relevance to program effectiveness. The socio-economic variables include various indicators of "development," such as income, literacy, urbanization, mortality, etcetera. The program inputs include personnel, service points, and expenditures net of compensation.[6]

Table B2 summarizes the results of the analysis. Column 1 shows the selected output measures used as dependent variables. Columns 2, 3, and 4 show the socio-economic variables selected through stepwise regression, significance levels of F for each regression and the corresponding R^2. The next three columns—5, 6, and 7—show stepwise regression results with program input variables. Columns 8, 9, and 10 show regression results with selected pools of socio-economic and input variables, one from each group, two from each group, etcetera. The decomposition of total explained variation into R_S^2, R_I^2 and R_{SI}^2 is shown in columns 11, 12, and 13.

The main conclusions from this analysis are:

1) The socio-economic variables, program input variables, and a combination of both explained a statistically significant proportion of variations in all measures of output. The amount of variation explained by independent variables increased sharply when two or more variables were considered.

2) On the whole, program input variables explained a higher proportion of the variation in program output than the socio-economic variables. The level of inputs can explain a larger proportion of interstate differences in acceptor rates than those in user rates.

Among the three measures of output, *acceptor rates* (including camp results) were most dependent on program inputs. Two inputs—locally run urban service points and rural field workers (both per one thousand

---

time after applying appropriate (estimated) continuation rates to IUD and sterilization acceptors and reducing conventional contraceptive acceptors to equivalent users. Acceptors, and also users, in India include those recruited through service points run by voluntary organizations and local bodies which appear to be a substantial proportion of total service points in urban areas for a number of states. Since the program coordinates and supports these activities, for all practical purposes the acceptor rate and the user rate in the Indian case may be taken as those relating to the program.

[6] The data on cumulated expenditures during 1966–1971 are not net of compensation and they have been used primarily in preliminary analyses. Personnel and service points have been considered separately for urban and rural areas.

Table B2

Results of Regression Analysis of Family Planning Performance in Sixteen Indian States

Dependent variable 1	Stepwise regression			Stepwise regression			Multiple regression			Decomposition of R^2		
	SEV 2	s.l. of F 3	R^2 4	PIV 5	s.l. of F 6	R^2 7	SEV+PIV 8	s.l. of F 9	R^2 10	R_S^2 11	R_I^2 12	R_{SI}^2 13
1	4	.01	.49	13	.001	.76	4, 13	.001	.78	.02	.29	.47
1	4, 6	.01	.56	13, 14	.001	.90	4, 6, 13, 14	.001	.93	.03	.37	.53
1	4, 6, 5	.01	.70	13, 14, 16	.001	.93	4, 6, 5, 13, 14, 16	.001	.96	.03	.26	.67
1	4, 6, 5, 8	.01	.76	13, 14, 16, 18	.001	.94	4, 6, 5, 8, 13, 14, 16, 18	.001	.97	.03	.21	.73
2	4	.001	.61	13	.01	.48	4, 13	.001	.66	.18	.05	.43
2	4, 5	.001	.68	13, 14	.001	.76	4, 5, 13, 14	.001	.87	.11	.19	.57
2	4, 5, 6	.001	.74	13, 14, 18	.001	.82	4, 5, 6, 13, 14, 18	.001	.95	.13	.21	.61
2	4, 5, 6, 7	.01	.79	13, 14, 16, 18	.001	.84	4, 5, 6, 8, 13, 14, 16, 18	.001	.98	.14	.19	.65
3	5	.001	.60	20	.025	.31	5, 20	.01	.60	.29	0	.31
3	5, 9	.001	.68	20, 14	.025	.44	5, 9, 20, 14	.01	.72	.28	.04	.40
3	5, 9, 12	.001	.74	20, 14, 15	.01	.62	5, 9, 12, 20, 14, 15	.01	.80	.18	.06	.56
3	5, 9, 12, 7	.001	.80	20, 14, 15, 18	.025	.65	5, 9, 12, 7, 20, 14, 15, 18	.025	.88	.23	.08	.57

Abbreviations: SEV=Socio-economic variables

PIV=Program input variables

s.l. of F=Significance level of F statistic.

Variable codes: 1=acceptor rate; 2=user rate; 3=birth rate; 4=electricity consumption; 5=death rate; 6=hospital beds; 7=female secondary school enrollments; 8=developed districts; 9=urbanization; 12=surfaced roads; 13=locally run urban service points; 14=rural field workers; 15=rural physicians; 16=state urban service points; 18=program expenditures; 20=cumulative service points.

Note: See Table B1 for details.

153

Table B3

Zero-Order Correlation Coefficients between Variables Used in Regression Analysis of Family Planning Program in Sixteen Indian States

Variable	No.	Correlation coefficients									
		1	2	3	4	5	6	7	8	9	10
Acceptor rate	1	1.000									
User rate	2	.912	1.000								
Birth rate	3	-.211	-.456	1.000							
Electricity consumption	4	.699	.781	-.521	1.000						
Death rate	5	-.472	-.594	.774	-.450	1.000					
Hospital beds	6	-.053	.176	-.640	.287	-.582	1.000				
Female school enrollment	7	.372	.513	-.558	.389	-.618	.651	1.000			
Developed districts	8	.595	.568	-.501	.611	-.503	.413	.709	1.000		
Urbanization	9	.361	.465	-.500	.743	-.290	.495	.344	.705	1.000	
Income per capita	10	.691	.663	-.355	.759	-.458	.221	.323	.731	.658	1.000
Literacy	11	.411	.595	-.633	.517	-.579	.498	.908	.682	.401	.416
Surfaced roads	12	.191	.375	-.625	.278	-.489	.504	.835	.580	.259	.117
Locally run urban service points	13	.869	.696	-.064	.679	-.336	-.129	.172	.588	.478	.732
Rural field workers	14	.528	.644	-.309	.258	-.539	.368	.616	.342	.092	.258
Rural physicians	15	.362	.496	-.464	.211	-.504	.423	.390	.296	.253	.102
State urban service points	16	-.249	-.191	.312	-.465	.432	-.350	-.426	-.632	-.567	-.507
Urban field workers	17	.030	-.004	.338	-.303	.289	-.510	-.514	-.520	-.534	-.246
Expenditure	18	.472	.608	-.229	.351	-.290	.326	.550	.471	.371	.213
Rural service points	19	.508	.649	-.437	.472	-.386	.413	.655	.619	.489	.301
Service point years	20	.389	.537	-.557	.283	-.713	.555	.763	.528	.226	.347
Cumulative expenditure	21	.681	.792	-.265	.442	-.459	.329	.633	.484	.322	.379
Variable No.		1	2	3	4	5	6	7	8	9	10

Note: Correlation coefficients for sixteen pairs of observations are significant at 5 percent level where their values exceed 0.491. Such significant coefficients are italicized in the above table. The variables are described fully in Table B1.

Table B3 (Continued)

Correlation coefficients

Variable	No.	11	12	13	14	15	16	17	18	19	20	21
Acceptor rate	1											
User rate	2											
Birth rate	3											
Electricity consumption	4											
Death rate	5											
Hospital beds	6											
Female school enrollment	7											
Developed districts	8											
Urbanization	9											
Income per capita	10											
Literacy	11	1.000										
Surfaced roads	12	.865	1.000									
Locally run urban service points	13	.222	−.060	1.000								
Rural field workers	14	.603	.563	.184	1.000							
Rural physicians	15	.202	.286	.111	.410	1.000						
State urban service points	16	−.424	−.258	−.451	−.111	.087	1.000					
Urban field workers	17	−.409	−.243	−.152	.099	−.012	.800	1.000				
Expenditure	18	.487	.572	.215	.490	.670	.037	.024	1.000			
Rural service points	19	.659	.749	.277	.681	.537	−.202	−.065	.851	1.000		
Service point years	20	.776	.751	.128	.873	.317	−.389	−.192	.461	.689	1.000	
Cumulative expenditure	21	.601	.538	.380	.804	.554	−.109	.018	.859	.818	.704	1.000
Variable No.		11	12	13	14	15	16	17	18	19	20	21

Note: Correlation coefficients for sixteen pairs of observations are significant at 5 percent level where their values exceed 0.491. Such significant coefficients are italicized in the above table. The variables are described fully in Table B1.

155

married women of reproductive age)—explained about 90 percent of the variation in acceptor rates. On the other hand, two socio-economic variables most correlated with acceptor rates together could explain only 56 percent of the variation. Even when four socio-economic variables were introduced, the total explained variation was not more than that explained by one input variable, namely locally run urban service points.

One socio-economic variable, namely electricity consumption per capita, could explain as much as 61 percent of the interstate variation in *user rates;* the best that an input variable—locally run urban service points—could accomplish was less than 50 percent of the variance. But when more variables were added, the explanatory power of the input variables was slightly greater than that of socio-economic variables.

Interstate variation in the *birth rate* is not as much related to program inputs as to socio-economic variables among which death rate alone can explain about 60 percent of the variation. The input variable most strongly correlated with crude birth rate (cumulated service points) can explain only about 31 percent of the variance.

Interdependence Between SEV and PIV

A part of the explained variation in output measures (Table B2) which cannot be attributed to either the SEV or the PIV gives an indication of the level of interdependence. Such interaction was more important than the effect of inputs or socio-economic variables alone. As more variables were considered, the interaction effects increased in absolute value.

A fair degree of interdependence is suggested also by the zero-order correlation coefficients between PIV and SEV. (Table B3). Thirty out of eighty-one possible pairs were significantly correlated at the 5 percent level. One input variable—cumulated service point years—appeared to be highly correlated with socio-economic variables: positively with literacy; female secondary school enrollment; surfaced roads; hospital beds and urbanization; and negatively with death rate. The second most correlated input variable was rural service points. Expenditure (net of compensation) was significantly but not very strongly correlated with female secondary school enrollment and surfaced roads.

The stepwise regression of five selected PIV on nine selected SEV up to four steps (Table B4) shows that neither cumulative expenditure during 1966–1971 inclusive of compensation, nor expenditure during 1971–1972 exclusive of compensation, was highly correlated with the socio-economic variables. However, physical inputs, such as service points in urban and rural areas, appeared to be rather strongly correlated with socio-economic variables. Evidently, the availability of funds had not so far provided all the critical variables for program develop-

Table B4

Interrelation Between Program Input Variables (PIV) and Socio-Economic Variables (SEV): Sixteen States in India

Dependent variable [1] (PIV)	Step 1 Selected variables	s.l. of F	R^2	Step 2 Selected variables	s.l. of F	R^2	Step 3 Selected variables	s.l. of F	R^2	Step 4 Selected variables	s.l. of F	R^2
13	10	.01	.54	10,6	.01	.63	10,6,4	.01	.69	10,6,4,8	.01	.72
18	12	.025	.33	12,9	.05	.38	12,9,11	n.s.	.39	12,9,11,7	n.s.	.43
19	12	.001	.56	12,9	.001	.65	12,9,6	.01	.67	12,9,6,11	.01	.68
20	11	.001	.60	11,5	.001	.71	11,5,4	.001	.75	11,5,4,10	.01	.76
21	7	.01	.40	7,4	.025	.45	7,4,6	n.s.	.46	7,4,6,8	n.s.	.47

Results of stepwise regression with SEV as independent variable

[1] Variable codes (see Table B1 for full description):

4 = electricity consumption
5 = death rate
6 = hospital beds
7 = female secondary school enrollment
8 = developed districts
9 = urbanization
10 = per capita income
11 = literacy
12 = surfaced roads
13 = locally run urban service points
18 = program expenditures
19 = rural service points
20 = cumulative service points
21 = cumulative expenditures

Abbreviations: SEV = Socio-economic variables.
PIV = Program input variables.
s.l. of F = Significance level of F-statistic.
n.s. = Not significant at 5 percent level.

ment. The explained variation in these inputs indicating the level of dependence reached a maximum of only about 76 percent.

FAMILY PLANNING PERFORMANCE IN SELECTED COUNTRIES [7]

Results of regression analysis for nineteen countries presented in Table B5 show that program user rates were best explained by the socio-economic and input variables. Service points alone accounted for 62 percent of the total variance. When the number of independent variables was raised to eight, the proportion of explained variance increased to 93 percent. For total user rates, two variables (crude death rate and service points) explained about 53 percent of the variance; the figure increased to about 85 percent with eight explanatory variables. Acceptor rates had relatively weaker linkages with socio-economic and input variables; the best R^2 with two variables (funds and urbanization) was only 0.38, and although it increased to about 0.65 with eight explanatory variables, the smaller degrees of freedom made it not significant at 5 percent level.

Inputs appeared to be the more important explanation of acceptor rates. The relative dominance of inputs over socio-economic variables held also in explaining variations in program user rates. With respect to variations in total user rates, however, socio-economic variables appeared to have greater explanatory power than program input variables although the difference was marginal.

Interdependence between Program Inputs and Socio-Economic Development

Interaction effects measured by R_{SI}^2 accounted on average for roughly about a third, or a little more, of the total variation. The zero-order correlation coefficients also suggested not very strong interdependence of program inputs and levels of socio-economic development. Out of twenty-four possible pairs—four inputs × six socio-economic variables—only four showed correlations significant at 5 percent level. (Table B6.) Service points were associated negatively with death rate; the availability of physicians was correlated positively with female education and

---

[7] The nineteen countries are: Egypt; Fiji; Guatemala; India; Indonesia; Iran; Kenya; Republic of Korea; Malaysia; Mauritius; Morocco; Nepal; Pakistan; Philippines; Sri Lanka; Taiwan; Thailand; Tunisia; and Turkey. Initially, Hong Kong and Singapore were also included in analysis, but preliminary investigations showed an improvement in results when they were excluded. The two exclusively urban programs are indeed not comparable with those in other countries.

For each country, the most recent year during 1970–1973, for which complete information was available, has been taken as the reference year. User rates are those of the following year. Data have been obtained mostly from the Population Council *Factbooks* (Nortman 1970–1973), supplemented by World Bank documents, IPPF status reports, and other available documents.

Table B5

Results of Regression Analysis of Family Planning Performances in Nineteen Countries

Dependent variable [1]	Stepwise regression			Stepwise regression			Multiple regression			R^2 decomposed		
	SEV	s.l. of F	R^2	PIV	s.l. of F	R^2	SEV + PIV	s.l. of F	R^2	R_S^2	R_I^2	R_{SI}^2
1	7	n.s.[2]	.18	13	.025	.32	7, 13	.025	.38	0.6	.20	.12
1	7, 8	n.s.	.27	13, 12	.025	.40	7, 8, 13, 12	n.s.	.46	*	*	*
1	7, 8, 5	n.s.	.28	13, 12, 10	.025	.51	7, 8, 5, 13, 12, 10	n.s.	.58	*	*	*
1	7, 8, 5, 6	n.s.	.29	13, 12, 10, 11	.025	.53	7, 8, 5, 6, 13, 12, 10, 11	n.s.	.65	*	*	*
2	6	.001	.51	10	.001	.62	6, 10	.001	.69	.07	.18	.44
2	6, 9	.01	.53	10, 12	.001	.74	6, 9, 10, 12	.001	.89	.15	.36	.38
2	6, 9, 5	.01	.54	10, 12, 13	.001	.74	6, 9, 5, 10, 12, 13	.001	.90	.16	.36	.38
2	6, 9, 5, 4	.025	.54	10, 12, 13, 11	.001	.74	6, 9, 5, 4, 10, 12, 13, 11	.001	.93	.19	.39	.35
3	6	.001	.49	10	.01	.38	6, 10	.01	.53	.15	.04	.34
3	6, 9	.01	.55	10, 12	.01	.52	6, 9, 10, 12	.001	.77	.25	.22	.30
3	6, 9, 8	.01	.60	10, 12, 13	.01	.54	6, 9, 8, 10, 12, 13	.001	.82	.28	.22	.32
3	6, 9, 8, 7	.01	.63	10, 12, 13, 11	.025	.54	6, 9, 8, 7, 10, 12, 13, 11	.01	.85	.31	.22	.32

Abbreviations: SEV=socio-economic variables

PIV=Program input variables

s.l. of F=significance level of F statistic

n.s.=Not significant at 5 percent level.

* Computations omitted since regression is not significant.

[1] Variable codes (See Table B1 for full description: 1=Acceptor rate; 2=User rate; 3=Total user rate; 4=Per capita GNP; 5=Female secondary school enrollment; 6=Death rate; 7=Urbanization; 8=Newspaper circulation; 9=Density; 10=Service points; 11=Personnel; 12=Physicians; 13=Funds.

Table B6
Zero-Order Correlation Coefficients Between Variables Used in Regression Analysis of Family Planning Programs in Nineteen Countries

Variable	No.	Correlation coefficients												
		1	2	3	4	5	6	7	8	9	10	11	12	13
Acceptor rate	1	1.000												
Program user rate	2	.507	1.000											
Total user rate	3	.419	.926	1.000										
GNP per capita	4	.297	.348	.397	1.000									
Female school enrollment	5	.382	.617	.639	.370	1.000								
Death rate	6	−.323	−.712	−.698	−.490	−.787	1.000							
Urbanization	7	.429	.411	.538	.661	.537	−.466	1.000						
Newspaper circulation	8	.387	.327	.194	.163	.329	.471	.227	1.000					
Density	9	.325	.423	.507	−.001	.374	−.397	.357	.366	1.000				
Service points	10	.194	.789	.620	.380	.383	−.657	.166	.169	.053	1.000			
Personnel	11	.232	.474	.359	−.042	.349	−.399	.261	.249	.330	.478	1.000		
Physicians	12	.400	.622	.578	.268	.597	−.267	.524	.136	.047	.380	.408	1.000	
Funds	13	.571	.520	.303	.467	.188	−.414	.354	.283	.133	.645	.510	.229	1.000
	Variable No.	1	2	3	4	5	6	7	8	9	10	11	12	13

Note: Correlation is significant at 5 percent level if absolute values of coefficients exceed 0.455. These are italicized. The variables are described in Table B1.

160

Table B7

Interrelations Between Program Input Variables (PIV) and Socio-Economic Variables (SEV); Nineteen Countries

Results of stepwise regression with SEV as independent variables *

Dependent Variable* (PIV)	Step 1			Step 2			Step 3			Step 4		
	Selected variables	s.l. of F	R^2	Selected variables	s.l. of F	R^2	Selected variables	s.l. of F	R^2	Selected variables	s.l. of F	R^2
10	6	.01	.431	6, 9	.01	.482	6, 9, 5	.025	.520	6, 9, 5, 8	.025	.537
11	6	n.s.	.159	6, 4	n.s.	.233	6, 4, 7	n.s.	.316	6, 4, 7, 5	n.s.	.321
12	5	.01	.356	5, 6	.01	.463	5, 6, 7	.01	.536	5, 6, 7, 9	.025	.571
13	4	n.s.	.218	4, 6	n.s.	.263	4, 6, 5	n.s.	.309	4, 6, 5, 8	n.s.	.321

* Variable codes: (See Table B1 for full description):

4 = per capita income
8 = newspaper circulation
12 = physicians
5 = female secondary school enrollment
9 = density
13 = funds
6 = death rate
10 = service points
7 = urbanization
11 = personnel

s.l. of F = Significance level of F statistic.

n.s. = Regression not significant at 5% level.

urbanization; funds correlated positively with GNP per capita. The association of service points and physicians with socio-economic variables reflected the interrelation between program development and socio-economic development.

The stepwise regressions of four input variables on the socio-economic variables (Table B7) confirmed that service points and physicians were significantly associated with socio-economic variables, but the degree of dependence was not very high. Funds and personnel are not dependent on socio-economic variables.

Summary and Discussion

1) Variations in the output of family planning programs are better explained by socio-economic and input variables in the Indian case than in the inter-country case. This may be primarily due to better data with uniform definitions and concepts for India. In a sense, the Indian case presents a more controlled situation where not only are the units of analysis more comparable in terms of size and program age, but the political and administrative framework and the broad population policy are comparable. The inter-country comparisons, however, also show a fairly strong relationship between output and inputs.

2) The relative influence of socio-economic and input variables is different for alternative measures of output. The acceptor rate is a short-term performance measure. The user rate on the other hand is a longer term cumulative result of acceptor rates and the relevant continuation rates. Acceptor rates are influenced more strongly by program inputs than by socio-economic variables, in both cases. Inputs remain a major determinant of user rates as well though their importance relative to SEV is less marked than for acceptor rates. The total user rates and birth rates are more dependent on SEV than on PIV.

3) The inter-dependence of PIV and SEV is stronger in the Indian case than in the international case. In both cases, however, physical facilities rather than expenditures are more dependent on SEV and suggest that program effectiveness may suffer in the absence of socio-economic development in spite of availability of funds.

The foregoing analysis is a cross-sectional areal analysis of data that may have serious limitations, especially in the inter-country case. The number of observations in both cases has been relatively small, and the consistency of results over different periods of time has not been evaluated. Many of the independent variables are significantly correlated. Nevertheless, program inputs seem to play an important role in bringing people to programs, either through short-term motivation or by cashing in on existing unmet demands. Socio-economic factors, however, assume an increasingly important role in the long-term effectiveness of programs by first sustaining the motivation of those who accepted and second by gradually broadening the demand in the form of increased non-program use. On the whole, both social change and family planning programs have a positive role in promoting increased contraceptive practice and a decline in fertility.

STATISTICAL ANNEX

Annex Figure 1

Trend in Specific Fertility Rates in Selected Countries of Asia

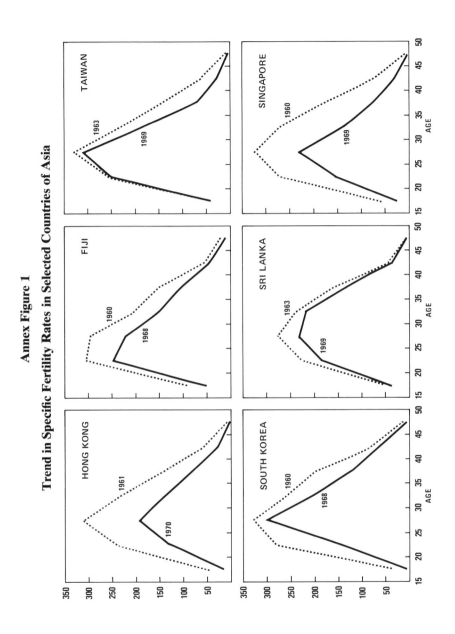

Annex Figure 2

Trend in Specific Fertility Rates in Trinidad & Tobago, Barbados, Mauritius, and Costa Rica

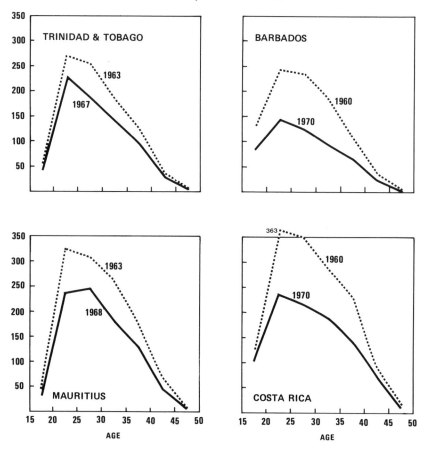

Annex

Annex Table 1
Population Growth Rates in the World and Major Regions Classified by Vital Rates

Regions	High birth rate; high death rate [a]	High birth rate; low death rate	Low birth rate; high death rate	Low birth rate; low death rate	Total
NUMBER OF COUNTRIES					
World	76	29	—	49	154
Africa	45	3	—	1	47
Asia	24	10	—	7	41
Latin America	6	14	—	10	30
Europe, North America, USSR, and Oceania	1	2	—	31	34
PERCENT OF TOTAL POPULATION					
World	40	30	—	30	100
Africa	98	2	—	—	100
Asia	49	45	—	6	100
Latin America	9	74	—	17	100
Europe, North America, USSR, and Oceania	..	..	—	100	100
POPULATION GROWTH RATE, PERCENT PER YEAR					
World	2.6	2.1 [b]	—	0.9	2.0
Africa	2.5	3.3	—	1.7	2.5
Asia	2.7	1.9 [b]	—	1.4	2.3
Latin America	2.8	3.1	—	1.6	2.8
Europe, North America, USSR, and Oceania	2.4	2.6	—	0.8	0.8

[a] Birth rates 30 or higher are classified as high. Death rates 15 or higher are classified as high.

[b] If the People's Republic of China is excluded, the annual rate of population growth in countries in this category would be 3.0 and 2.7 percent in the world as a whole and in Asia, respectively.

.. Indicates less than one percent.

Source: Population Reference Bureau. *1973 World Population Data Sheet.* Washington, D.C.: P.R.B.

Annex Table 2

Expectation of Life at Birth, 1936–1939 and 1950–1970, by Five-Year Intervals, in Major Areas and Regions of the World

Region	1935–1939	1950–1955	1955–1960	1960–1965	1965–1970
WORLD TOTAL [a]	40	46.6	49.1	51.2	53.1
Developed regions	56	64.6	67.8	69.2	70.4
Developing regions	32	41.7	44.4	47.0	49.0
South Asia	30	40.6	43.4	46.1	48.8
Middle South Asia	30	39.5	42.4	45.4	48.3
South East Asia	—	42.8	45.2	47.5	49.7
South West Asia	—	44.0	46.4	48.8	51.4
East Asia	30	44.8	47.1	49.6	52.2
Mainland region	—	42.9	45.5	48.1	50.5
Japan *	49	61.9	66.9	69.0	70.9
Other East Asia	—	50.6	53.1	55.6	60.3
Europe	58	65.4	67.9	69.6	70.9
Western Europe *	62	67.6	69.3	70.7	71.7
Southern Europe *	53	63.3	66.4	68.2	69.8
Eastern Europe *	54	63.2	66.5	68.7	70.6
Northern Europe *	63	69.4	70.6	71.3	71.9
Africa	30	36.4	38.6	40.9	43.3
Western Africa	—	32.3	34.5	36.8	39.2
Eastern Africa	—	35.0	37.5	40.0	42.3
Northern Africa	—	42.3	44.8	47.3	49.8
Middle Africa	—	34.5	35.7	36.9	39.3
Southern Africa	—	43.0	45.3	47.3	48.0
Soviet Union *	—	61.7	67.4	68.9	70.3
North America *	62	68.7	69.7	70.0	70.5
Latin America	40	52.3	55.3	57.9	60.2
Tropical South America	—	52.0	54.6	57.2	59.7
Middle America	40	49.5	54.0	57.6	60.3
Temperate South America *	51	60.4	61.9	63.3	64.6
Caribbean	—	52.0	54.7	56.7	58.5
Oceania	—	58.0	60.5	62.9	64.8
Australia and New Zealand *	66	64.3	66.8	69.3	71.8
Melanesia	—	39.8	42.3	44.8	47.3
Polynesia and Micronesia	—	54.2	56.9	59.2	61.4

* These regions are those considered as "developed."

[a] Developed regions and Middle America according to interpolated and averaged values of life tables in United Nations. *Demographic Yearbook 1967*, Table 29. Developing regions from rough estimates corresponding to estimated levels of the death rate.

Source: United Nations. May 3, 1973. Demographic Trends in the World and its Major Regions 1950–1970. E/Conf. 60/BP/1.

Annex Table 3
Birth Rates, 1935–1939 and 1950–1970, by Five-Year Intervals, in Major Regions of the World

Regions	Birth rate per 1,000 population				
	1935–1939 a	1950–1955	1955–1960	1960–1965	1965–1970
WORLD TOTAL	34–38	36.7	36.4	35.1	33.8
Developed regions	24.9	22.9	21.9	20.5	18.6
Developing regions	40–45	43.9	43.6	42.0	40.6
South Asia	40–45	46.7	46.3	45.1	44.3
Middle South Asia	40–45	47.0	46.5	45.4	44.4
South East Asia	—	46.2	45.9	44.6	44.2
South West Asia	40–45	46.4	46.0	44.0	43.6
East Asia	40–45 b	37.3	36.6	34.0	31.5
Mainland region	—	39.4	39.0	36.1	33.1
Japan *	29.3	23.7	18.2	17.2	18.0
Other East Asia	—	37.0	42.1	39.1	35.0
Europe	20.4	19.8	19.2	18.7	18.0
Western Europe *	17.3	17.7	17.7	18.2	17.5
Southern Europe *	24.3	21.2	20.8	20.7	19.4
Eastern Europe *	23.1	23.7	21.4	17.5	17.3
Northern Europe *	15.8	16.8	16.7	17.9	17.6
Africa	40–45	47.3	47.0	46.9	46.8
Western Africa	—	48.8	48.8	49.0	48.8
Eastern Africa	—	47.2	46.8	46.4	46.6
Northern Africa	—	48.0	47.5	47.5	46.9
Middle Africa	—	45.5	45.2	45.0	45.3
Southern Africa	—	41.6	42.0	40.3	40.7
Soviet Union *	36.0	26.4	25.3	22.4	17.9
North America *	18.1	24.8	24.9	22.7	19.3
Latin America	40–45	41.3	40.4	39.1	38.4
Tropical South America	—	43.4	42.0	40.7	39.8
Middle America	—	47.0	46.2	44.6	43.7
Temperate South America *	27.6	29.2	28.2	26.8	26.3
Caribbean	—	38.1	37.8	36.7	35.0
Oceania	—	28.2	27.9	27.1	24.5
Australia and New Zealand *	17.6	23.5	23.3	22.6	20.2
Melanesia	—	43.3	43.1	42.4	41.7
Polynesia and Micronesia	—	45.4	44.6	41.5	39.7

* These regions are those considered as "developed."
a Developed Regions According to United Nations. 1966. *World Population Prospects as Assessed in 1973.* ST/SOA/Ser. A/41.
Developing Regions According to United Nations. 1949. *World Population Trends 1920–1947.* ST/SOA/Ser. A/3.
b Includes South East Asia, but not Japan.

Source: United Nations. May 3, 1973. Demographic Trends in the World and its Major Regions 1950–1970. E/Conf. 60/BP/1.

Annex Table 4
Composition of Changes in Birth Rate

Country	Period	Change in birth rate	Age-sex composition	Marital status	Marital fertility	Total
			Percentage of change due to:			
Korea, Rep. of	1957/61–					
	1962/67	−8.2	6	33	61	100
	1960–1970	−14.3	5	35	60	100
Taiwan	1960–1970	−11.6	13	24	63	100
Malaysia (West)	1960–1969	−8.3	5	67	28	100
Singapore	1957–1966	−14.1	0	63	37	100
Hong Kong	1961–1965	−6.7	79	10	11	100
	1965–1967	−4.2	13	0	87	100
Sri Lanka	1953–1963	−4.8	57	43	0	100
	1963–1968	−2.5	−31	131	0	100
	1968–1970	−2.7	−21	31	90	100
Tunisia	1965–1968	−4.8	19	42	39	100
Barbados	1960–1970	−12.8	15		85[a]	100
Trinidad and Tobago	1960–1970	−13.2	−2		102[a]	100
Jamaica	1960–1970	−7.9	87		13[a]	100
Mauritius	1960–1970	−12.5	4		96[a]	100

[a] Combined effect of changes in marital status distribution and marital fertility.

Sources: Lapham, R. J. and W. P. Mauldin. March 1972. National Family Planning Programs: Review and Evaluation. In *Studies in Family Planning.* New York: The Population Council. Also estimates from World Bank data.

Annex Table 5
Fertility Decline by Age Group

Country	Period	Ages 15–29	Ages 30–49	All ages
		Average annual fertility decline (percentages)		
Trinidad and Tobago	1963–1967	5.4	5.9	5.6
United States	1963–1968	5.0	6.0	5.3
Mauritius	1963–1968	4.7	5.9	5.3
Singapore	1960–1969	4.2	5.9	5.0
Hong Kong	1961–1972	4.8	4.7	4.7
Canada	1960–1969	4.1	5.4	4.5
Barbados	1960–1970	4.1	4.4	4.2
Korea, Rep. of	1960–1968	3.8	3.5	3.7
Costa Rica	1960–1970	3.4	3.4	3.4
Fiji	1960–1968	3.2	3.4	3.3
Taiwan	1963–1969	0.7	6.9	3.2
Sri Lanka	1963–1969	3.0	2.1	2.6
West Germany	1963–1967	1.2	3.8	1.8
England and Wales	1960–1970	0.5	2.4	1.4

Source: Estimated from World Bank data.

Annex Table 6
Urban and Rural Population in 1950 and 1970 and Average Rate of Growth in Both the World and Eight Major Areas

Area	Urban population (millions) 1950	Urban population (millions) 1970	Rural population (millions) 1950	Rural population (millions) 1970	Annual change 1950–1970 (percent) Urban population	Annual change 1950–1970 (percent) Rural population
WORLD TOTAL	*703.2*	*1,358.3*	*1,782.5*	*2,275.9*	*3.29*	*1.22*
Developed regions	439.2	699.1	418.0	390.1	2.32	−0.34
Less developed regions	264.0	659.2	1,364.5	1,885.8	4.58	1.62
South Asia	112.5	233.1	585.9	892.7	3.64	2.11
East Asia	100.8	274.9	556.2	655.0	5.02	0.82
Europe	208.9	293.7	183.1	168.4	1.70	−0.42
Africa	30.5	76.7	186.8	267.7	4.62	1.80
Soviet Union	71.2	138.6	108.9	104.0	3.33	−0.22
North America	105.8	169.1	60.3	58.5	2.34	−0.15
Latin America	65.7	159.2	96.7	124.1	4.42	1.25
Oceania	7.8	13.1	4.8	6.2	2.62	1.31

Source: United Nations. May 3, 1973. *Demographic Trends in the World and Its Major Regions, 1950–1970.* E/Conf.60/BP/1. Table 10. P. 32.

Annex Table 7
Percentage and Number of Illiterate Persons Ages 15 and Over in the Developed and Developing Countries of the World, 1950–1970

	Persons Number (million)	Persons Percent	Males Number (million)	Males Percent	Females Number (million)	Females Percent
World						
1950 *	705.0	44.0	N.A.	—	N.A.	—
1960	735.0	39.3	307.0	33.5	428.0	44.9
1970	783.0	34.2	315.0	28.0	468.0	40.3
Developed countries						
1960	33.0	4.9	11.6	3.6	22.3	6.2
1970	27.3	3.5	9.3	2.5	18.0	4.3
Developing countries						
1960	701.1	59.2	295.4	49.6	405.7	68.9
1970	756.0	50.2	306.0	40.4	450.0	60.2

* Figures for 1950 pertain to the midpoint of the estimated range.

Source: U.N. Educational, Scientific and Cultural Organization. 1963. 1972. *Statistical Yearbook.* Paris: United Nations.

Annex Table 8

Dependency Ratios for Different Regions and Selected Countries, 1950, 1960, and 1970

(percent)

	Youth dependency: Persons ages 0–14 as percent of those ages 15–64			Old age dependency: Persons ages 65+ as percent of those ages 15–64			Total dependency: Persons ages 0–14 and 65+ as percent of those ages 15–64		
	1950	1960	1970	1950	1960	1970	1950	1960	1970
World	61.4	64.8	64.1	8.4	8.5	9.0	69.7	73.4	73.1
Developed regions	43.3	45.6	42.3	11.7	13.4	15.1	55.0	59.0	57.4
Developing regions	72.4	75.5	74.8	6.4	5.8	6.0	78.7	81.4	80.8
Selected developed countries									
Japan	59.4	46.9	34.8	8.3	8.9	10.1	67.7	55.9	44.9
Federal Republic of Germany	35.0	32.0	38.1	13.8	15.6	20.6	48.8	47.6	58.7
Hungary	37.2	38.6	30.9	10.8	13.8	16.2	48.0	52.3	47.0
Sweden	35.3	33.3	32.3	15.4	18.1	21.5	50.8	51.4	53.8
USSR	47.1	49.0	45.3	9.5	10.8	10.9	56.7	59.8	56.5
United States	41.5	52.0	45.2	12.5	15.4	16.1	54.0	67.4	61.3
Australia	40.6	49.0	46.0	12.4	13.8	13.8	53.0	62.8	58.7
Selected developing countries									
Hong Kong	45.2	72.6	62.7	3.8	5.0	6.8	49.0	77.5	69.5
India	68.7	73.6	76.4	6.0	5.4	5.4	74.8	79.0	81.8
Iraq	88.7	89.7	102.1	5.2	4.8	10.6	93.9	94.5	112.8
Syria	76.4	85.7	94.0	8.1	7.3	6.0	84.5	93.0	100.0
Algeria	72.3	83.5	94.0	7.9	7.4	6.0	80.2	90.9	100.0
Mexico	82.1	89.1	92.0	6.8	6.4	8.0	88.9	95.5	100.0
Jamaica	60.8	77.2	95.8	6.9	8.0	12.5	67.7	85.1	108.3

Sources: United Nations Population Division. May 1970 Population Estimates by Legions and Countries, 1950–1960: Total Population, Age-Sex Structure and Urban-Rural Distribution. ESA/P/WP.31.

Nortman, Dorothy. 1973. Population and Family Planning Programs: A Factbook. Reports on Population/Family Planning. New York: Population Council.

Population Reference Bureau. 1973. World Population Data Sheet. Washington, D.C.: P.R.B.

World Bank. Various dates. Fact Sheets on Social Indicators.

Annex Table 9
Recent Unemployment Rates in Selected Countries of Asia

SELECTED COUNTRIES OF ASIA

Country	Period	Age groups covered	Urban Areas			Rural areas		
			Persons	Males	Females	Persons	Males	Females
Malaysia (West)	1967–1968	15+	9.9	7.7	15.2	5.4	5.4	5.5
Philippines	1968	10+	9.1	8.8	9.5	7.4	5.0	12.6
India	1966–1967	All ages	1.6	1.5	1.8	2.7	1.8	4.3
Thailand	1969	11+	1.3	1.5	1.0	0.1	0.2	—

SRI LANKA (1967–1968)

Age group	Urban		Rural		All island	
	Males	Females	Males	Females	Males	Females
15–19	42.0	53.8	31.8	37.6	34.7	30.6
20–24	30.4	51.7	24.1	39.7	23.4	28.8
25–29	10.7	28.5	9.2	25.9	8.4	15.9
30–34	5.2	11.4	4.1	10.5	3.9	6.9

Sources: Malaysia: Department of Statistics. 1970. *Socio-Economic Sample Survey of Households—Malaysia 1967–68: Employment and Unemployment, West Malaysia.*
Philippines: Bureau of the Census and Statistics. 1968. *BCS Survey of Households Bulletin.* Series 26.
India: Visaria, Pravin. 1971. The Level and Composition of Labor Force in India. In *Employment and Unemployment Problems of the Near East and South Asia, Vol. 1.* Edited by Ronald G. Ridker and Harold Lubell. Delhi: Vikar Publications.
Thailand: National Statistical Office, Office of the Prime Minister. 1969. *Final Report of the Labor Force Survey, Whole Kingdom.* July–September.
Sri Lanka: Srivastava, R. K. 1973. The Unemployment Problem with Special Reference to the Rural Sector. *Marga.* 2:2.

Annex Table 10

Size and Rate of Growth of Labor Force in Developed, Developing, and All Countries of the World, 1950–1970, and Projections Up to 2000

	World labor force (million)	Developed countries labor force (million)	Developing countries labor force (million)	World		Developed countries		Developing countries	
				Decennial increases (million)	Annual rate of growth (percent)	Decennial increases (million)	Annual rate of growth (percent)	Decennial increases (million)	Annual rate of growth (percent)
Total									
1950	1,066.8	392.2	674.6	—	—	—	—	—	—
1960	1,276.5	439.4	837.1	209.7	1.79	47.2	1.14	162.5	2.16
1970	1,500.8	487.8	1,012.9	224.3	1.62	48.4	1.04	175.8	1.91
1980	1,785.4	542.3	1,243.1	284.6	1.74	54.5	1.06	230.2	2.05
1990	2,115.0	588.0	1,527.0	329.6	1.69	45.7	0.81	283.9	2.06
2000	2,528.0	627.0	1,901.0	413.0	1.78	39.0	0.64	374.0	2.19
Males									
1950	725.8	249.2	476.6	—	—	—	—	—	—
1960	829.2	273.1	556.1	103.4	1.33	23.9	0.92	79.5	1.54
1970	981.8	301.1	680.6	152.6	1.69	28.0	0.98	124.5	2.02
1980	1,179.7	333.8	845.9	197.9	1.84	32.7	1.03	165.3	2.17
1990	1,410.0	361.0	1,049.0	230.3	1.78	27.2	0.78	203.1	2.15
2000	1,686.0	380.0	1,306.0	276.0	1.79	19.0	0.51	257.0	2.19
Females									
1950	341.0	143.0	198.0	—	—	—	—	—	—
1960	447.3	166.3	281.0	106.3	2.71	23.3	1.51	83.0	3.50
1970	519.0	186.7	332.3	71.7	1.49	20.4	1.16	51.3	1.68
1980	605.6	208.5	397.2	86.6	1.54	21.8	1.10	64.9	1.78
1990	705.0	227.0	478.0	99.4	1.52	18.5	0.85	80.8	1.85
2000	842.0	247.0	595.0	137.0	1.76	20.0	0.84	117.0	2.19

Source: International Labour Organization. 1974. Labour Force Projections. Geneva: I.L.O. Unpublished.

Annex Table 11
Distribution of Countries and World Population Per Capita GNP, 1960 and 1971

Per capita GNP (US$)	1960			1971		
	No. of Countries	Population (millions)	Total GNP (US$1,000 millions)	No. of Countries	Population (millions)	Total GNP (US$1,000 millions)
0–99	38	1,517	124.4	17	332	26.0
100–199	24	168	23.9	26	1,578	220.3
200–299	26	243	52.9	18	221	53.4
300–399	10	92	27.7	15	142	48.9
400–599	16	415	203.9	13	193	88.7
600–799	5	58	40.6	11	122	88.0
800–999	5	50	46.5	7	39	31.9
1,000–1,249	3	21	23.9	6	81	93.2
1,250–1,499	8	162	215.6	6	289	402.3
1,500–1,999	5	26	42.0	3	60	110.1
2,000–2,999	3	199	549.8	12	238	552.8
3,000+	—	—	—	10	366	1,618.0
Grand Total	143	2,993	1,351.0	144*	3,675	3,333.6

* The number of countries in 1971 was greater than in 1960 because of the addition of Bangladesh.

Sources: United Nations. *Demographic Yearbooks* (various dates); *Yearbook of National Accounts Statistics, 1970, Vol. 2, International Tables.*
World Bank. 1973. *World Bank Atlas.*
Notes:
1. In cases of incomparability between total and per capita GNP estimates, which were especially frequent for countries with incomes under $300–350, per capita GNP figures took precedence over total figures.
2. The 1960 figures for centrally planned economies were obtained by projecting 1971 figures backwards in accordance with the recorded growth rates. A deflation factor was then applied to correct for the change in the value of the U.S. dollar. The resultant figures should be taken as approximations.
3. The GNP estimates are mostly at market prices, though some figures at factor cost had to be used. GNP in market prices was almost 11 percent higher than GNP at factor cost.

Annex Table 12

Average Annual Percentage Rates of Growth in Population and Aggregate as Well as Per Capita Food and Agricultural Production in Developed and Developing Countries, 1948–1971

	Period		
	1948–52 to 1959–61	1959–61 to 1969–71	1948–52 to 1969
Population			
World	1.88	2.04	1.96
Developed regions	1.29	1.14	1.22
Developing regions	2.26	2.62	2.44
Aggregate food production			
World	3.27	2.66	2.96
Developed regions	3.18	2.61	2.90
Developing regions	3.39	2.79	3.09
Aggregate agricultural production			
World	3.18	2.54	2.86
Developed regions	3.09	2.43	2.76
Developing regions	3.47	2.70	3.09
Per capita food production			
World	1.32	0.64	0.98
Developed regions	1.80	1.53	1.66
Developing regions	1.02	0.19	0.60
Per capita agricultural production			
World	1.32	0.46	0.89
Developed regions	1.71	1.30	1.50
Developing regions	1.11	0.09	0.60

Source: Food and Agricultural Organization. 1972. *Monthly Bulletin of Agricultural Economics and Statistics.* 21: 1. Tables 1 and 2.

Annex Table 13

Indices of Population and Aggregate and Per Capita Agricultural and Food Production, in Different Regions of the World, and Average Annual Rates of Growth

	Average Index (1952–1956 = 100)			Average annual growth rate (percent)		
	1948–1952	1959–1961	1969–1971	1948–52 to 1959–61	1959–61 to 1969–71	1948–52 to 1969–71
Population						
World [1]	93	112	137	1.88	2.04	1.96
Developed regions	95	108	121	1.29	1.14	1.22
Western Europe	97	105	114	0.80	0.82	0.81
Eastern Europe and USSR	95	109	122	1.38	1.13	1.26
North America	93	111	127	1.78	1.36	1.57
Oceania	91	115	141	2.37	2.06	2.21
Other developed countries [2]	94	108	123	1.40	1.31	1.35
Developing regions	92	115	149	2.26	2.62	2.44
Latin America	90	118	157	2.74	2.90	2.82
Near East, excl. Israel	90	117	153	2.66	2.72	2.69
Far East, excl. Japan	92	114	147	2.17	2.57	2.37
Africa, excl. South Africa	91	115	148	2.37	2.55	2.46
Food production						
World [1]	87	120	156	3.27	2.66	2.96
Developed regions	87	119	154	3.18	2.61	2.90
Western Europe	84	116	151	3.28	2.67	2.98
Eastern Europe and USSR	83	134	177	4.91	2.82	3.86
North America	92	110	137	1.80	2.22	2.01
Oceania	92	120	167	2.69	3.36	3.02
Other developed countries [2]	81	123	175	4.26	3.59	3.93
Developing regions	86	120	158	3.39	2.79	3.09
Latin America	87	119	162	3.18	3.13	3.16
Near East, excl. Israel	81	122	162	4.18	2.88	3.53
Far East, excl. Japan	87	122	161	3.44	2.81	3.12
Africa, excl. South Africa	86	114	142	2.86	2.22	2.54
Agricultural production						
World [1]	87	119	153	3.18	2.54	2.86
Developed regions	87	118	150	3.09	2.43	2.76
Western Europe	84	116	149	3.28	2.54	2.91
Eastern Europe and USSR	82	132	174	4.87	2.80	3.83
North America	93	109	130	1.60	1.78	1.69
Oceania	89	122	162	3.20	2.88	3.04
Other developed countries [2]	81	122	169	4.18	3.31	3.74
Developing regions	86	121	158	3.47	2.70	3.09
Latin America	87	123	157	3.52	2.47	3.00
Near East, excl. Israel	82	123	166	4.14	3.04	3.59
Far East, excl. Japan	87	122	160	3.44	2.75	3.09
Africa, excl. South Africa	85	117	149	3.25	2.45	2.85

Annex Table 13 (Continued)

	Average index (1952–1956 = 100)			Average annual growth rate (percent)		
	1948–1952	1959–1961	1969–1971	1948–52 to 1959–61	1959–61 to 1969–71	1948–52 to 1969–71
Per capita food production						
World [1]	93	106	113	1.32	0.64	0.98
Developed regions	92	110	128	1.80	1.53	1.66
Western Europe	87	111	131	2.47	1.67	2.07
Eastern Europe and USSR	87	122	145	3.44	1.74	2.59
North America	99	99	107	0	0.78	0.39
Oceania	102	104	119	0.19	1.36	0.77
Other developed countries [2]	87	114	143	2.74	2.29	2.52
Developing regions	94	104	105	1.02	0.19	0.60
Latin America	97	100	104	0.30	0.39	0.35
Near East excl. Israel	96	105	106	1.55	0.09	0.82
Far East, excl. Japan	94	107	109	1.30	0.18	0.74
Africa, excl. South Africa	94	104	106	1.02	0.19	0.60
Per capita agricultural production						
World [1]	93	106	111	1.32	0.46	0.89
Developed regions	92	109	124	1.71	1.30	1.50
Western Europe	87	110	130	2.37	1.68	2.03
Eastern Europe and USSR	87	121	144	3.35	1.76	2.55
North America	99	97	101	−0.20	0.40	0.10
Oceania	99	107	116	0.78	0.81	0.80
Other developed countries [2]	87	113	137	2.65	1.94	2.30
Developing regions	94	105	106	1.11	0.09	0.60
Latin America	97	104	100	0.70	−0.39	0.15
Near East, excl. Israel	91	105	109	1.44	0.37	0.91
Far East, excl. Japan	95	106	108	1.10	0.19	0.64
Africa, excl. South Africa	93	101	101	0.83	0	0.41

[1] Excluding People's Republic of China.
[2] Israel, Japan, and South Africa.

Annex Table 14

Distribution of Developing Countries and Rate of Growth of Their Population According to (1) Relationship Between Rates of Growth of Food Production and Estimated Demand for Food, and (2) Adequacy of Food Supply With Respect to Caloric Requirements, 1971

Rate of growth of food production vs. rates of growth of population and demand for food, by adequacy of food supply with respect to caloric requirements	Number of countries	Population in 1971		Rate of population growth, 1961–71
		million	percent	
All				
Total	73	2,435.92	100.00	2.22
(a) Supply < requirement	45	1,974.19	81.00	2.10
(b) Supply ≥ requirement	28	461.73	19.00	2.72
Food production increased as much as or more than estimated demand				
Total	25	348.00	14.3	2.89
(a) Supply < requirement	11	77.14	3.2	2.68
(b) Supply ≥ requirement	14	270.86	11.1	2.95
Food production increased less than estimated demand but more than population				
Total	18	1,654.01	67.9	2.07
(a) Supply < requirement	11	1,486.31	61.0	2.03
(b) Supply ≥ requirement	7	167.70	6.9	2.44
Food production increased less than population				
Total	21	397.72	16.3	2.27
(a) Supply < requirement	16	381.49	15.7	2.27
(b) Supply ≥ requirement	5	16.23	0.7	2.31
Countries having negative growth rates				
Total	9	36.19	1.5	2.06
(a) Supply < requirement	7	29.25	1.2	2.11
(b) Supply ≥ requirement	2	6.94	0.3	1.87

Source: Food and Agricultural Organization. August 3, 1973. *Population, Food Supply and Agricultural Development.* E/CONF. 60/BP/5. Annexes IV and V.

Annex Table 15

Cropland in Relation to Population by Countries About 1970

Country	Cropland hectares (thousands)	Total population (thousands)	Agricultural population (thousands)	Hectares of cropland per person of: Total population	Hectares of cropland per person of: Agricultural population
Africa					
Angola	900	5,501	3,568	.16	.25
Ghana	2,835	8,832	4,840	.29	.59
Ivory Coast	8,859	4,916	3,986	1.80	2.22
Nigeria	21,795	76,795	45,423	.32	.48
Rwanda	704	3,609	3,277	.20	.21
Uganda	4,888	8,549	7,342	.57	.67
Zaire	7,200	17,493	13,701	.41	.53
Asia					
China, P. Rep.	110,300	850,406	568,921	.13	.19
" (Taiwan)	867	14,520	6,171	.06	.14
Japan	5,510	103,540	21,329	.05	.26
Korea, Dem. P. Rep.	1,894	13,674	7,275	.14	.26
" , Rep.	2,311	32,422	17,300	.07	.13
Burma	18,941	27,584	17,570	.69	1.08
Indonesia	18,000	119,913	83,230	.15	.22
Malaysia	3,524	10,931	6,176	.32	.57
Philippines	8,977	38,493	26,752	.23	.34
Thailand	11,415	35,814	27,398	.32	.42
Vietnam, Dem. Rep.	2,018	20,757	16,108	.10	.13
" , Rep.	2,918	18,332	13,620	.16	.21
Bangladesh	9,500	71,000	60,000	.13	.16
India	164,610	550,376	372,605	.30	.44
Nepal	2,090	11,040	10,112	.19	.21
Pakistan	24,000	60,000	35,000	.40	.69
Latin America					
Cuba	3,585	8,407	2,755	.43	1.30
Guatemala	1,498	5,180	3,246	.29	.46
Haiti	370	4,867	3,754	.08	.10
Mexico	23,817	50,670	23,617	.47	1.01
Puerto Rico	236	2,784	387	.09	.61
Argentina	26,028	24,353	3,704	1.07	7.03
Bolivia	3,091	4,931	2,873	.63	1.08
Brazil	29,760	93,565	40,869	.32	.73
Chile	4,632	9,780	2,484	.47	1.86
Colombia	5,258	21,117	9,541	.25	.55
Peru	2,843	13,586	6,189	.21	.46
Uruguay	1,947	2,886	482	.67	4.04
Venezuela	5,214	10,997	2,887	.47	1.81

Annex Table 15 (Continued)

Country	Cropland hectares (thousands)	Total population (thousands)	Agricultural population (thousands)	Hectares of cropland per person of:	
				Total population	Agricultural population
Europe					
Italy	14,930	53,667	9,735	.28	1.53
Portugal	4,370	9,630	3,523	.45	1.24
Spain	20,601	33,290	11,222	.62	1.84
Yugoslavia	8,205	20,527	9,651	.40	.85
Hungary	5,594	10,310	2,484	.54	2.25
Poland	15,326	32,805	9,940	.47	1.54
Romania	10,512	20,253	10,503	.52	1.00
USSR	232,809	242,768	77,322	.96	3.01
Denmark	2,678	4,921	595	.54	4.50
Germany, Fed. Rep.	8,075	61,682	3,514	.13	2.30
" , Dem. Rep.	4,806	17,257	2,133	.28	2.25
Sweden	3,053	8,046	754	.38	4.05
United Kingdom	7,261	55,711	1,540	.13	4.71
North America					
Canada	43,404	21,406	1,712	2.03	25.4
United States	176,440	205,395	8,216	.86	21.5
Oceania					
Australia	44,610	12,552	1,049	3.55	42.53

Source: Devring, Folke. 1973. Land Reform: Ends and Means: A Background Study to the World Bank Policy Paper on Land Reform. Prepared for Seminar on Land Reform. Washington, D.C.: World Bank. Mimeo.

Annex Table 16
Distribution of the World's Population by Government Policy on Population and Family Planning Activities

Government Position	TOTAL WORLD Number of Countries	TOTAL WORLD Population[a] (thousands)	TOTAL DEVELOPED COUNTRIES Number of Countries	TOTAL DEVELOPED COUNTRIES Population[a] (thousands)	TOTAL DEVELOPING COUNTRIES Number of Countries	TOTAL DEVELOPING COUNTRIES Population[a] (thousands)
All positions	171	3,665,682	36	1,089,510	135	2,576,172
1. Use of contraceptives prohibited	—	—	—	—	—	—
2. Sales illegal	2	36,927	2	36,927	—	—
3. Sales allowed; advertising illegal	2	24,308	2	24,308	—	—
4. Pronatalist incentives	4	96,546	4	96,546	—	—
5. Laissez faire	71	635,341	8	327,853	63	307,488
Pronatalist	(13)	(373,016)	(2)	(248,079)	(11)	(125,937)
Neutral	(53)	(243,150)	(6)	(79,774)	(47)	(163,376)
Antinatalist	(5)	(18,175)	—	—	(5)	(18,175)
6. Official support of voluntary programs	26	259,018	7	115,265	19	143,753
7. Official program	32	661,162	13	488,611	19	172,551
8. Official program including motivation campaign	31	615,726	—	—	31	615,726
9. Official program & economic incentives	1	547,368	—	—	1	547,368
10. Curtailment of rights & privileges with excess children	1	2,110	—	—	1	2,110
11. Restrictions on marriage	—	—	—	—	—	—
12. Restrictions on number of children	1	787,176	—	—	1	787,176
13. Involuntary fertility control	—	—	—	—	—	—
Information unavailable	3[b]	17,796[b]	—	—	3[b]	17,796[b]

[a] Based on 1971 estimate of population; if unavailable, based on latest available estimate, usually 1970. Taken from International Planned Parenthood Federation. *Family Planning in Five Continents* 1973. London: IPPF.

[b] No information available for Albania, Mongolia, and Democratic Republic of Korea; excluded from totals.

Annex Table 16 (Continued)

	DEVELOPING COUNTRIES							
Africa		Latin America		Asia		Oceania		
Number of Countries	Population [a] (thousands)	Number of Countries	Population [a] (thousands)	Number of Countries	Population [a] (thousands)	Number of Countries	Population [a] (thousands)	
53	359,305	36	260,483	40	1,954,747	6	1,637	
								1.
—	—	—	—	—	—	—	—	
—	—	—	—	—	—	—	—	2.
								3.
—	—	—	—	—	—	—	—	
—	—	—	—	—	—	—	—	4.
37	134,367	8	102,350	17	70,652	1	119	5.
(8)	(29,119)	(2)	(96,144)	(1)	(674)	—	—	
(26)	(97,192)	(6)	(6,206)	(14)	(59,589)	(1)	(119)	
(3)	(7,786)	—	—	(2)	(10,389)	—	—	
								6.
6	89,059	8	26,914	5	27,780	—	—	
3	59,338	13	94,098	1	18,332	2	783	7.
								8.
7	76,541	7	37,121	14	501,329	3	735	
								9.
—	—	—	—	1	547,368	—	—	
								10.
—	—	—	—	1	2,110	—	—	
—	—	—	—	—	—	—	—	11.
								12.
—	—	—	—	1	787,176	—	—	
								13.
—	—	—	—	—	—	—	—	
—	—	—	—	—	—	—	—	

Sources: International Planned Parenthood Federation 1969–1974, *Situation Reports*. London: IPPF.

U.S. Agency for International Development, Office of Population 1972. *Population Program Assistance*. Washington, D.C.: Government Printing Office.

International Planned Parenthood Federation. 1973. *Family Planning in Five Continents*. London: IPPF.

U.N. Social and Economic Council. 1969. *World Population Situation*. Geneva: U.N.

McIntyre, Robert J. 1973, Pronatalist Policies in European Socialist Countries. General Conference, International Union for the Scientific Study of Population, Liege, Belgium, 1973. University Park Pennsylvania: Pennsylvania State University. Mimeo.

Annex Table 17

Assistance to Population Programs by Region and Type of Activity, 1971 and 1972

(thousands of U.S. dollars)

1971

Activity	South Asia		East Asia		Africa		Oceania		Latin America		Interregional		International assistance* net total	
	Amount	(Percent)	Amount	(Percent)	Amount	(Percent)	Amount	(Percent)	Amount	(Percent)	Amount	(Percent)	Amount	(Percent)
Demography[a]	5,296	(14.2)	730	(13.9)	3,316	(15.5)	15	(4.3)	5,322	(17.9)	4,208	(9.0)	18,887	(13.5)
Biomedical research[b]	2,518	(6.8)	539	(10.3)	1,418	(6.6)	50	(14.5)	5,982	(20.2)	15,386	(33.0)	25,893	(18.4)
Family planning	29,407	(79.0)	3,974	(75.8)	16,660	(77.9)	280	(81.2)	18,339	(61.9)	27,076	(58.0)	95,736	(68.1)
Total to region	37,221	(100.0)	5,243	(100.0)	21,394	(100.0)	345	(100.0)	29,643	(100.0)	46,670	(100.0)	140,516	(100.0)

Administrative costs excluded from net total

1972

Demography[a]	2,023 (2.7)	127 (3.5)	3,069 (16.4)	— (0)	1,476 (5.2)	10,471 (18.6)	17,166 (9.4)
Biomedical research[b]	5,076 (6.8)	424 (11.8)	4,624 (24.7)	93 (23.0)	5,354 (18.8)	19,109 (33.9)	34,680 (19.0)
Family planning[c]	67,896 (90.5)	3,036 (84.6)	11,019 (58.9)	311 (77.0)	21,736 (76.0)	26,851 (47.5)	130,849 (71.6)
Total to region	74,995 (100.0)	3,587 (100.0)	18,712 (100.0)	404 (100.0)	28,566 (100.0)	56,431 (100.0)	182,695 (100.0)
Administrative costs, excluded from total							15,744 —

* Includes assistance given for general purposes—such as international conferences, seminars, publications, and films—and funds allocated by governments to enable special institutions in the donor countries to develop expertise and undertake research in the population field.

[a] Includes assistance for advisors, surveys and censuses, training, research, and general purposes.

[b] Includes assistance for research in the physiology of human reproduction and the practical application in the development of contraceptives.

[c] Includes assistance for advisers, training, research, and general purposes.

Source: Organization for Economic Cooperation and Development, Development Center. 1974. Assistance for Population Programmes in 1972. Paris: OECD. Table 3. Mimeo. Also 1973. Development Assistance for Population Activities in 1971. Paris: OECD Table 5. Mimeo.

Annex Table 18

Assistance for Population Activities by Selected Major Donors 1960–1972.

(thousands of U.S. dollars)

Year	TOTAL c	NET TOTAL d	United States	Australia	Canada	Belgium	Denmark	Finland	Fed. Rep. of Germany	Japan	Netherlands	New Zealand	Norway	Sweden	Switzerland	U.K.
										Governments						
1972	268,484	182,695	120,000	357	4,681	18	1,953	293	2,435	2,196	3,041	77	5,539	12,668	191	6,681
1971	208,575	154,050	95,868		3,911	147	1,917	263	1,657	2,090	1,539		3,870	9,194	168	2,521
1970	161,949	126,663	74,506				1,349	75	1,525	378	1,408		990	6,522		434
1969	111,859	85,855	45,440				296	50	250	199	338		225	5,474		261
1968	68,996	58,038	34,750											3,056		
1967	40,748	29,489	4,445											2,322		
1966	44,299	34,311	3,892											1,364		
1965	19,333	17,515	2,134											571		
1964	19,615	15,853												532		
1963	11,929	10,722												241		
1962	5,523	4,684												91		
1961	6,452	6,445												91		
1960	3,198	2,148												91		
Before 1960 b	(8,238)	(5,038)												(93)		
Subtotal	970,960	728,468	381,035	357	8,592	165	5,515	681	5,867	4,863	6,326	77	10,624	42,217	359	9,897
TOTAL	970,960	728,468					476,575									

Annex Table 18 (Continued)

Year	Multilateral organizations										Private organizations				
	World Bank	UN	FAO	WHO	UNESCO	ILO	UNICEF	UNDP	UNFPA	Other	IPPF	Population Council	Ford Foundation	Rockefeller Foundation	Other
1972	34,400	3,704	271	2,205	1,384	1,280	1,460	1,074	4,049	5,200	19,523	9,171	13,673	6,560	4,400
1971	7,800	913	504	4,015	852	285	3,125	133	7,262ᵃ	5,200	19,294	14,084	15,221	2,865	3,877
1970	2,000	1,942		1,669	16		6,407		6,716		9,077	16,717	15,094	15,124	
1969		2,060		1,048	49		5,492		1,160		5,406	17,778	17,519	8,814	
1968		3,773			12				882		820	11,323	12,513	1,867	
1967											807	8,412	19,478	5,284	
1966											211	7,383	27,243	4,206	
1965											271	5,437	9,843	1,077	
1964											108	2,832	13,340	2,803	
1963											84	2,412	9,192		
1962											72	2,412	2,948		
1961											69	1,655	4,637		
1960												1,500	1,607		
Before 1960 ᵇ												(4,200)	(3,945)		
Subtotal	44,200	12,392	775	8,937	2,313	1,565	16,484	1,207	20,069	10,400	55,742	101,116	162,308	48,600	8,277
TOTAL	118,342										376,043				

ᵃ Includes funds allocated to U.N. Industrial Development Organization and U.N. Office of Technical Cooperation.
ᵇ Figures within brackets are not included in the totals.
ᶜ Including double-counting of interchanging transfers.
ᵈ After deductions of double-counting of interchanging transfers.

Sources: Organization or Economic Cooperation and Development, Development Centre. 1973. Development Assistance for Population Activities in 1971. Table I and IV. Also 1973. Table II. Mimeo.

Annex Table 19

Assistance to Population Programs by Type of Activities, 1972

(thousands of U.S. dollars)

Donors	Demography							Biomedical research	Family planning						Donor total
	Advisers	Surveys-Censuses	Training	Demography	Research in economic and social demography	General	Subtotal		Advisors	Training	Research	Supplies	General	Subtotal	
Bilateral															
Belgium													7	7	7
Canada		17			394	183	594	735			251		28	279	1,608
Denmark												257	358	615	615
Germany, Fed Rep.													83	83	83
Japan										103		93		196	196
Netherlands													341	341	341
Norway								1,052				194		194	1,246
Sweden										300		2,824	466	3,590	3,590
United Kingdom					6		6	74	25		1	226	2,571	2,824	2,904
United States		379	1,749	1,232	2,066	3,931	9,357	12,864	1,519	2,788	1,500	4,476	41,731	52,014	74,235
Total		396	1,749	1,232	2,466	4,114	9,957	14,725	1,544	3,192	1,752	8,080	45,585	60,143	84,825
Multilateral organizations															
UN	482	1,090	203	506	57	431	2,769		51	208	251		425	935	3,704
UNFPA		65				65	65	1,000							1,065
FAO	13					119	132						139	139	271
UNESCO			151	35		20	206		318	140	46	82	592	1,178	1,384

ILO	50		20			103			138	28	8	23	359	525	1,280
UNDP		98			37	191	376		82	25	97	35	560	698	1,074
WHO	22	45		21	33	34	110	670	107	103	519	85	1,083	1,425	2,205
UNICEF					632	755	81						775	1,379	1,460
World Bank													34,400	34,400	34,400
Other													5,200	5,200	5,200
Total	567	1,233	374	527	794	999	4,494	1,670	696	504	921	225	43,533	45,879	52,043
Private agencies															
Ford Foundation			365					5,439	190	133	3,039		507	3,869	9,673
IPPF							365	6,987		1,645	3,133	3,243	4,215	12,536	19,523
Population Council	25	19	577	138		807	1,986	3,850	590	455	441	97	1,752	3,335	9,171
Rockefeller Foundation							364	2,009		113	301		273	687	3,060
Other													4,400	4,400	4,400
Total	25	19	942	138	784	807	2,715	18,285	780	2,346	6,914	3,340	11,447	24,827	45,827
Total by activity	592	1,648	3,065	1,897	4,044	5,920	17,166	34,680	3,020	6,042	9,587	11,635	100,565	130,849	182,695

Source: Organization for Economic Cooperation and Development, Development Centre, 1974. Assistance for Population Programmes in 1972. Table 1. Paris: OECD. Mimeo.

Annex Table 20

Assistance for Family Planning and Population Programs by Selected Major Donors and Disposal of Funds, 1972

(thousands of U.S. dollars)

	Donors									Total to recipient
	Governments				Private Agencies					
	UN	World Bank	USA	Other	Ford Foundation	IPPF	Council Population	Rockefeller Foundation	Other	
Total budget	16,816		123,265	40,155		24,935	14,776	6,608		
Headquarters programs and administrative cost	1,389		3,265	25		5,412	5,605	48		
Total available funds	15,427	34,400	120,000	40,130	13,673	19,523	9,171	6,560	9,600	
Recipient donor agencies[a]										
UN Agencies			29,040	22,198	900					52,138
IPPF	1,990		8,000	6,556						16,546
Population Council			4,725		3,100			3,500		11,325
Other private agencies	994		4,000	786						5,780
Subtotal	2,984		45,765	29,540	4,000			3,500		85,789

Recipient regions for programs

										Total to recipient	
										Amount	Percent
Developing world programs[b]											
Africa	1,763	—0—	10,992	1,024	50	3,308	1,242	33	300	18,712	(10.3)
South Asia	6,874	34,400	16,694	7,683	533	5,146	1,246	119	2,300	74,995	(41.0)
East Asia	129	—0—	552	642	—0—	1,263	749	52	200	3,587	(2.0)
Oceania	10	—0—	—0—	97	—0—	297	—0—	—0—	—0—	404	(0.2)
Latin America	1,093	—0—	9,250	842	1,170	9,509	1,735	167	4,800	28,566	(15.6)
Subtotal	9,869	34,400	37,488	10,288	1,753	19,523	4,972	371	7,600	126,264	(69.1)
Inter-Regional Programs[c]	2,574	—0—	36,747	302	7,920	—0—	4,199	2,689	2,000	56,431	(30.9)
Total distribution to recipient regional programs	12,443	34,400	74,235	10,590	9,673	19,523	9,171	3,060	9,600	182,695	(100.0)

[a] The funds received by these agencies contribute to their total budgets for the year.

[b] East Asia includes only Hong Kong, the Republic of Korea, and Taiwan. South Asia includes many of the other developing countries in Asia, except for the People's Republic of China. A complete listing of the countries included in each region is found in Development Assistance for Population Activities in 1971. OECD (1973, Paris: OECD, mimeo), pp. 10–12.

[c] Under this heading is classified assistance given for general purposes (such as international conferences, seminars, publications, and films), and funds allocated by governments to institutions in the donor country to undertake population research and family planning activities.

Source: Organization for Economic Cooperation and Development, Development Center. 1974. Assistance for Population Programmes in 1972. Paris: OECD. Table 2. Mimeo.

Annex Table 21
Annual Support for Research and Training in Reproductive Biology,* 1967–1973

(thousands of U.S. dollars)

Agency	1967	1968	1969	1970	1971	1972	1973 a
Total	15.1	16.3	27.5	33.5	47.9	61.1	61.4
U.S. National Institutes of Health—Center for Population Research (NIH)	7.1	7.1	9.8	13.5	23.0	31.1	31.4
National Science Foundation	—	0.3	0.4	0.1	0.4	0.4	0.5
Ford Foundation	6.3	6.2	7.7	7.7	9.9	9.8	10.3
Rockefeller Foundation	—	0.1	0.7	2.3	3.0	4.2	4.4
U.S. Agency for International Development (AID)	0.3	0.5	6.4	7.4	6.4	8.3	5.3
Population Council b	0.4	1.0	1.0	1.0	1.0	1.4	1.1
Swedish International Development Authority	—	—	0.1	0.1	2.5	3.0	4.0
Other overseas assistance agencies c	—	—	—	—	—	0.6	2.0
University budgets d	1.0	1.1	1.4	1.4	1.7	2.3	2.4

* Excluded from this table are grants and inhouse and developmental expenditures by pharmaceutical firms. The table contains slight discrepancies from earlier tables published by the authors. See Research in Reproductive Biology and Contraceptive Technology: Present Status and Needs for the Future. 1970. *Family Planning Perspectives.* 2:3, p. 5. Also Research in Contraception and Reproduction: A Status Report. 1971. *Family Planning Perspectives,* 3:3, p. 15.

a 1973 figures are estimated.

b Net of Ford Foundation, Rockefeller Foundation, NIH and AID contributions.

c Canadian International Development Authority, International Development Research Centre (Canada); NORAD (Norway); Danida (Denmark).

d Estimated at 15 percent non-government support.

Source: Harkavy, Oscar, and John Maier. 1973. Research in Contraception and Reproduction, A Status Report, 1973. *Family Planning Perspectives.* 5:4, Table 1, p. 213.

Annex Table 22

Percentage of Married Women Ages 15–44 Using Contraceptives by Source of Supplies for Selected Countries, 1973

	Program supplies and service	Private sector supplies and service	Total
Egypt	15.8	4.9	20.7
Fiji	28.9	4.4	33.4
Guatemala	2.7	1.1	3.8
Hong Kong	27.1 [a]	25.2	52.3 [a]
India	13.6	u	u
Indonesia (1972)	3.3	u	u
Iran (1971)	9.3 [b]	u	u
Kenya (1971)	2.2	—	2.2
Korea, Rep. of (1972)	24.0	6.0	30.0
Malaysia (West)	9.3	u	u
Mauritius (1972)	16.8	4.3	21.2
Morocco	2.1	3.5	5.6
Nepal	2.5	u	u
Pakistan (1971)	12.0 [c]	u	u
Philippines	11.0	—[d]	11.0
Singapore [e]	18.3	—[d]	18.3
Taiwan	27.0	30.0	57.0
Thailand	17.7	8.0	25.7
Tunisia	6.4	u	u
Turkey	2.5	u	u

u—Unavailable.

[a] Sterilization acceptors are not considered program acceptors.

[b] More than the figure shown, but not known exactly.

[c] Includes only sterilized persons and IUD users.

[d] Included in program.

[e] Includes only sterilized persons and oral users.

Note: Program plus private does not add up to total because of rounding.

Source: Nortman, Dorothy. 1972 and 1973. "Population and Family Planning Programs: A Factbook." In *Reports on Population/Family Planning.* No. 2. Table 16. New York: The Population Council.

Annex Table 23

Percentage of Married Women Ages 15–44 Using Contraceptives

	1969	1970	1971	1972	1973
Egypt	10.0	8.0 e	9.0	11.0 e	20.7
Fiji	—	—	—	—	33.4
Ghana	—	2.0	—	—	—
Guatemala	—	—	—	7.0	3.8
Hong Kong	42.0	50.0	51.0	54.0	52.3
India	8.0	12.0	—	13.2 p	13.6 p
Indonesia p	0.1	0.2	0.8	3.3	—
Iran	3.0	11.2 e	9.3 e	—	—
Kenya	1.0	1.0	2.2	—	—
Korea, Rep. of	25.0	32.0	42.0	30.0	—
Malaysia (west)	6.0	7.0	8.0	8.0 p	9.3 p
Mauritius	—	—	25.0	21.2	—
Morocco	1.0	1.0	3.0	4.0	5.6
Nepal p	0.3	0.7	2.5	—	—
Pakistan	17.0 p	11.0 p	12.0 e	—	—
Philippines	—	—	—	8.1	11.0
Singapore	37.0	45.0	25.0 p	18.4 p	18.3 e p
Sri Lanka	5.5	8.2	—	—	—
Taiwan	32.0	36.0	44.0	56.0	57.0
Thailand	7.4	7.6	9.6	18.7	25.7
Tunisia	8.2	10.0	12.0	6.0 p	6.4 p
Turkey	3.0	3.0	4.4 e	—	2.5 p

e Estimated from data available. Does not include all methods.
p Program only.

Source: Nortman, Dorothy. 1969–1973. Population and Family Planning Programs: A Factbook. In *Reports on Population/Family Planning.* No. 2. Table 12, 1969; Table 15, 1970–71; and Table 16, 1972–73. New York: The Population Council.

Annex Table 24

Number of Acceptors of Family Planning Program Services in Selected Developing Countries and Percentage Change, 1968–1972

(acceptors in thousands)

	1968	1969	1970	1971	1972	Percent change 1968–1972
Bangladesh [a]	1374	1303	346	185	119	−91
Chile	99	89	63	83	63	−36
Colombia	50	99	125	155	164 [b]	228
Egypt	134	148	206	221	237	77
Fiji [a]	3	2	3	3	3	—
Hong Kong	25	28	28	29	30	20
India	3115	3411	3782	5000	5615	80
Indonesia	25	53	181	519	1039 [b]	4056
Iran [a]	122	231	304	385	u	i
Jamaica	2	28	19	22	22 [b]	1000
Kenya	9	26	31	41	43	378
Korea, Rep. of [d]	488	702	743	671	630	29
Malaysia (west)	70	66	56	55	56 [b]	−20
Mexico	11	20	25	29	45 [b]	309
Morocco	9	19	23	26	25	178
Nepal	16	27	32	u	u	u
Pakistan [a]	1324	1167	318	u	136	−90
Philippines [b]	43	85	192	409	590	1272
Singapore	36	37	27	22	24 [b]	−33
Sri Lanka	43	55	55	53	71	65
Taiwan [c]	123	114	160	187	173 [b]	41
Thailand [b]	52	117	203	364	404	677
Tunisia	16	20	23	27	31 [b]	94
Turkey	68	77	66	54	43 [b]	−37

[a] Estimated from data available. Does not include all methods.

[b] Includes acceptors in the International Postpartum Family Planning Program.

[c] Includes acceptors at the private Family Planning Association clinic.

[d] Estimated sum of all methods; acceptors who had a reinsertion six or more months after terminating earlier IUD use are duplicated in this count.

i—Incomplete data.

u—Unavailable.

Source: Nortman, Dorothy. 1973. *Population and Family Planning Programs: A Factbook.* In *Reports on Population/Family Planning.* No. 2. Fifth ed., Table 13. New York: The Population Council.

Annex Table 25

Acceptors of Family Planning Program Services per Thousand Women Ages 15–44, 1968–1972

	1968	1969	1970	1971	1972
Bangladesh a, f	—	—	—	12.3	6.0
Dominican Republic	4.2	17.6	19.1	21.9	22.6
Fiji a	27.3	18.2	27.3	25.0	25.0 b
Ghana	—	1.4	4.2	11.4	15.2
Guatemala	6.9	11.4	19.3	15.1	13.9
Hong Kong	32.1	35.0	35.0	35.1	37.5
India	28.0	29.9	32.6	43.5	47.6
Indonesia	1.1	2.3	6.7	17.9	35.8 b
Iran a	23.5	43.6	56.3	70.0	3.2 e
Jamaica	4.9	63.6	40.4	44.0	55.0 b
Korea, Rep. of d	75.1	104.8	116.1	98.7	95.4
Laos	—	0.5	1.2	2.3	6.2
Malaysia (West)	33.7	31.4	26.7	27.5	26.7 b
Mauritius	54.2	50.0	57.6	56.5	44.6
Morocco	3.0	6.3	7.4	8.1	8.1
Nepal	5.9	9.6	11.4	15.0	NA
Pakistan a	58.8	50.7	12.7	14.0	10.5 g
Philippines b	5.8	11.2	24.6	49.3	73.8
Singapore	90.0	92.5	58.7	46.8	49.0 b
Taiwan	43.5	40.7	53.3	56.7	52.4 b
Thailand b	7.5	16.2	28.2	47.3	49.9
Tunisia	16.7	20.0	23.0	27.0	28.2 b
Turkey	9.6	10.5	8.8	7.2	5.4b

a Estimated from data available. Does not include all methods.

b Includes acceptors in the International Postpartum Family Planning Program.

e Includes acceptors at the private Family Planning Association clinics.

d Estimated sum of all methods; acceptors who had a reinsertion six or more months after terminating earlier IUD use are duplicated in this count.

e Acceptors of IUD only, approximately 3 percent of total.

f Formerly East Pakistan.

g Formerly West Pakistan.

Source: Nortman, Dorothy. 1969–1972. Population and Family Planning Programs: A Factbook. In *Reports on Population/Family Planning.* No. 2. Tables 4 and 11, 1969; Tables 4 and 14, 1970; Tables 4 and 13, 1971; Tables 4 and 13, 1972; Tables 4 and 13, 1973. New York: The Population Council.

Annex Table 26

Median Age and Parity of Women Who Are Acceptors and of Wives of Men Who Are Acceptors

Country	Year	All methods		IUD		Oral		Sterilization	
		Age	Parity	Age	Parity	Age	Parity	Age	Parity
Bangladesh	1965–1966	—	—	30.4	4.7	—	—	—	—
	1967–1968	—	—	—	—	—	—	31.6	4.8
Brazil	1971*	28.4	3.1	30.0	3.8	29.9	2.6	—	—
Colombia	1971*	26.8	3.2	26.7	3.3	26.6	3.1	—	—
	1972	25.7	2.8	26.4	3.1	24.6	2.4	—	—
Dominican Republic	1972	—	—	25.9	3.5	24.1	2.7	—	—
Ghana	1971*	31.4	4.2	31.1	3.9	—	—	—	—
Honduras	1971*	24.2	2.0	27.3	3.0	23.4	1.7	—	—
Hong Kong	1966–1968	—	—	—	—	28.9	2.7	—	—
	1968	—	—	32.4	3.6	—	—	—	—
	1970	27.9	—	—	—	24.6	—	32.8	—
	1971*	27.0	1.9	—	—	—	1.4	—	—
	1972	26.5	—	29.5	2.9	25.5	1.5	—	—
Indonesia	1971*	30.3	4.4	30.2	4.5	29.3	4.0	36.2	7.1
	1972	29.2	3.8	29.7	—	28.7	—	—	—
Iran	1971*	26.6	3.4	25.9	3.4	26.5	3.3	—	—
	1972	—	—	29.8	4.7	30.7	4.2	—	—
Jamaica	1968–1971	27.9	3.2	—	—	25.5	—	—	—
Kenya	1970	—	—	29.3	4.8	28.0	4.1	—	—
Korea, Rep. of	1966	—	—	38.6	4.4	—	—	—	—
	1969	—	—	33.2	3.8	34.0	3.9	—	—
	1972	—	—	32.8	3.6	—	—	34.2	3.7
Malaysia (West)	1969	28.8	—	—	—	—	—	—	—
	1971	27.7	—	—	4.5	—	3.1	—	5.7
Mexico	1971*	29.8	3.5	—	—	29.5	3.6	—	—
	1972	—	—	28.5	4.0	27.0	3.7	—	—
Nigeria	1971*	32.3	4.8	32.5	4.8	—	—	—	—
Pakistan	1965–1966	—	—	34.6	5.0	—	—	—	—
	1967–1968	—	—	—	—	—	—	33.8	4.4
Philippines	1970	—	—	30.5	4.3	29.9	4.1	—	—
	1971*	27.9	3.2	28.3	3.4	26.0	2.4	—	—
Singapore	1967–1968	—	—	—	—	29.4	3.0	—	—
	1972	25.5	—	24.5	—	—	—	—	—
Sri Lanka	1970	28.8	3.8	—	—	—	—	—	—
	1972	28.4	3.8	—	—	—	—	—	—

Annex Table 26 (Continued)

Country	Year	All methods Age	Parity	IUD Age	Parity	Oral Age	Parity	Sterilization Age	Parity
Taiwan	1967–1968	—	—	—	—	31.1	3.6	—	—
	1968	—	—	31.6	3.7	—	—	—	—
	1971	—	—	30.2	3.3	29.7	3.3	—	—
Thailand	1965	—	—	28.0	3.8	—	—	—	—
	1968–1969	—	—	28.8	3.4	—	—	—	—
	1971	—	—	29.2	3.6	29.4	3.4	—	—
	1971 *	28.6	3.4	28.2	3.2	26.9	2.4	30.9	4.3
Tunisia	1966	—	—	33.4	5.1	—	—	—	—
	1969	—	—	31.4	4.6	—	—	35.6	5.8
	1970	—	—	31.5	4.5	—	—	—	—
Turkey	1968	—	—	30.4	3.8	—	—	—	—
	1969	—	—	29.7	3.6	—	—	—	—
	1970	—	—	29.6	3.5	—	—	—	—
	1971	—	—	29.2	3.4	—	—	—	—
Venezuela	1971 *	26.2	3.7	26.6	3.8	24.7	3.4	34.4	7.3

* International Postpartum Family Planning Program.

Source: Nortman, Dorothy. September 1973. Population and Family Planning: A Factbook. In *Reports on Population/Family Planning*. No. 2. Fifth edition. New York: The Population Council.

Annex Table 27

Distribution of Acceptors by Method in Selected Countries, Latest Year Available

Country	Year	Percentage by method				
		IUD	Oral	Sterili-zation	Other	Total
Bangladesh	1972	7.2	4.1	0.4	88.3	100
Chile	1972	56.1	36.9	3.0	4.0	100
Colombia a	1972	48.3	47.2	0.0	4.5	100
Egypt	1972	35.9	32.5	0.0	31.6	100
Fiji a	1972	48.5	0.0	51.5	0.0	100
Hong Kong	1972	1.9	72.7	1.3	24.1	100
India	1972	5.9	0.0	53.8	40.3	100
Indonesia a	1972	35.7	55.6	0.0	8.7	100
Iran	1971	3.7	96.3	0.0	0.0	100
Jamaica a	1972	9.0	46.0	0.0	45.0	100
Kenya	1972	10.9	79.1	0.0	10.0	100
Korea, Rep. of a	1972	48.9 b	22.5	3.7	24.9	100
Malaysia (West) a	1972	1.9	86.8	6.9	4.4	100
Mexico a	1972	31.0	51.9	0.0	17.1	100
Morocco	1972	19.3	70.2	0.0	10.5	100
Pakistan	1969	31.8	0.0	2.4	65.8	100
Philippines a	1972	14.1	57.3	0.0	28.6	100
Singapore a	1972	0.8	40.6	26.0	32.6	100
Sri Lanka	1972	26.0	44.7	13.4	15.9	100
Taiwan	1972	58.3	38.6	0.0	3.1	100
Thailand a	1972	19.9	73.0	7.1	0.0	100
Tunisia a	1972	36.5	36.2	7.0	20.3 c	100
Turkey a	1972	89.4	10.6	0.0	0.0	100

a Includes acceptors in the International Postpartum Family Planning Program.
b Reinsertions six or more months after terminating earlier IUD use are duplicated in the count.
c Includes "social abortion."

Source: Nortman, Dorothy. September 1973. Population and Family Planning: A Factbook. In *Reports on Population/Family Planning.* No. 2. Fifth edition. Table 13. New York: The Population Council.

Annex Table 28
Continuation Rates Twelve Months After Acceptance, for Selected Countries

	Method	
Country	IUD	Orals
Chile	73 g	—
Colombia a	75	56
Hong Kong a	64	38 b
India	78 f	53 e
Indonesia a	86	
Iran a	63 b	54
Korea, Rep. of	58 g	—
Mexico a	78	42
Pakistan a	59 b	—
Philippines a	82	56
Puerto Rico a	72	58
Singapore	68 c	—
Sri Lanka	—	76 d
Taiwan	60	42
Thailand a	79	72
Trinidad & Tobago	57	91
Turkey a	67	38
Tunisia	75 g	—
Venezuela a	87	56

a First-method continuation rates for total program.

b Continuation rates based on fewer than 750 estimated acceptors at the beginning of the ordinal month.

c Continuation (net) rates with reinsertion in Kandang Kerban Maternity Hospital.

d Three tea estates.

e Bombay.

f Cumulative retention rates per 100 IUD acceptors with reinsertions in a field program in Delhi.

g Cumulative retention rates per 100 IUD acceptors without reinsertions.

Sources: Sivin, Irving. 1971. Fertility Decline and Contraceptive Use in the International Postpartum Family Planning Program. *Studies in Family Planning.* 2:12. pp. 248–256.

Mauldin, W. Parker et al. 1967. Retention of IUDs: An International Comparison. *Studies in Family Planning,* No. 18.

Jones, Gavin W. and Parker W. Mauldin. 1967. Use of Oral Contraceptives: With Special Reference to Developing Countries. *Studies in Family Planning.* No. 24.

Forrest, Jacqueline E. 1971. Postpartum Service in Family Planning: Findings to Date. *Reports on Population/Family Planning* No. 8. New York: The Population Council.

de Souza, C. Mahabir. 1969. Comparative Study Between IUCD and OC. In *Medical Report.* pp. 57–61. Trinidad and Tobago: Family Planning Association of Trinidad & Tobago.

World Bank data.

Annex Table 29

Indicators of Mass Media Coverage * for Selected Countries

	Newspapers per thousand people	Radios per thousand people	TVs per thousand people
Chile	109 (1971)	103 (1971)	41 (1971)
Colombia	89 (1971)	143 (1970)	51 (1970)
Egypt	22 (1969)	132 (1971)	16 (1970)
Fiji	30 (1970)	98 (1971)	—
Hong Kong	485 (1969)	170 (1970)	110 (1971)
India	16 (1971)	21 (1970)	0.08 (1971)
Iran	12 (1971)	93 (1969)	12 (1971)
Indonesia	7 (1965)	114 (1969)	0.80 (1971)
Jamaica	114 (1971)	230 (1969)	38 (1971)
Kenya	14 (1970)	48 (1969)	1.50 (1970)
Korea, Rep. of	138 (1971)	126 (1970)	13 (1970)
Malaysia	63 (1971)	57 (1970)	18 (1971)
Mexico	116 (1965)	294 (1971)	67 (1971)
Morocco	16 (1971)	66 (1971)	15 (1971)
Nepal	3 (1971)	—	—
Pakistan	18 (1965)	14 (1971)	0.90 (1970)
Philippines	21 (1971)	45 (1969)	11 (1971)
Singapore	174 (1971)	150 (1971)	75 (1971)
Sri Lanka	42 (1971)	39 (1971)	—
Taiwan	8 (1971)	16 (1970)	0.40 (1970)
Thailand	24 (1970)	79 (1971)	7 (1969)
Tunisia	16 (1969)	77 (1970)	10 (1970)
Turkey	41 (1969)	107 (1971)	3 (1971)

* Number in parentheses indicates year of latest available data.

Source: United Nations Educational, Scientific, and Cultural Organization. 1973. *UNESCO Statistical Yearbook 1972.* Tables 9.1, 12.2., and 13.2. Paris: U.N. Education, Scientific and Cultural Organization.

Annex Table 30
Health Care Indicators in Selected Developing Countries

Country [b]	Population per physician 1969 [a]	Population per nursery & mid-wifery personnel 1969 [a]	Government health expenditures per capita [b] 1970–1971 [a] (U.S. dollars)	GNP per capita market prices 1970 (U.S. dollars)
Rwanda	53,540	7,280	$ 0.45	$ 60
Ethiopia	71,800	—	0.67	80
India	5,240	5,650	0.83	110
Sri Lanka	3,690	1,460	3.76	110
Kenya	12,140	3,140	0.14	150
Thailand	8,410	2,360	1.38	200
Philippines	10,220	5,100	1.06	210
Morocco	13,160	2,760	2.80	230
Korea, Rep. of	2,310	1,630	1.33	250
Algeria	7,860	2,460	4.53	300
Colombia	2,160	—	2.04	340
Malaysia (west)	4,230	830	7.18	380
Trinidad & Tobago	2,320	360	14.27	860
Jamaica	4,140	550	20.44	670
Chile	2,440	4,330	7.10	720
Venezuela	1,100	460	19.64	980

[a] Or recent years.

[b] Refer also to country notes below.

Sources: World Bank. 1972. *World Bank Atlas.* Washington, D.C.: World Bank.

World Health Organization. 1973. *World Health Statistics Annual, 1969.* Geneva: WHO.

World Bank. 1974. A Bank Approach to Health Policy. Draft, March 5, 1974. Washington, D.C.: World Bank, Population and Human Resources Division, Development Economics Department.

Notes:

Rwanda: Expenditures financed with foreign sources do not enter into the budget. Public sector health expenditures financed with foreign aid amounted to 145.0 million francs. The central government is almost the sole supplier of public services. "Welfare" is included in "Health."

Ethiopia: Both central and provincial governments are responsible for provision of public health services but the extent of provincial expenditure is not known.

India: Medical and public health services are mainly provided by the state governments.

Kenya: Medical services in Kenya are free. The service is shared by municipal and county councils.

Thailand: Foreign financed expenditures are outside the budget. Medical services are provided by the central government. Municipalities and sanitary districts provide some public-health services, but major capital expenditures and a large part of current expenditures are financed by the central government.

Philippines: Foreign loan financed expenditures are included in the budget. The central government is the main provider of public health services. It operates about one-half of the country's hospitals. The service for rural areas is provided through the Department of Health's rural health units.

Morocco: The Ministry of Public Health is the major supplier of medical and health services. Some municipalities also provide these services but their expenditures are partly financed with subsidies from the central government.

Korea, Rep. of: Health services are mainly provided by the local governments.

Algeria: Medical and health services are rendered by the central government through health centers, dispensaries and hospitals. Some municipalities also operate hospitals.

Colombia: Public medical-health service is shared by the Ministry of Public Health and decentralized agencies including the social security institutions. The decentralized agencies receive grants from the national government.

Malaysia (West): Most health services are the responsibility of the federal government, but local authorities share public health services. Medical services in government hospitals are free.

Trinidad & Tobago: Almost all public medical and health services are provided by the central government. Local governments make some expenditures for environmental health services, but these are financed largely with the central government grants.

Jamaica: Almost all public medical and health services are financed by the central government. However, the training hospital of the University of the West Indies Medical School provides medical services, which are financed largely from other sources.

Venezuela: The social security system and local governments provide medical services in their own medical establishments.

Annex Table 31

Medical Resources Devoted to Family Planning Programs for Selected Countries, 1972

Country	Physi-cians *	Other health personnel *	Field workers *	Physical facilities *	Mobile units
Bangladesh	1,000	4,020	11,045 c, d, e	454	0
Chile	360	588	u	u	0
Colombia	370	1,150	2,300 b	573	0
Egypt	3,850	6,000	1,800 a	3,187	0
Fiji	30	118	u	140	13
Hong Kong	6	48	52	57	0
India	5,107	31,988	5,338 e	39,416	855
Indonesia	813	2,641	3,774	2,067	0
Iran	1,111	1,314	1,746 a, d	988	405
Jamaica	1	37	u	147	1
Kenya (1970)	60	30	u	250	12
Korea, Rep. of	1,614	920	1,473	1,866	10
Malaysia (West) (1971)	6	232	u	472	0
Mexico	u	u	u	112	1
Morocco	538	7,407	—	167	0
Nepal (1971)	11	440	—	86	2
Pakistan	1,363	234	19,747 c, e	963	0
Philippines	1,933	6,839	u	1,495	8
Singapore	8	50	2 a	53	0
Sri Lanka	4	4	u	490	1
China, Rep. of	837	782	464	1,062	10
Thailand	599	7,123	90	4,777	4
Tunisia	26	56	u	372	15
Turkey	1,184	3,657	u	570	5

* A part-time worker is considered as equivalent to one-half of a full-time worker.
a Social workers.
b Rural health promoters.
c Including distributors of conventional contraceptives.
d Women's health corps.
e Includes lady family planning visitors.
u—Unavailable

Source: Nortman, Dorothy. 1973. Population and Family Planning Programs Reports on Population/Family Planning. No. 2. Fifth edition. New York: The Population Council. Table 7.

206

Annex Table 32

Annual Mortality Rate Due to Family Planning Techniques, Abortion, and Pregnancy

Family Planning Techniques	Per million users
Oral Contraceptives: estrogen/progestin formulations	
age group 20–24	13
age group 35–44	34
continuous dosage progestin (mini-pill)	—
IUD	..
Sterilization	
tubal ligation	10–20 [a]
vasectomy	—
Abortion	Per million abortions [b]
Legal	6–400
Criminal	500–1000
Pregnancy	Per million births
England and Wales, in 1966	
all ages	223
age group 35–44	576
Colombia, in 1963	
all ages	7,250
Ceylon, in 1963	
all ages	2,959
USSR	320
United States	310

— No evidence of lethal effects.

.. Mortality known but not measured.

[a] Estimated.

[b] The range reflects variations in the method (e.g., vacuum aspiration vs. hysterectomy) as well as timing (first vs. later trimesters of pregnancy) of procedure.

Source: Gillie, Oliver. 1970. Safety of the Pill. *Science Journal.* July, Table 1, p. 57.

Annex Table 33

Costs Per Acceptor of Family Planning Programs in Selected Countries [1]

(U.S. dollars)

	1965	1966	1967	1968	1969	1970	1971	1972
Dominican Republic	—[d]	—	—	43	10	17	14	9
Fiji [a]	—	—	—	28	57	39	49	u
Ghana	—	—	—	—	—	158	44	18
Guatemala	—	—	—	—	—	—	—	39
Hong Kong	—	—	11	8	10	11	13	15
India	—	10	12	13	14	17	17	15
Indonesia	—	—	—	29	61	27	14	9 [b]
Iran [a]	—	—	—	5	20	u	18	u
Jamaica	—	—	—	330	20 *	38 *	49 *	u
Korea, Rep. of	3	4	5	12	6	6	9	9
Malaysia (West)	—	—	38	17	12	14	14 *	13 * [b]
Mauritius	15	10	15	22	22	22	28	—
Morocco *	—	—	—	19	14	13	11	14
Nepal	—	—	—	3	7	12	u	u
Pakistan [a]	40	10	15	15	19	u	u	u
Philippines [b]	—	—	6	7	11	7	7	10
Taiwan [c]	3	4	4	5	6	6	5	6 [b]
Thailand [b]	—	—	—	20	14	13	9	12
Tunisia	—	—	—	55	39	30 [a]	33	44 [b]
Turkey	112	33	35	39	40	18	25	42 [b]

[1] Since information is not available on what is included under costs, figures may not be comparable between countries or over time.

* Government cost.

[a] Estimated from data available.

[b] Includes acceptors in the International Postpartum Family Planning Program.

[c] Includes acceptors at the private Family Planning Association clinic.

[d] Estimated sum of all methods, which include acceptors who had a reinsertion six or more months after terminating earlier IUD use, are duplicated in this count.

[e] IUD only, approximately three percent.

u Unavailable.

Source: Nortman, Dorothy. September 1973. Population and Family Planning Program: A Factbook. In Reports on Population/Family Planning. No. 2. Fifth edition. Tables 13 and 17. New York: The Population Council.

208

REFERENCES

Agarwala, S. N. 1972. A Study of Factors Explaining Variability in Family Planning Performance in Different States in India. In, Proceedings of 1972 All India Seminar on Family Planning Problems in India. Deonar (Bombay): International Institute for Population Studies.

Ahluwalia, Montek S. Forthcoming 1974. Income Inequality: Some Dimensions of the Problem. In *Redistribution with Growth*. Hollis B. Chenery; Montek Ahluwalia; C. L. G. Bell; John H. Duloy; and Richard Jolly. London: Oxford University Press.

Anand, Sudhir. 1973. *The Size Distribution of Income in Malaysia, Part I.* Washington, D.C.: Development Research Center, World Bank. Mimeo.

Arthur D. Little, Inc. 1972. Commercial Distribution of Contraceptives in Colombia, Iran, and the Philippines. *Reports on Population/Family Planning.* No. 11. New York City: The Population Council.

Balfour, M. C. 1962. A Scheme for Rewarding Successful Family Planners. New York City: The Population Council. Mimeo.

Becker, Gary S. 1960. An Economic Analysis of Fertility. In *Demographic and Economic Change in Developed Countries.* Universities National Bureau Committee for Economic Research. Princeton: Princeton University Press.

Becker, Gary S. 1973. A Theory of Marriage: Part I. *Journal of Political Economy.* 81:4, 813–846.

Bilsborrow, Richard E. 1973. Dependency Rates and Aggregate Saving Rates: Corrections and Further Analyses. Chapel Hill: University of North Carolina. Mimeo.

Boserup, Ester. 1965. *The Conditions of Economic Growth.* Chicago: Aldine Publishing Co.

Callahan, D. 1971. *Ethics and Population Limitation.* New York City: The Population Council.

Chow, L. P. 1970. Family Planning in Taiwan, Republic of China: Progress and Prospects. *Population Studies.* 24:3, 339–352.

Chow, L. P. 1971. A "Positive" Incentive Scheme Encouraging Family Planning Practice in Rural Areas—Draft Proposal. Baltimore: Department of Population Dynamics, The Johns Hopkins University. Mimeo.

Chow, L. P. and R. Gillespie. 1966. Taiwan, Experimental Studies. *Studies in Family Planning.* 1:13, 1–5.

Chow, L. P. and I. Sirageldin. 1972. Study on the Feasibility of a Monetary Incentive Scheme to Encourage Fertility Control Practices. Baltimore: Department of Population Dynamics, The Johns Hopkins University. Mimeo.

Clark, Colin. 1967. *Population Growth and Land Use.* New York City: St. Martin's Press.

Coale, Ansley J. 1973. The Implications of Prospective Trends of Economic and Social Development for Demographic Change: The Demographic Transition. In *International Population Conference, Liege, 1973. Vol. 1.* Liege: International Union for the Scientific Study of Population.

Conning, A. 1973. Latin American Fertility Trends and Influencing Factors.

In *International Population Conference. Liege, 1973. Vol. 2.* Liege: International Union for the Scientific Study of Population.

Dandekar, V. M. and Nilakantha Rath. 1971. *Poverty in India.* Poona: Indian School of Political Economy.

David, Henry P. Forthcoming 1974. Abortion Research in Transnational Perspective: An Overview. In *Abortion Research Reader,* edited by Henry P. David. Lexington, Massachusetts: Lexington Books.

Dixon, Ruth. 1972. Explaining Cross-Cultural Variations in Age at Marriage and Proportions Never Marrying. *Population Studies.* 25:2, 215–233.

Eizenga, W. 1961. *Demographic Factors and Savings.* Amsterdam: North-Holland.

Enke, S. 1960. The Gains to India from Population Control: Some Money Measures and Incentive Schemes. *Review of Economics and Statistics.* 42: May.

Elliot, Charles. 1973. *Distributional Patterns of Development and Welfare: A Case Study of Zambia.* Paris: United Nations Educational, Scientific and Cultural Organization.

Finkle, Jason L. 1971. Politics, Development Strategy, and Family Planning Programs in India and Pakistan. *Journal of Comparative Administration.* 3:3, 259–295.

Finnigan, Oliver D., III. 1972. Testing Incentive Plans for Moving Beyond Family Planning. Manila: U.S. Agency for International Development/ Philippines. Mimeo.

Finnigan, Oliver D., III and T. H. Sun. 1972. Planning, Starting and Operating an Educational Incentives Project. *Studies in Family Planning.* 3:1.

Freedman, Ronald, et al. 1969. The Family Planning Program for All of Taiwan. In *Family Planning in Taiwan.* R. Freedman and J. Y. Takeshita. Princeton: Princeton University Press.

Hajnal, J. 1965. European Marriage Pattern in Perspective. In *Population in History,* edited by D. V. Glass and D. E. C. Eversley. Chicago: Aldine Publishing Co.

Harbison, Frederick Harris; Joan Maruhnic; and Jane R. Resnick. 1970. *Quantitative Aspects of Modernization and Development.* Research Report No. 115. Princeton: Department of Economics, Industrial Relations Section, Princeton University.

Hartfield, V. J. 1971. The Role of the Nurse in Family Planning Programs. *Contraception.* 3:2, 105–114.

Hermalin, Albert I. 1972. Taiwan: Appraising the Effect of a Family Planning Program through an Areal Analysis. Population Paper No. 2. Nankang, Taiwan: Institute of Economics, Academia Sinica.

Hulka, J. F. 1969. A Mathematical Model Study of Contraceptive Efficiency and Unplanned Pregnancies. *American Journal of Obstetrics and Gynecology.* 104:3, 443–447.

India National Sample Survey. 1971. *Tables with Notes on the Fertility and Mortality Rates in Urban Areas of India, Sixteenth Round: July 1960–August 1961.* No. 180. New Delhi: Cabinet Secretariat.

International Institute for Population Studies. 1969. *Newsletter,* No. 30. Bombay: International Institute for Population Studies.

Jain, Anrudh K. and D. V. N. Sarma. 1974. Some Explanatory Factors for Statewise Differential Use of Family Planning Methods in India. New York City: The Population Council. Mimeo.

Jain, Sagar C. 1971. Comparative Study of the Effective and Non-Effective Family Planning Program in India: Report of the Feasibility of Study Design. Chapel Hill, North Carolina: Carolina Population Center. Mimeo.

Jain, S. 1969. Estimation of Population Growth Under Family Planning Programme. *Journal of Family Welfare* (Bombay). 16:1, 33–47.

Jain, S. and A. Tiemann. 1973. The Size Distribution of Income: Compilation of Data. Discussion Paper No. 4. Washington, D.C.: World Bank. Mimeo.

Kavalsky, Basil. 1973. An Experimental Program for Population Control and Social Security in Bangladesh. Washington: World Bank. Mimeo.

Kim, T. R. 1970. *National Intra-Uterine Contraception Report.* Seoul: National Family Planning Center.

King, Timothy. 1971. Private Savings. In *Financing Development in Latin America,* edited by Keith Griffin. London: Macmillan.

Kirk, Dudley. 1946. *Europe's Population in the Interwar Years.* Princeton: Princeton University Press.

Kirk, Dudley. 1960. The Influence of Business Cycles on Marriage and Birth Rates. In *Demographic and Economic Change in Developed Countries,* prepared by Universities-National Bureau Committee for Economic Research. Princeton: Princeton University Press.

Kirk, Dudley. 1971. A New Demographic Transition. In *Rapid Population Growth,* prepared by National Academy of Sciences. Baltimore and London: The Johns Hopkins Press.

Kocher, James. 1973. *Rural Development Income Distribution and Fertility Decline.* New York City: The Population Council.

Kwon, E. Hyock. 1971. Use of the Agent System in Seoul. *Studies in Family Planning.* 2:11, 237–240.

Lapham, R. J. 1970. Family Planning and Fertility in Tunisia. *Demography.* 7:2, 241–253.

Lapham, R. J. and W. P. Mauldin. 1972. National Family Planning Programs: Review and Evaluation. *Studies in Family Planning.* March, 29–52.

Leff, Nathaniel H. 1969. Dependency Rates and Savings Rates. *American Economic Review.* 59:5.

Little, I. M. D. and J. A. Mirrlees. 1969. *Manual of Industrial Project Analysis in Developing Countries. Vol. 2.* Paris: Organization for Economic Cooperation and Development, Development Centre.

Matsumoto, Y. Scott; Akira Koizumi, and Tadahiro Nohara. 1972. Condom Use in Japan. *Studies in Family Planning.* 3:10, 251–255.

Mauldin, W. Parker; William Watson, and Louisa Noe. 1970. *KAP Surveys and Evaluation of Family Planning Programs.* New York City: The Population Council.

Misra, Bhaskar D. 1973. Family Planning: Differential Performance of States. *Economic and Political Weekly.* 8:33, 1769–1779.

Mueller, Eva. 1967. *Incentive Payments for Family Planning.* New Delhi: U.S. Agency for International Development. Mimeo.

Nortman, Dorothy. 1970, 1971, 1972, 1973. Population and Family Planning Programs: A Factbook. *Reports on Population/Family Planning.* New York City: The Population Council.

Organization of American States. 1971. *Employment and Growth in the Strategy of Latin American Development: Implications for the Seventies. Structure of the Product and of Employment in Latin America, Annex 4.* Panama: Organization of American States.

Oshima, Harry D. 1971. Labor Absorption in East and Southeast Asia: A Summary with Interpretation of Postwar Experience. *Malayan Economic Review*. 16:2, 55–77.
Palmore, James and Ariffin bin Marzuki. 1969. Marriage Patterns and Cumulative Fertility in West Malaysia: 1966–1967. *Demography*. 6:4, 383–401.
Pohlman, Edward. 1971. *Incentives and Compensations in Birth Planning*. Monograph 11. Carolina Population Centre. Chapel Hill: University of North Carolina.
Potter, R. E. 1972. Additional Births Averted When Abortion Is Added to Contraception. *Studies in Family Planning*. 3:4, 53–59.
Potts, D. M. 1973. The Implementation of Family Planning Programmes. *British Journal of Hospital Medicine*. March, 288–294.
Repetto, Robert. 1968. India: A Case Study of the Madras Vasectomy Program. *Studies in Family Planning*. 1:31, 8–16.
Repetto, Robert. 1971. *Time in India's Development Programmes*. Cambridge: Harvard University Press.
Repetto, Robert; Thomas Reese, and Suyono Haryono. 1973. *Indonesia's Family Planning Delivery System: A Preliminary Multivariate Statistical Enquiry*. Technical Report Series, Monograph No. 7. Jakarta: BKKBN (National Family Planning Coordinating Body).
Repetto, Robert, and Dr. S. Suyatne, Chief, Field Worker Bureau, BKKBN (National Family Coordinating Body). 1973. Analysis of Field Worker Characteristics and Performance. Private communication, April.
Research and Marketing Services. 1970. A Study on the Evaluation of the Effectiveness of the TATA Incentive Program for Sterilization. Bombay: R.M.S. Unpublished.
Revelle, Roger. 1973. Will the Earth's Land and Water Resources Be Sufficient for Future Populations? Presented at the Symposium on Population, Resources and Environment, Stockholm. New York City: United Nations. Mimeo.
Rich, William. 1973. *Smaller Families Through Social and Economic Progress*. Washington, D.C.: Overseas Development Council.
Ridker, Ronald. 1969. Synopsis of a Proposal for a Family Planning Bond. *Studies in Family Planning*. No. 43.
Ridker, Ronald. 1971. Savings Accounts for Family Planning, An Illustration from the Tea Estates of India. *Studies in Family Planning*. 2:7, 150–152.
Ridker, R. G. and R. J. Muscat. 1973. Incentives for Family Welfare and Fertility Reduction: An Illustration from Malaysia. *Studies in Family Planning*. 4:1, 1–11.
Robinson, Warren C. 1969. Evaluating the Economic Benefits of Fertility Reduction. *Studies in Family Planning*. No. 39. New York City: The Population Council.
Rosenfield, A. 1971. Family Planning: An Expanded Role for Paramedical Personnel. *American Journal of Obstetrics and Gynecology*. 110:7, 1030–1039.
Rosenfield, Allan G.; Winich Asavasena, and Jumroon Mikhanorn. 1973. Person-to-person Communication in Thailand. *Studies in Family Planning*. 4:6, 145–149.
Ross, John A. et al. 1972. Findings from Family Planning Research. *Reports on Population/Family Planning*. No. 12. New York City: The Population Council.
Ross, J. A. and J. E. Forrest. 1971. Program Effects on Fertility. New York City: The Population Council. Unpublished.

Sauvy, Alfred. 1969. *General Theory of Population.* Translated by Christopher Campos. New York City: Basic Books.

Schultz, T. Paul. 1969. *Effectiveness of Family Planning in Taiwan: A Methodology for Program Evaluation.* Santa Monica: Rand Corporation.

Schultz, T. Paul. 1973. Determinants of Fertility: A Micro-Economic Model of Choice. Minneapolis: University of Minnesota. Mimeo.

Schultz, T. Paul and Julie Da Vanzo. 1970. *Analysis of Demographic Change in East Pakistan: Retrospective Survey Data.* No. R-564-AID. Santa Monica: The Rand Corporation.

Segal, Sheldon J. 1973. Revised and forthcoming 1974. The Case for Both Fundamental and Applied Studies in the Search for New Contraceptives. Woods Hole, Massachusetts: The Population Council. Background paper to *World Population Conference, Bucharest, 1974.* New York City: United Nations.

Simmons, G. B. 1971. *The Indian Investment in Family Planning.* New York City: The Population Council.

Simon, Julian. 1969. Money Incentives to Reduce Birth Rates in Low Income Countries. A Proposal to Determine the Effect Experimentally. Urbana: University of Illinois. Mimeo.

Sinzarinbum, Masri and Chris Manning. 1973. Fertility in Mojolama. Jogjakarta: Institute of Population Studies, University of Gadjah Mada. Mimeo.

Sirageldin, I. and S. Hopkins. 1972. Family Planning Programs: An Economic Approach. *Studies in Family Planning.* 3:2, 17–23.

Speidel, J. Joseph; R. T. Ravenholt; and Mary E. Irvine. 1974. Liberalized Policies for Distribution of Oral Contraceptives. *Studies in Family Planning.* 5:2, 62–67.

Srikantan, K. S. 1974. Comparative Analysis of Family Planning Programs in the Context of Socio-Economic Infrastructure: States of India. New York City: The Population Council. Mimeo.

Taylor, Howard C., Jr. and Bernard Berelson. 1971. Comprehensive Family Planning Based on Maternal/Child Health Services. *Studies in Family Planning.* 2:2, 21–54.

Taylor, Howard C., Jr. and Robert J. Lapham. 1974. A Program for Family Planning Based on Maternal/Child Health Services. *Studies in Family Planning.* 5:3, 71–72.

United Nations. 1965. *Population Bulletin of the United Nations, No. 7, 1963.* New York City: United Nations.

United Nations. 1971. *World Economic Survey, 1969–1970; The Developing Countries in the 1960s: The Problem of Appraising Progress.* New York City: United Nations.

United Nations Economic and Social Council. 1969. *World Population Situation.* Geneva: United Nations.

van der Tak, Jean. Forthcoming 1974. *Abortion, Fertility, and Changing Legislation: An International Review.* Lexington, Massachusetts: Lexington Books.

van de Walle, Etienne, and John Knodel. 1967. Demographic Transition and Fertility Decline: The European Case. In *Sydney Conference: Contributed Papers.* Liege: International Union for the Scientific Study of Population.

Williamson, J. G. 1968. Personal Savings in Developing Nations: An Intertemporal Cross Section from Asia. *Economic Record.* June.

World Bank. 1974. The Management Problem in Family Planning Programmes. Prepared for U.N. World Population Conference, 1974, Bucharest. E/Conf/60/CBP/12. New York City: United Nations.

World Health Organization. 1974. Research on the Biomedical Aspects of Fertility Regulation and on the Operational Aspects of Family Planning Programmes. World Population Conference, Working Paper No. 19. New York City: World Health Organization. Mimeo.

Wray, Joe D. 1971. Population Pressure on Families: Family Size and Childspacing. In *Rapid Population Growth,* prepared by National Academy of Sciences. Baltimore and London: The Johns Hopkins Press.

Yen, C. H. 1972. Taiwan. *Studies in Family Planning.* 4:5. 118–123.

A.L. OLIVEIRA MEMORIAL LIBRARY

3 1782 00092 4429

HB885 .I58 1974
Population policies and economi
c development; a World Ba 1974